Who are you
MEANT
to be?

A Groundbreaking
Step-by-Step Process for Discovering
and Fulfilling
YOUR TRUE POTENTIAL

Anne Dranitsaris, PhD
Heather Dranitsaris-Hilliard

tors of the Striving Styles™ Personality System

sourcebooks

Published by Sourcebooks, Inc.
P.O. Box 4410, Naperville, Illinois 60567-4410
(630) 961-3900
Fax: (630) 961-2168
www.sourcebooks.com

Library of Congress Cataloging-in-Publication Data

Dranitsaris, Anne.
   Who are you meant to be? : a groundbreaking step-by-step pr
covering and fulfilling your true potential / Anne Dranitsaris, Ph
Dranitsaris-Hilliard. — 1st Edition.
      pages cm
   Includes bibliographical references.
   (trade paper : alk. paper) 1. Personality. 2. Behavioral assess
consciousness (Awareness) I. Dranitsaris-Hilliard, Heather. II.
   BF698.D6773 2013
   158.1–dc23

                              2012034698

            Printed and bound in the United States of Ame
                    VP 10 9 8 7 6 5 4 3 2 1

*This book is dedicated to everyone who strives to live
their lives in the pursuit of their potential.*

CONTENTS

INTRODUCTION

What Were You Born For?

The potential of the average person is like a huge ocean unsailed, a new continent unexplored, a world of possibilities waiting to be released and channeled toward some great good.

—*Brian Tracy*

HAVE YOU NOTICED THOSE people who seem to have it all together? They look like they don't have a worry in the world. After all, most of us are just trying to figure it out as we go. It's not that we aren't looking for ways to live authentically, as our best selves. We just get so caught up focusing on our faults, trying to figure out what's wrong with us or being upset about the unfair advantage that other people have over us, that we fail to see our own gifts, our unique abilities, and our own capacity to experience the fulfillment of living life as who we are meant to be.

We tend to fill our minds with incessant, negative chatter that drives us down the road to depression and anxiety. We tell ourselves what we should be doing; what we didn't do well enough; and how our looks, our bodies, our friends, and so forth, aren't good enough. We have an underlying sense of impending danger and spend so much time worrying that we undermine our confidence. Feeling anxious, insecure, or indecisive, we don't seem to have the skills and capacity to look inward for answers, or even reassurance. We often end up with some degree of persistent, unfocused anxiety about ourselves and a sense of hopelessness about what we can do about it.

We, as authors and experts in the field of human development, believe that each person has a potential to fulfill and a unique inner journey to take. We all hold the promise of who we are meant to be within us, just waiting to be embraced and manifested in our daily lives. Our potential has to do with living life authentically, as our best selves. Who you are meant to *be* does not mean "What are you meant to do?" *Being* is a state, not an activity. It represents how we feel and the quality of our experience as we go about the activities of our lives. So it's not so much about what we do but about how we feel about ourselves as we do it.

Achieving your potential and living who you are meant to be is a process, not a destination. It's not as if you realize one day, "Gosh, I think I have achieved my potential." If that's the case, what do you do then? Lie down and die? Regress so you can do it again? It is living each day with self-awareness, working at and striving to be your best self, that ultimately leads us to being who we are meant to be. Remember the old Zen saying, "*Before enlightenment, chop wood, carry water. After enlightenment, chop wood, carry water.*" Who we are meant to be is experienced; it's not a utopian palace at the end of the road of life. You can start living it now.

We all have the capacity to fulfill our potential as human beings if we focus on our experiences and take care to produce the ones that support us to live as our best selves. For us to achieve our potential and to become who we are meant to be requires us to:

1. acquire self-knowledge and self-awareness
2. know our brains and the mechanics of our mind
3. create an inner state of well-being by observing our thoughts and feelings

4. know when we are creating disease with our thoughts, actions, and inactions
5. live from the experience of love, not fear
6. focus on the quality of our experiences rather than the quantity
7. care for and about ourselves
8. empathize with and share ourselves with others
9. do work that is meaningful and aligned with our authentic selves
10. be honest with ourselves and express ourselves authentically

We have written this book to show you how to fill the gap between what you know and what you do; to teach you how to live your life from the inside out; and to encourage you to experience your life instead of worrying or being afraid of what might happen if… We have written this book so you can achieve your potential and become who you are meant to be.

Getting Past the Aha Moment

We have all had it—that moment of insight and discovery, where everything suddenly becomes clear. We know what we have to do, and we get excited about the prospect of doing it and what we will look like, feel, and experience when it is done. Then, one of two things happens: we actively engage in making the insight a reality, or we go back to the way we were before we had the aha experience.

We have seen many lives changed when people get past the excitement of their aha moment and actively work on breaking the habit that has been limiting them or interfering with their experiencing real happiness and satisfaction in their lives. For some it has meant leaving a job or getting out of an abusive relationship. For others it has been realizing that they don't have to feel or create distress for themselves; they can create the feeling state they want to live.

As lovely as an aha moment is, it is simply an endorphin rush that gives us a temporary high from the experience of making the discovery. We researched this extensively, looking for the reasons that caused people not to change despite a real desire to do so. Our answer emerged from studying the physiology of the brain and how it develops and changes because of its neuroplastic makeup—its ability to shape and reshape itself based on experience.

What we have found is that unless we make what we know into an actual experience, we can't expect permanent change, as the brain needs experiences to build new habits of mind. Habits of mind and patterns of brain functioning change with repeated experience over time. Otherwise, we automatically revert to the behavioral patterns that the brain has always used. When we don't realize that the work we are doing is changing the neural patterns in our brain, we give up and say things like, "Thinking positive doesn't work—I tried it all week but I am still unhappy," or "I tried meditation once and nothing happened." Despite what we like to believe, we can't just learn about something or try it a couple of times and expect our behavior to change. We have called the process of learning without changing *inactive knowing*. Inactive knowing happens when the area of the brain responsible for thinking and knowing ("I know I should get my taxes done") is at odds with the emotional area or our emotional brain ("I hate doing taxes. I saw a cute pair of shoes on my way home today. I think I'll go shopping instead."). In a fully integrated brain, where both thought and experience matter (both sensing and emotional experiences), action follows thought.

Our Experience Exposed the Problem

After talking with thousands of struggling individuals over the past three decades in our roles as clinical psychotherapist, corporate therapist, and organizational development consultants, we discovered a serious disconnect between clients' self-awareness and their ability to put into practice new modes of behavior that made the most of their innate skills and preferences. Although they wanted to know what was wrong with them and they wanted to change, they could not bring themselves to do it.

Most of our clients assumed that if they and other people had information about themselves and they understood what they had to do to succeed or develop, they would. In practice, we didn't see this happening. Even when we gave our clients personality assessments that promised to change behavior, people learned about themselves, but their behavior didn't change unless the change would somehow meet their needs. We were seeing inactive knowing in action.

Why didn't these clients change their behavior? Suppose that you take a series of psychological tests, and one of the things the tests determine is that when you are emotionally upset, you tend to binge eat. You'll probably agree that the mere knowledge of this fact does not stop you the next time you feel the impulse. If anything, now that you have a "reason" for your behavior, you may see the reason as a justification for remaining helplessly attached to bingeing as a source of comfort. It doesn't draw attention to the emotions or frustrated needs that are causing you to act on your impulse to eat like you were never going to see another meal.

Nowhere could we find an assessment or approach to help our clients that would truly shed light on what was behind behaviors like this, behaviors that are seemingly counter to what is in a person's best interests. We wanted a system that considered the full human experience—emotions, needs, behavior, and personality. At the same time, it had to have a clear Roadmap for helping people develop in order to sustain behavioral change.

How We Tackled the Problem

We have always been concerned with how we could best help people break through limitations to achieve their potential. We chose careers in which we could do this, both in organizations and in clinical practice. Heather first approached it as an organizational effectiveness and leadership development consultant, while Anne came from a clinical psychotherapy and executive coaching background. Our first business together was based on the integrated business model "People, Systems, Results." The main scope of our work was with the assessment and development of leaders, teams, the organization and its culture, or a group of individual employees. Our approach included looking at the organization of an individual's personality, using the Myers-Briggs Type Indicator® (MBTI®) which determines a persons personality type and a four-letter code. The MBTI sorts people into sixteen personality types and provides insight into their strengths and weaknesses. We also determined an individual's emotional intelligence, using the Emotional Quotient Inventory®, a self-scoring assessment that looks at emotional functioning on five different scales of emotional functioning. Various leadership assessments, such as the Leadership Skills Profile and our own Leadership Competency Profile were used in our leadership development programs. These predicted how well a leader was performing, using forty-two behavioral competencies.

None of the assessments available created a whole picture for the client. Each provided only a portion of the picture. We became aware of a gaping hole in modern approaches to analyzing personality. It was too disconnected. You could find out your type, your color, or even your conflict style, but that didn't connect to your emotions. Or you could discover you weren't empathetic and had little self-awareness, but not what it meant relative to your personality. We found existing personality tests to be inadequate: they simply failed to bring emotions, brain physiology, development, and brain specialization into the equation. And they lacked a system for development to help people go from knowing to experiencing to changing their behavior and developing their brains.

As new research about the brain emerged, we became fascinated by how it could be used to help people. For example, research in emotional intelligence was demonstrating that people who developed emotional intelligence by using both the emotional and rational parts of the brain were happier, healthier, and more successful than those who did not. In addition, single-photon emission computed tomography (SPECT) imaging technology allowed us to observe the functional areas of the brain and their relationship with an individual's personality type. We were excited about how these developments could improve our ability to help our clients.

We looked at the brain and personality the same way we would approach any other organ system of the body. We considered its structure, function, and purpose, and the idea that *psychological needs* are the driving force for behavior behind each of the functional areas of the brain emerged. What we found was that when employees' needs were satisfied by the work they were doing, morale and productivity both increased. When leaders stopped trying to adapt to an ideal version of how they should behave and instead looked at their fears, their personality organization, and their own needs, they were able to more authentically lead their employees and teams. When individuals in therapy stopped blaming others and began putting their energy into meeting their own needs, they started achieving their goals and spent less time focusing on their emotions and their story.

Our Solution: The Striving Styles Personality System

It became clear to us that to really help our clients, we had to create something that was inclusive of emotions and personality styles to close the gap between knowing and doing, thereby moving clients from *inactive knowing* to *active knowing* to achieve greater results. In 2007, we began creating an assessment and development system with the same type of substantial reports we had been customizing for our clients. We combined the most up-to-date research on how different parts of the brain function and the role of emotions in learning and development with psychological type, needs, brain dominance theories, and mindfulness to create the Striving Styles Personality System, or SSPS. The SSPS blends new brain science with Carl Jung's century-old personality system to show how the brain functions and how key areas of our brain operate in our personality. It shows why most people live in "survival mode," using behaviors, thinking patterns, and beliefs that keep them there.

Having used the system successfully in our consulting business and personal lives for the past five years, we became increasingly excited about how successful and powerful it is when used as directed. We have had the opportunity to use it extensively with leaders and teams, in personal and relationship counseling, and to improve the mental health of our clients. Through our personal experiences with raising children and supporting their learning challenges including attention deficit/hyperactivity disorder (ADHD), we have begun helping parents and teachers to put this practical framework to use. It has been invaluable to us as we navigated personal opportunities and challenges. It was our desire to bring our approach to achieving potential to a larger audience that led to the writing of *Who Are You Meant to Be?*

Our book introduces you to the SSPS, which builds your understanding of how your brain is organized and how it is intended to be used. Most important, you will discover which of eight possible Striving Styles is truest to your brain's natural makeup and how the other Styles function in your personality. Our book brings you benefits that are unique to the SSPS: you will learn how to harness the power of your emotions, enhance the functioning of your brain as a whole, and create a clear, step-by-step Roadmap for becoming who you are meant to be.

The Organization of the Book

This book is organized into three parts and takes you from learning how your brain functions to getting to know the eight Striving Styles, and then to building your personal Roadmap for becoming who you are meant to be. The book is filled with stories and examples to bring the theory and the Styles to life for you. All the examples have been taken from our work in clinical and organizational practice, as well as from our personal experiences. For the explanations of the brain, the Striving Styles, and other theoretical elements of the SSPS, we have tried to use simple, everyday language to make them easy for everyone to understand. The scientific foundation for the SSPS is built on a body of established knowledge and well-accepted theories that we touch upon here in brief; however, you will find a complete bibliography of those authors and theorists in the back of the book.

Part 1: Who Are You Meant to Be?

In the first chapter, we cover our current reality, the fact that we aren't yet living consciously, and some of the reasons why. We discuss why our culture places little value on becoming acquainted with our selves, our needs, and our emotions, and therefore most of us receive no systematic training in how to do so. This chapter also explains how excessive adaptation causes us to live in survival mode and how that gets in the way of becoming who we are meant to be.

Chapter 2 introduces you to the theory behind the Striving Styles and the key elements of how they function. It also provides a brief description of each of the eight Styles and their predominant need. It shows why it is so important for needs to be satisfied and what happens when they are not.

Chapter 3 gives an overview of the anatomy of the four quadrants of the brain and the Striving Styles Squad, and how they work together. This chapter explains how the quadrants function so that you begin to understand the mechanics of your mind. In addition to providing information about the quadrants of the brain, the chapter lists the activities that each quadrant is most efficient and least efficient at performing.

Chapter 4 discusses how the human brain develops. It also introduces Dr. Paul MacLean's triune brain theory and a very important component of the SSPS—the self-protective and self-actualizing systems of the brain. This chapter helps you understand how at birth, the brain is the most undifferentiated organ in the body, which means that it is still raw material waiting to be formed, molded, and developed during our childhood and adolescence. This perspective on brain development brings new awareness to the reasons for both growth-oriented, or self-actualizing, behaviors and defensive, or self-protective, behaviors. It also demonstrates how your brain's development can get stalled and why despite this you can continue to develop your brain no matter what your age.

Chapter 5 contains the Striving Styles Self-Assessment. Taking the assessment lets you discover your own Predominant Striving Style. This chapter gives instructions on how best to answer the questions to pinpoint your Style and what to do if your results don't match your idea of yourself. It also helps you narrow down what your three Associate Striving Styles might be.

Part 2: The Eight Striving Styles

The eight chapters in this section contain descriptions of each of the Striving Styles. As you will see, each style is represented as a character, and you will learn about its patterns of behavior in relationships, social activities, and communication. Each chapter highlights how each individual Style gets its predominant need satisfied and what happens if it is not. You will learn about each Style's blind spots and what each can do to make sure they are using self-actualizing behaviors rather than self-protective ones.

Part 3: Becoming Your Best Self

Part 3 is the working, practical section of the book. It includes the SSPS Roadmap for Development, a comprehensive, step-by-step approach to achieving your potential based on your Predominant Striving Style. Full of exercises for you to complete, this part of the book gives you all the tools you need to understand your brain, chart a course for your development, and move to action.

Chapter 14 lets you immerse yourself in learning about your Predominant Striving Style and helps you figure out how often you get your predominant need met. It has a series of charts for you to fill in, which will help you reflect on your current state as well as determine which activities you can use to help you strengthen your Self-Actualizing System.

Chapter 15 takes you to the next step in the process and includes the Who Are You Meant to Be Planner. The planner leads you through the process of brainstorming your desired future state by identifying both the fears that will block your progress and the action steps required to achieve your potential. It also includes specific habits to incorporate to support your success as you move to action.

You Don't Have to Leave Your Future to Chance

The unexamined life is not worth living.

—Socrates

Who Are You Meant to Be? reveals an entirely new way of understanding human behavior and, most significantly, a way to help us realize our own potential to live a happy, fulfilled life by breaking free of behaviors that limit our growth. It provides insight into how we can use our natural abilities and inclinations to achieve what we were born for. It also invites us to get our hands a little dirty by becoming a mechanic of our own brain, learning how to fine-tune it for optimal performance. It teaches us to recognize and redirect powerful instinctive and emotional energies into constructive actions, which will help us shift gears from just surviving to becoming who we are meant to be.

This book emphasizes that the key to lasting change lies in self-awareness, which gives us the ability to make conscious choices about our behavior and how we react to the behavior of others— and the book also shows readers how to take these critical steps toward self-actualization. As the SSPS reveals, when we are able to acknowledge our internal motivation and then consciously engage our whole brain to move us to action, we feel in line with our best selves: we are becoming who we are meant to be.

We would like to give thanks to all of the people who have influenced the writing of this book, whose needs, behavior, and openness to following our advice and coaching have led us to deeper levels of understanding how the functioning of the brain affects whether we become who we are meant to be. In particular, we are grateful to our husbands, children, family, and close friends who have lived with us in our personal petri dish as we developed the Striving Styles. They gave us real-life experiences to experiment with and learn from, because we don't just write and talk about our subject; we live it.

As our experiences shape and develop the structure of our brains, we altered our brains during the development of the Striving Styles. We brought the Styles to life through envisioning and imagining; structuring and building the system; sharing our emotional experiences and witnessing each other's; and experiencing the moment of completion with a combination of joy, relief, and excitement. We hope that our story inspires you to step out of your comfort zone and take the challenge to live your own life as authentically as possible.

PART I
WHO ARE YOU MEANT TO BE?

Resolve to be thyself: and know that he who finds himself, loses his misery.

—*Matthew Arnold*

RESEARCH SHOWS THAT GREATER self-awareness leads to increased fulfillment in life, and that this journey happens by looking inside of us. Unless we have first done the inner work, getting to know our inner landscape, we end up wandering through life forever in search of ourselves. In Western society, we are encouraged to look outside of ourselves for affirmation and approval. We then judge ourselves on the basis of these external standards or measures of success, good behavior, and societal values. We build an idea or image of who we are over time and constantly evaluate whether we are good or bad according to these mental constructs. We feel the need to protect ourselves, and we see ourselves as limited human beings who are merely surviving.

Part 1 of *Who Are You Meant to Be?* explores the reasons we tend to go searching for ourselves in all the wrong places rather than setting our own course to become our best selves. It provides insight into how both society and our brain development contribute to our living on autopilot without really understanding the mechanics of our mind.

The Striving Styles Personality System sheds light on how our brains work, marrying approaches from psychology with brain anatomy and physiology. Until recently, the brain has been ignored when it came to studying psychology, and our psyche has been treated as a mysterious terrain needing to be explored in the privacy of a therapist's office and without reference to its functionality, composition, or purpose. Part 1 makes the brain and emotions less mysterious by providing a clear picture of how our emotions and needs affect our behavior. It explains how the brain is organized, how it develops, and what it needs to develop and perform optimally. This part teaches the basic mechanics of the mind, the functional areas of the human brain, and how each of the Striving Styles is most likely to behave to a model for becoming who you are meant to be.

Chapter One
THE WAY WE LIVE

Once the soul awakens, the search begins and you can never go back. From then on, you are inflamed with a special longing that will never again let you linger in the lowlands of complacency and partial fulfillment. The eternal makes you urgent. You are loath to let compromise or the threat of danger hold you back from striving toward the summit of fulfillment.

— *John O'Donohue,* Anam Cara: A Book of Celtic Wisdom

THINK OF A TIME when you truly felt connected to yourself. You knew what you were aiming for, knew you were on target, knew what you needed, and had a plan to get it. All the while, you were brimming with passion about the whole enterprise. You were fully engaged, working with strong determination and purposefulness. You were infused with a feeling of well-being and power. If you've ever experienced this feeling, even for a short time, you have a sense of what it means to live authentically as who you are meant to be. It's a wonderful feeling—like driving a finely tuned race car on a smooth track with the finish line clearly in your sights. But for most of us, the better-fitting analogy is white knuckling the wheel of a sputtering old jalopy, hanging on for dear life as we bounce over an endless series of potholes toward an uncertain destination.

Too often, we try to figure out what we are meant to be (good mother, loving husband, dutiful son) or what we are meant to do (scientist, teacher, engineer) without really knowing who we are. In other words, we get in the car and drive with only a vague notion of where we are going or why. We seem to define ourselves and live our lives from the outside in, looking outside for answers to questions that can only be answered from within. This approach leads to a lack of self-knowledge and self-awareness and is one of the reasons that so many of us suffer from anxiety, depression, addictions, and other problems. And even if we see our lives as moving along fairly well (maybe not like a high-performance race car, but not like a bucket of bolts either), imagine the benefit we could enjoy if we had an "owner's manual" that could show us how to prevent some of our most frustrating situations and how to stay tuned up and running more smoothly. Imagine that there was a Roadmap to help you emerge as the person you are meant to be. Well, here it is!

Who Are You Meant to Be? is for everyone who wants to thrive—to step up and face the challenges of living life authentically, feeling the power that comes from living unafraid to be themselves. However, doing so doesn't mean that we have to drop out of society. The Striving Styles help us understand what it means to live our life authentically and thrive as a result. This book can be of benefit to everyone. It helped a nine-year-old girl learn at school rather than being labeled "unfocused" and "rebellious"; it helped the couple who stopped fighting and blaming each other for their unhappiness and started working together to create a more loving relationship; it helped the employee who stopped complaining about work and asked for a transfer when he realized that his job was not meeting his needs; and it helped the leader who was no longer afraid to hold his employees accountable and stopped hiding out in his office. It has the potential to help every one of us who has ever felt empty, has been afraid to show who we are, has been dissatisfied with a career or relationship, or has been simply living anything less than our potential.

Life on Autopilot

> There is only one success: to be able to spend your life in your own
> way, and not to give others absurd maddening claims upon it.
>   —*Christopher Morley,* Where the Blue Begins

With all the advances that have been made in understanding the
human brain, and the hundreds of volumes that have been written
on the ins and outs of personality, emotions, and behavior, how can
it be that most of us know more about the basic features of our
televisions or computers than we do about our own thoughts and
feelings? A quick scan of the self-help section of any bookstore
confirms it: we have more information at our fingertips on how to
create the life we are meant to live than we could ever read in a lifetime. We read the information—some of us obsessively—yet few of
us actually use it to make significant changes in our lives. Ironic, isn't
it, that in a culture so attached to the success of the individual, we
walk right past the opportunity to get into the race car and instead
climb behind the wheel of the jalopy again and again, going down
the same dead ends and making the same wrong turns?

Often, we don't even know there's a problem. If we don't love
our jobs, if we feel stifled in a relationship, if we get impatient with
those we love, or if we just have a restlessness we can't quite define,
we may write it off as "normal." But the truth is that most of us
don't understand our own needs, feelings, and habits of mind very
well, so we sabotage ourselves by living life at less than full throttle.
Over time, we may accept this compromised situation as living,
when, unknown to us, all we are really doing is surviving.

When we feel insecure or indecisive, we don't seem to have the
skills and capacity to look inward for answers, or we are too afraid
or embarrassed to seek help. We often end up with some degree
of persistent, unfocused anxiety about ourselves. We keep pushing

ourselves to do more and have more or are in pursuit of a perfect state of being that always seems to elude us. We live our lives on autopilot doing what is expected of us because we are too afraid we will disappoint or upset others should we reveal our human qualities or perceived limitations.

Take Suzanne as an example.

Suzanne is a working mother who spends whatever free time she has with her three young children. She has regular evening and bedtime routines with the kids because she read that this was important to their development. She has little time with her husband and even less to spend on herself.

Although she had never been much of a crafter, she felt pressured to accept a request by her youngest child's teacher to plan and set up a large bulletin board display for Halloween. Despite not having the time or inclination to do this, she didn't feel that she could say no. Suzanne felt increasingly panicked and resentful as Halloween drew closer. During the entire week before she delivered the bulletin board, she lost her patience with the kids and toiled away on the project as her husband made dinner and carried out the pre-bedtime rituals without her. In spite of being an early-to-bed sort of person, she stayed up well past midnight on the final night to finish. When she saw the final product, all she could think of was how someone else could have done it better.

Like Suzanne, we can get so caught up trying to do what others expect of us that we become a "human doing," stretching ourselves so thin that we end up running on empty. We make decisions that are inconsistent with our own values, and we forget that we have a self to take care of. We don't always think of the consequences of this, and if we do, those thoughts probably come in the form of negative self-talk. For example, "Why did I say that I would help Ted move? I am so stupid. My wife is going to be so angry with me. I keep doing the same thing over and over again. When am I ever going to learn? I am hopeless." This type of self-talk only serves to make us feel defeated as we go from activity to activity, without awareness of the price we pay when we are just surviving our day-to-day lives.

Why do we stretch ourselves beyond all reasonable limitations or repeatedly fail to say what we really want? Simply put, we do it out of fear for the way it will make us or someone else feel. We let our fear define and decide what experiences we will have and what we will say, because we are afraid of stirring up emotions in others or ourselves. We don't want to risk causing those whose love and approval we desire to feel disappointment, frustration, or anger when we fail to meet their expectations. We are also afraid of the feelings we might have—such as anxiety, embarrassment, or shame—when we don't measure up to our own expectations. We adapt excessively, looking outside of ourselves to let us know who we should be and how we should act.

Looking Outside of Ourselves for the Answers

You can succeed if nobody else believes it, but you will never succeed if you don't believe in yourself.

—*William J. H. Boetcker*

Looking outside of ourselves to get to know who we are or who we should be doesn't make sense. It's like looking through an open window when what we really need is a mirror. When we depend on others' approval to determine what we will do with our lives, we live in a narrow, distorted version of ourselves. The same thing happens when we compare ourselves to others. We don't realize how much we weaken our self-esteem by making these comparisons, as they tend to make our own perceived shortcomings appear even worse. Whenever we look outside for acceptance and approval, we move further away from our true nature and become more and more dependent on others to validate us. Asking others who they think we are meant to be is like calling out through the open window, saying, "I'm searching for myself. Have you seen me anywhere?"

Too often, the way we come to realize that we aren't traveling on our own path or we are failing to meet our potential is that we finally get tired of listening to ourselves complain and we start doing something about our situation. We might also wake up to the fact that we've been waiting for something or someone else to change, believing that this will allow us to have the life we really want. Some of us hit a life crisis, such as a divorce, children leaving home, or losing a job we hated anyway, before we take stock of ourselves and how much we have denied ourselves in order to feel safe and accepted by others. "I should have gone back to school," "I don't know why it took me so long to leave that man," or in Suzanne's case, "Why can't I ever just say no?" These are common statements from people who are stuck on the bumpy back roads of life, unable to find the route to the true home within themselves. Regrets abound when these people reach their later years and recognize that they have been too afraid to do anything other than what was expected of them. Even when they do get in touch with what they want to do to fulfill their potential, they may still sabotage themselves by believing that they are too old or that it's too late!

Bonnie Ware has written a book called *The Top Five Regrets of the Dying*. This book is significant, as it shows how people feel when they don't live their lives as the person they were meant to be. People are not born to regret not having really lived their lives authentically, yet many do just that. Unfortunately, it's often not until later in life that they realize they have lived the life others expected them to because they didn't have the courage to live a life true to themselves. They look at their wasted potential, all of the things that they failed to do, and the dreams they didn't make come true because of their choices. People also regret working so hard to avoid conflict with others and wish they'd had the courage to express their emotions. They regret not letting themselves be happier because they wouldn't believe, or they never learned that happiness is a choice. Instead, they got stuck using automatic negative patterns of thinking and habits of mind. Living in fear, they survived by pretending to others, and to their selves, that they were okay. They lived their life on automatic pilot, adapting instead of thriving.

Whether we realize it or not, fear is the greatest barrier to achieving our potential. Fear is aroused when we feel threatened, whether the threat is real or imagined, and it is a nervous system response to some stimulus. It doesn't matter whether we care to admit our fear, fear is a response designed to let us know when something will take us out of our physical or emotional safety zone. We are hardwired to survive, and fear is the early warning system that our survival (physical or psychological) is being threatened. For example, how often has something like this happened to you?

Mike's boss asked him to come to her office. He immediately felt his stomach clench, as his mind wildly raced over everything he might have done wrong or failed to deliver on time. By the time he got to her office, his breath was shallow and his palms were sweating. He stood nervously waiting to be told the inevitable bad news. The boss invited Mike to sit down, and said she wanted to ask him whether he was interested in working on a special project with her that required his particular skill set. Without asking—or even thinking—about project specifics or his own interests and needs, Mike said yes simply because he was enormously relieved that he wasn't in trouble.

When we live life in survival mode, depending on others to like and approve of us in order to feel okay about ourselves, we are poised to react from fear, catastrophizing about worst-case scenarios, rather than from the confident core of who we really are—our authentic self. But most of the time, we don't know that we are just surviving. We live life on automatic pilot, never questioning events such as the one in Mike's example. We think these situations are normal because everyone else seems to experience them; however, this is not the case. We can lift ourselves above the fear and actually thrive in our life.

Growing up in a society that encourages us to not need anyone, we try really hard to pretend that we don't, despite that need being an authentic human quality. In fact, we learn that not needing anybody is an admirable quality. We take pride in being insensitive toward ourselves and others, working hard to not let on that we feel anything. Should we be upset or need sympathy or reassurance, we call ourselves "needy" and scold ourselves. Here's an example of how this shows up in daily life.

Selma was communicating sympathy to her son-in-law, Percy, following the loss of his father. Percy had always been close to his dad, and Selma knew how difficult the loss of his father must be for Percy. Much to Selma's surprise, he replied, "It's fine. He had a good run." Selma was appalled at Percy's insensitivity and lack of emotion. During the following months, he gained thirty-five pounds and sunk into a depression, which he worked hard to cover up with false joviality and a lot of good wine.

Percy was not connected to himself; instead, he was behaving the way he thought others expected him to behave. In his mind, he was being rational and strong, cutting himself off from expressing his emotions. It took him several months of therapy to start to glimpse the need to express himself authentically, and to release the pain he had buried for most of his life.

Learning to Survive

You are not responsible for the programming you picked up in childhood. However, as an adult, you are one hundred percent responsible for fixing it.

—*Ken Keyes Jr.*

It has taken thousands of years for us to evolve to our present industrialized cultures, in which we typically don't have to devote all of our energy to the basic life-or-death tasks of finding food and shelter. Our brain and nervous system, however, still have these built-in survival instincts to ensure our physical and psychological survival. This means that we emerge from the womb prewired to battle for our *physical* survival. Infants and young children are driven by internal cues that trigger emotional responses designed to get their needs met. A baby's experience is something like this: "I am hungry, so I cry. If you don't come fast enough, my crying will be infused with fear and rage. If I am content, I will wriggle with pleasure." The internal world of the infant and small child is where the action is. They are all about their experiences and emotions. Caretakers are just objects to satisfy their needs.

Our psychological appetites and needs demand satisfaction as well, and as infants and young children, we go through this same process of seeking to ensure these needs get met. Babies and young children cry when they are afraid or when they need connection, touch, or comfort for any other reason. If their needs are consistently met during childhood and their early bonding experiences are loving, nurturing, and without disruption, they form a secure attachment to their primary caregiver. With this solid bond established, it is much easier for them to learn that they don't have to constantly worry about getting their needs met. The same is true for us as adults: if we are secure and confident that our basic needs are being met in a consistent way, we don't feel pressure to adapt our personalities to fit into a prescribed societal role so that people will like us, accept us, and make us feel good about ourselves. Instead, we set out to become who we are meant to be.

If a caregiver doesn't attend to a child's needs consistently, the child doesn't build a strong bond of trust with the caregiver, and the child's sense of security does not develop normally. The child forms an insecure attachment to his caregiver and doesn't feel safe in the environment. The child is stuck in its instinctual survival mode. Such children become adults who are ever cautious of the perceived and imagined threats to their psychological well-being. They become hypervigilant, looking outside of themselves for cues about whether they are okay. They get locked into a system where they survive by adapting to what is expected of them or using their emotions to keep them safe—like the time when you were three and your overzealous Aunt Betty's attempt to give you a hug sent you running from the room screaming. Some of us have discovered the hard way that the tactics we used to feel safe at the age of three just don't work as well once we are old enough to tie our own shoes and pay income taxes.

When we live in survival mode instead of looking inside of ourselves for cues and clues about who we are meant to be and what we desire, we look outward to see what we *should* have, how we *should* behave; in other words, we try to be like others so that we feel safe. Or we look for things that might explain why we feel anxious and dissatisfied with our lives, our work, or our relationships, blaming ourselves and being obsessed with finding out what's wrong with us. We compare ourselves to others instead of accepting and getting to know who we are and what gives us pleasure. We may abandon bold and courageous aspirations we once held ("I want to quit my job and work for the Peace Corps") and start obsessing about desires that are born of fear ("I want to get a nose job so people won't stare at me anymore"). We can never accept and live from our authentic self when we are constantly looking out the window, a vantage point that never lets us see what's in the mirror. Unknown to us, we are using emotional reasoning rather than logic. Is it really logical to get a nose job because you don't have the courage to quit your job? Of course not. But there's no limit to how creative we can be when we are rationalizing our emotional decisions.

Development—From Emotion to Reason

Feelings or emotions are the universal language and are to be honored. They are the authentic expression of who you are at your deepest place.

—*Judith Wright*

We don't have to think too much about how any of the organs of our body develop, because for the most part, we are born with them ready to function In the same way, many people believe that our brains will grow on a preset course as we age and that it really doesn't matter what we do, think, or experience. We think that our brain and emotions are sort of like fruit: with age, they naturally mature. Most people also believe that, with a few exceptions, everyone's brain is the same, humming along on its track like a well-oiled locomotive, passing predictable milestones along the way—I call the process the Brain Train to Adulthood. It goes something like this:

Observe the stop called Three Years Old, where you are too old to wet your bed or want to sleep with your mother. Then move along to stop Six Years Old, where you should master reading and writing. All aboard! At Eight, enter Big-Girl-and-Boy-Ville—no more temper tantrums or crying over hurt feelings! At Thirteen, drop off all childish baggage such as playing with dolls or hugging your parents in public. At Eighteen, please select the college major that will determine what you do with the rest of your life, then proceed at full speed to Twenty-One, where you debark from Childhood and are handed your transfer ticket to Full-Fledged Adulthood. Now get off the train and, whether you are ready or not, pick a life partner, get in your jalopy, and fasten your seat belt. It's definitely going to be a bumpy ride!

If you don't follow this route as you grow up, your parents and other adults might call you "immature," "lazy," or even "stupid." They may say things like, "Why can't you be more like Janie? She doesn't go crying to her mother every time she hurts herself!" Parents can shame or guilt children for not staying on track with school or career choices. In a family therapy session I had a number of years ago, a mother said to her seventeen-year-old son, "You've always been such a good student. I don't know what's wrong with you that you want to take a year off to decide what you want to do in college. You are going to end up a lazy bum like your Uncle Ted." The son didn't know what he wanted to do and didn't want to waste his and his parents' money. He was being rational but his parents were on autopilot, afraid that if he didn't stay on track he wouldn't survive. In their minds, you don't get off the train before you finish high school and go to college. If you do, there is something seriously wrong with you—end of story.

Our brains actually develop through experience, stimulation, and engagement. When we are allowed to explore, interact with, and master activities in an environment of consistency, predictability, and loving parenting, we arrive in adulthood ready to work at becoming who we are meant to be. However, our development can just as easily take a detour in its trajectory and become temporarily (or permanently) stunted, so that instead we arrive in adulthood in search of ourselves or trying to be what others want us to be. We go to a certain college because our friends are going there or our parents want us to. Or we don't go to college because we don't know what we want to do or don't really want to work that hard. Having limited life experiences because of overprotective parents causes some young adults to take whatever job or relationship keeps them close to home, so that they don't have to leave their comfort zone. Before they know it, they're stuck in Rutsville, just getting by day to day, unfulfilled but safe.

While we all need to adapt to the society we live in, the brain develops best when we aren't forced to conform excessively, as this leads to a perpetual state of discontent with ourselves. We end up never feeling that we are fully measuring up to all the "shoulds," "musts," and "ought-tos" that we have learned to believe will make us a "good" or "nice" person. Playing it safe rather than living our lives to the fullest, we use our precious energy to obsess about what is wrong with us, to seek help for our perceived shortcomings, or to pretend that we don't feel as empty as we do. This leaves us perpetually searching outside of ourselves to fill the emptiness we feel inside.

Instead of mining the vast treasures that are waiting in our more evolved brain centers, we continue with primitive behaviors such as "hunting and gathering," because this is what we know how to do. We go to shopping malls to hunt and gather the biggest, the best, and the latest goods available. We want to know what our neighbors have, so we gather information from TV, the Internet, newspapers, and those mobile devices that we can't seem to do without. We gather friends on Facebook; we gather DVDs for our home library; we gather experiences and credentials for our résumés (the more the better); we hunt for bargains, for love, for the perfect body and the perfect mate. These instinctual and emotional impulses find their outlets in overeating, overworking, overconsumption of alcohol, and compulsive gambling, among other problems. Of course, none of these behaviors brings us closer to understanding our true selves and our deep needs. In fact, studies show that the more affluent a society becomes, the unhappier its people.

Living life on autopilot takes us off our own path and moves us to one that someone else predetermined for us. However, it is possible for us to get back on track, beginning by taking stock of our needs and emotions. Without experiencing and using our emotions effectively, we have no fuel to engage in our lives and to stay on our own path when life becomes difficult. Getting to know our emotions, the role they play in our lives, and how we can best use them can prevent us from getting hijacked while on the road to who we are meant to be.

Emotions Drive Behavior

Emotions operate on many levels. They have a physical aspect as well as a psychological aspect. Emotions bridge thought, feeling, and action—they operate in every part of a person, they affect many aspects of a person, and the person affects many aspects of the emotions.

—*John D. (Jack) Mayer*

Our emotions alert us to how we experience what is happening and how we feel about how things are going in our lives. Emotions influence what happens in our brain and motivate us to behave and act in certain ways. Additionally, they affect our physical body as much as they do our thinking and feeling. When we repress, ignore, deny, vent, or act out our emotions, it has a negative impact on both our mind and our body. We don't always understand why we feel the way we do because we haven't taken the time to process our emotions. Like food we can't digest, unprocessed emotions get stored, compartmentalized, or simply rejected, rather than being life-enhancing sources of information and understanding about ourselves and the world around us. Either their energy stays with us or we release it indirectly through our behavior and our life choices. Unknowingly, we set off a chain of chemical reactions in the body that lead to chronic states of depression, anxiety, and discontent.

Biologically, our emotions arise because of our interactions with the world. Unless you live alone in a remote cave, someone, at some time, is going to upset you. (And even a cave-dwelling hermit can be vexed occasionally—for example, by a hungry tiger!) Your partner, child, coworker, or boss is going to do something that provokes anger, fear, sadness, or any of the full range of other so-called negative emotions. When we pay attention to our emotions, especially the more difficult ones such as anger, anxiety, and helplessness, we have a great opportunity to look at ourselves and realize what is causing us to feel the way we do. Then, with increased self-awareness, we can respond to the situation authentically, working through the challenges that may have led to the negative emotional state in the first place.

However, in the quick-fix culture we live in, we look for the fastest way to stop the feelings; we act out our emotions; or we lose ourselves in emotionally engaging characters in books, on TV, and at the theater. We often choose to repress or displace our feelings rather than really investigate them, because we see emotions as problems rather than authentic expressions of our experiences.

For example, imagine that your household finances are tight and your partner decides to splurge on an expensive luxury item, which makes you feel angry. You can respond to this emotion in several ways. You could express it: "I feel angry because you spent that money on a luxury we can't afford." You could act out the emotion by shouting, locking your partner out of the house, or buying something even more outrageously extravagant, such as a Tilt-A-Whirl amusement ride for your front lawn. Or you could deny the emotion, telling yourself that mature people don't allow themselves to get angry, or that because anger is a harmful emotion, you'd rather not feel it. If you choose any of these methods of dealing with your anger and you still feel upset, you might go on to compound your bad feelings by scolding yourself for having them. But emotions exist no matter how much we deny them or their effect on us.

We don't realize that most of the time we are motivated by our feelings, not our thoughts. I know we like to think that as grown-ups we are completely rational beings, but how does that account for our flipping off the driver who makes us angry? How does it square with being rude to the cashier when we're in a hurry and she has to change the tape in her register? Or when we know we need to do the laundry but instead lie down on the couch and enjoy a few movies with that tub of rocky road ice cream? We like to do what gives us pleasurable feelings. We also do things to avoid pain. This doesn't mean that we are going to be happy with ourselves—quite the opposite, in fact. We find ourselves perplexed when, rather than doing what we said we would (e.g., going to the gym, balancing the checkbook), we choose more self-indulgent or self-destructive behaviors.

Suzanne, from our earlier example, knows that she's not artistic, that she needs to be with her children, and that her time is very limited. Yet she agrees to a project that requires artistic ability, takes her away from her children, and uses time she can't spare. In an attempt to protect herself from the disapproval of others, Suzanne acts from her feelings. She opts to protect herself, reacting to her primitive instincts and impulses that say there is danger in failing to please everyone. Suzanne (and many of us) will end up having the same frustrating experiences again and again, feeling helpless to do anything about it. We live so much of our lives trying to protect ourselves from the emotional discomfort that we feel when we don't live up to our own or others' expectations. We try to avoid feeling embarrassed or guilty when we can't do it all, and we try to be what others want so they never get upset, angry, or disappointed with us. We end up trying to bypass emotional land mines on the landscape of our lives for fear of something blowing up.

When was the last time you let feelings stop you from doing or saying something? Think about it, because it happens all the time whether you are aware of it. It's possible that you don't register feeling afraid or you don't want to admit when you feel this way. Instead, you probably tell yourself you don't feel like doing an activity, or that people who do such things are crazy, stupid, or irresponsible. Many of us don't want to admit how often we let fear define our lives. It can be something as simple as "I didn't go to the movies with my friend last night because I was afraid I'd be tired today," or something more significant, like "I didn't apply for the position at work, even though I desperately want the job, because I was afraid I wouldn't get it." We rationalize and talk ourselves out of doing what we want to do or trying something different because it will make us feel uncomfortable. We let our fear govern our choices and how we live our lives. This means that we know what we want and know our potential but are afraid to take a risk. Some people fear that others will judge or envy them, and so they don't try. Others are afraid of "living large," so instead they just overeat and become physically large, underachieving and devaluing themselves, going along for the ride in life, and using fear to keep them in their "safe place."

Although fear and anxiety are emotions that can impede living life to the fullest, the thing we seem most afraid of is thinking that we are "crazy," that we have problems with the functioning of our emotions. This fear causes some of us to press the mute button on our feelings with a few glasses of wine a day, a shopping spree that gives us something "real" to feel anxious about because of how much money we spent, or a fight with a loved one so that we can "dump our emotional bucket." Temporary relief? Yes. But the problem in our heads is still there the next day!

Our Problems Are All in Our Heads!

Feelings are not supposed to be logical.
Dangerous is the man who has rationalized his emotions.

—*David Borenstein*

People dread hearing that their problems are "all in their head." After all, this is just another way of saying that problems are a result of the brain not functioning optimally. Emotional and relationship problems, lack of motivation, depression and anxiety disorders, inability to focus, poor impulse control, addictions—they all originate in the brain and are usually the result of obstructed development. When we don't take the time to know and understand how our brain, mind, and emotions work, we remain vulnerable to the emotional distress that arises from living on autopilot.

When clients come to me for the first time, many say, "So, Doc.

Am I crazy? I think my problem is all in my head and I shouldn't even be here. It's stupid." They are often anxious and ashamed because they believe they are doing something wrong or that they should be able to control or stop how they feel. I always tell them, "Yes, it's all in your head. Emotional problems stem from the brain." Clearly, if it were their liver, they wouldn't come to see me. We want to believe we can "cure" our emotional problems without letting anyone know about them, yet if it were the pancreas we were having trouble with, no one would suggest that we just put on a happy face, get over it, and move on with our life. Many receive this advice (sometimes even from health professionals) regarding difficulties that originate in our most complex organ: the brain.

When people come to therapy or for coaching, it usually isn't because they want to get to know themselves; they come to try to fix what is wrong with them or simply to rid themselves of unpleasant feelings. Turning away from the mirror, they want to stay at the window, applying some cosmetics and disguises to give those outside a nicer view. Many believe that looking deeply at our own emotions is self-indulgent and a waste of time at best and a terrifying prospect at worst. Psychological theories of emotions and personality are often seen as "pseudoscience," and our fear that there is something "wrong" with us inhibits us from exploring this unknown territory. It's all too easy to see our emotions as a Pandora's box that is better left closed. The truth is that we could be diverting this fearful energy to the constructive act of getting to know more about ourselves.

It's time to change the way we think about our emotions, to make sure we develop our brains as nature intended, and to become who we are meant to be. Emotions are a part of our experience as humans. They are biochemical events that occur in the brain in response to a stimulus, causing a series of reactions throughout our body. We feel our way through life, either through our senses or through our emotions. Yet in our society, we remain squeamish and uncomfortable about discussing our emotions. We then pass this discomfort on to our children. And with the types of things we say to children about their emotions, is it any wonder they grow up confused about what they are feeling? For example, "What do you mean you're afraid of going upstairs alone? Don't be stupid. There is nothing to be afraid of." "What are you crying for? For heaven's sake, stop being so sensitive about everything." "You should be able to control your temper, young lady. How many times do I have to tell you that it's not nice to get angry at people?" Or "Don't say you hate your sister because she kicked you. You bad boy! Apologize to her right now and tell her you love her." These are all examples of how parents influence children's experience of their emotions.

Ignoring or manipulating emotions leads only to greater mental distress and dysfunction. Ironically, today there is more information available about how to deal with problems related to emotions than ever before. In order to take care of our emotional health, we have to meet the problems head on, taking responsibility for the smooth and efficient functioning of our miraculous brains!

Our Brain (Mental Health) Is Our Responsibility

Whatever any man does he first must do in his mind, whose machinery is the brain. The mind can do only what the brain is equipped to do, and so man must find out what kind of brain he has before he can understand his own behavior.

—*Gay Gaer Luce and Julius Segal (from* Sleep, *1966)*

Many of us don't consider our mental health to be our responsibility, or even as something we can influence. Even when we do, the stigma of mental health problems can be a powerful disincentive for people seeking help. According to a 2010 report by the Substance Abuse and Mental Health Services Administration (SAMHSA), the majority of Americans who experience some form of mental disorder do not seek professional help. The SAMHSA report states that while one in five American adults (45.9 million) experienced some form of mental illness in 2010, only about 39 percent of these individuals received some form of treatment. Among those who do access treatment, most turn to prescription drugs to try to eliminate the symptoms rather than look for the cause of their mental illness.

Statistics also indicate that there is a dramatic rise in the rate of depression and anxiety among young people in America. Today, high school and college students are five to eight times more likely to meet the criteria for diagnosis of major depression and/or an anxiety disorder than students were a half a century or more ago. Fear continues to stop people from reaching out and getting the help they need. In fact, statistics also show that the number of people who opt to commit suicide rather than get help is on the rise. That's because most of us grow up without a realistic understanding of mental illness—not knowing how normal and natural it is to experience emotional distress or that seeking professional help is the wise choice in the same way as going to a doctor for an irritable bowel.

Repressing emotions or pretending they don't exist is like having an eccentric relative living in our basement. We find her outrageous and amusing but embarrassing, and we don't want to talk about her or let anyone else know she's there. The more we pretend she's not there, the more energy we expend hiding her and devising stories about why people can't come over. Because she's not allowed in our lives, she's gets more outrageous and demanding, yet we still pretend she doesn't exist because we're afraid of what people will think about us if they meet her or know she's there. What we really need to do is bring her upstairs, give her a room in the house, and bring her into our life.

As you can see, our conditioned beliefs and the way we relate to our emotions and mental health are a primary impediment to our development because they keep us in survival mode. Until now, there has been no systematic approach to creating mental health that could be used to help people understand the mechanics of their mind, their needs, and their emotions. In the next chapter, we introduce the Striving Styles Personality System and examine how psychological needs have to be satisfied in order for us to develop our brains and escape from survival mode.

CHAPTER TWO
STRIVING STYLES
PERSONALITY SYSTEM

I am here for a purpose and that purpose is to grow into a mountain, not to shrink to a grain of sand. Henceforth will I apply all my efforts to become the highest mountain of all and I will strain my potential until it cries for mercy.

—*Og Mandino*

THE STRIVING STYLES PERSONALITY SYSTEM (SSPS) is a neuropsychological approach to understanding the mechanics of the mind. It is a comprehensive "user manual" for people. It shows how our brain is organized, how our needs and emotions influence our behavior, and how we can strengthen our authentic self to become who we are meant to be. It provides an approach to development based on the satisfaction of psychological needs.

What Are Striving Styles?

Our personality has a style that includes the way we think and process information, our attitudes, the way we express our feelings, our needs and strivings, our behavior and actions, and our manner of interacting with others. Our Striving Style is expressed in a predictable and dynamic fashion.

Based on neuroscience and a seamless integration of the work of leading theorists in the area of brain dominance and specialization, such as Carl Jung, Roger Sperry, Ned Hermann, and Katherine Benziger, to name a few, the SSPS provides a way for us to understand and integrate the functioning of our brain. Jung's work is particularly important to the development of the SSPS, as he was the first to capture the four functions of the brain into a theory of psychological type. He believed that people operate from different psychological frameworks and orientations that are identifiable through observation.

For the past century, Jung's psychological type theory has strongly influenced the way we understand mental functions and their roles in our personalities. Jung also believed that humans are driven by a need for individuation, which we can think of as a sense of wholeness or full understanding of ourselves. He saw emotions as agents that could cause us to act in psychologically healthy or unhealthy ways. His careful observations over the years resulted in significant advances in understanding and predicting behavior, particularly with respect to differences in people's ideas, responses, and actions.

We have built the SSPS on Jung's psychological type theory, incorporating recent developments in neuroscience that show that Jung's proposed mental functions correspond to the brain's physiology. Brain scanning technologies such as positron-emission tomography (PET) and magnetic resonance imaging (MRI) have connected Jung's theory with those of prominent brain scientists by showing that there is a specialized area of the brain for each of the eight Striving Styles.

The following is an overview of the key components of the Striving Styles. It sets out how the brain is organized to do the work it has to do in our personalities. It introduces the basic physiology of the brain and the functions that reside in the different brain areas. As well, this section introduces the Striving Styles, what they are called, and where they reside in the brain.

We have four quadrants in our brain. The brain has two hemispheres, each with a front and back section, for a total of four quadrants. The front of each hemisphere is called the prefrontal cortex, the most highly evolved part of the brain and the one that synthesizes experiences and information to try to make sense of them. The two back sections of each hemisphere have more neural connections to the limbic system or primitive brain, which is more involved with our emotions and pure sensations. Each quadrant has a specific function that it performs in our personality, which you will learn more about later in this chapter.

Each quadrant performs its function in the external and the internal world. Each brain quadrant or functional region is divided into two distinct areas of operation: one that focuses its efforts on the external world and the other that favors the internal world. Each of the eight functional areas is purposeful and has its own biological mandate that it must fulfill. We call each of these eight areas of brainpower or intelligence Striving Styles.

There are eight Striving Styles. Each Style performs specific tasks and behaves in predictable ways in our personality. We call them Striving Styles because each has an ability to help us to strive toward achieving our potential. However, each Striving Style has a distinct way of fulfilling its biological mandate; in other words, each has its own agenda. Each Style performs specific functions either in the outer world of activities and interactions with others or in our inner world of thoughts and feelings. We all have the energetic potential of all eight Striving Styles available to us, with all the natural talents, abilities, and patterns of behavior that go with them. However, some of the striving energies are more active than others are and will play a more dominant role in our personality.

Each Striving Style is represented by an archetype or avatar. These eight avatars are commonly recognized models of people, behaviors, or personalities that are easy to understand and apply to daily life. We consider each Style as complex and multidimensional as humans are, with motivations, needs, and patterns of behavioral and emotional responses. As we move through the Striving Styles and their corresponding avatars, we will undoubtedly find similarities to those near and dear (and perhaps not so dear) to us. More important, however, the Striving Styles presents a mirror in which we can get a good look at ourselves.

Eight Striving Styles

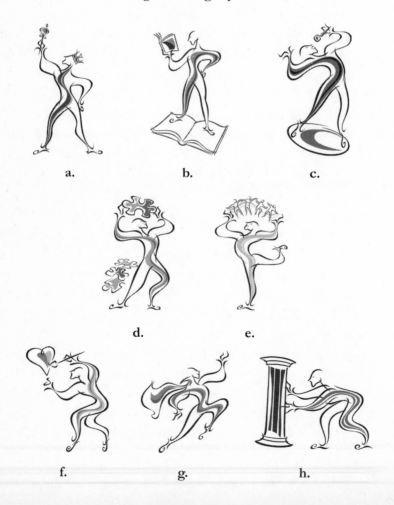

a.

b.

c.

d.

e.

f.

g.

h.

Striving Style	Predominant Need	Key Characteristics
Leader (a.)	To be in control	Analytical, driven, goal oriented, organized, takes initiative, seeks authority and order
Intellectual (b.)	To be knowledgeable	Information oriented, focused, independent, factual, seeks knowledge and competence
Performer (c.)	To be recognized	Enthusiastic, forward thinking, competitive, achievement oriented, seeks novelty and opportunities
Visionary (d.)	To be perceptive	Innovative, imaginative, esoteric, revolutionary, seeks global understanding and awareness
Socializer (e.)	To be connected	Sociable, outgoing, affable, sentimental, seeks personal and social success
Artist (f.)	To be creative	Authentic, self-critical, enigmatic, self-contained, seeks emotional intensity and originality

Striving Style	Predominant Need	Key Characteristics
Adventurer (g.)	To be spontaneous	Adventurous, impulsive, straightforward, risk taking, seeks sensation and pleasurable experiences
Stabilizer (h.)	To be secure	Mechanical, loyal, dutiful, authoritarian, seeks routine and stability

Each of the Striving Styles has a predominant need (biological mandate). There is a psychological need or appetite that motivates each of the Styles to behave in a certain way to satisfy that need, depending on which of the four quadrants of the brain the Style resides in. Like other human appetites, the need "hungers" for satisfaction and is distressed when that hunger is not satisfied. The quadrant of the brain in which the need resides determines how we will behave to get that need met. Each of us has a hierarchy of needs, with one of them being strongest. This is our predominant need. This need is nonnegotiable because it provides the foundation for our psychological balance and security. The more aware we are of our predominant need and how to meet it, the more consciously we can strive to get the need met.

Our other psychological needs are not essential in the same way our predominant one is, and they are therefore negotiable. We can get along without having them met and can put them aside as we pursue meeting our predominant need. They don't "make or break" us, as our predominant need has the potential to do if it is not met. And because the predominant is stronger and must be met, it tends to win over the others. For example, if your predominant need is to be recognized and you also have a need to be secure, you are more likely to follow your impulse to go to an event where there is the potential to get recognition than to stay home and garden so that you feel secure. You can delay or ignore gratifying the need to be secure as you seek the recognition that your predominant need craves.

We have one Striving Style that is the "alpha." We are hard-wired from birth to favor one of the Striving Styles over the others. We call this our Predominant Striving Style. It is the functional area of the brain that houses our predominant need, which must be met for us to develop and grow toward our potential. The Predominant Striving Style is the area of the brain that we naturally use the most, and that works the most efficiently. As discussed later in this chapter, it is estimated that the quadrant of the brain where our Predominant Style resides operates roughly one hundred times more efficiently than the other three quadrants do. It's easy to use our Predominant Style because it takes much less energy to operate than the other Styles do. We generally feel energized when we are using it, and we use it for long periods of time without feeling fatigued. Imagine how much energy you would waste if you spent your whole life trying to walk on your hands instead of using your feet. It's likely that you'd feel exhausted much of the time, you'd have trouble fitting in, and you'd wonder why everyone else seemed so different. This is what it's like when you are not living authentically according to your Predominant Style and your natural abilities.

The types of activities performed with your Predominant Style are very specific to the quadrant of the brain where the Style is located. That means that you will naturally excel at those activities and will learn new skills easily when they relate to that quadrant. This explains why some activities come easily to us and others don't. When you understand the nature of the quadrant of the brain where your Predominant Style resides, you can predict what activities are going to come most naturally and truly capitalize on those strengths and abilities.

Your Predominant Striving Style's psychological need must be satisfied in order for you to live in the most authentic, healthy, and growth-oriented way possible. Your natural striving to meet the need of your Predominant Style will be expressed in just about everything you do: if you are not having the need met directly, then its expression will take place indirectly through your behavior. In one way or another, it will make itself known.

You will find out your Predominant Style when you take the Striving Styles Self-Assessment in chapter 5.

We have access to three other Styles called Associate Styles. In addition to our Predominant Style, we have three Associate Styles, residing in the three other quadrants of the brain that take various roles in our personality. Associate Styles have different functions, talents, and abilities and complement the functioning of the Predominant Style (more about this in chapter 3). Use of the Associate Styles requires more energy because they don't have as many naturally occurring neural pathways as the Predominant Style has. However, with time and use, they become easier to access as you strengthen the connections from the Predominant Style and become more skilled in the behaviors that are most natural for the Associate Styles to perform.

Anatomically, two of the Associate Styles have direct physical contact with the Predominant Style, and these two Associates have neural connections that allow them to communicate directly with the Predominant Style. The fourth Style—the one that is diagonally opposite the Predominant one—has no direct connection to the Predominant Style and must communicate via the two Associates that reside next to the Predominant Style. This Associate Style often operates in opposition to or independent of the other Styles and is most difficult to access. You can get a clearer picture of the relationships among the Styles if you imagine four neighbors whose properties form a square.

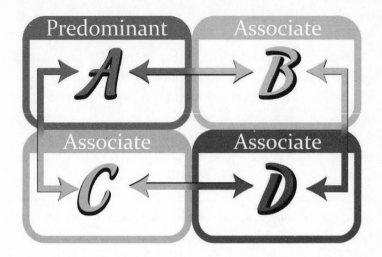

The picture above shows that the four neighbors (A, B, C, and D) have walls around their properties, but there are some gates that connect them. The gates allow Neighbor A to communicate easily with B and C, but not with D. If A and D want to communicate, they have to go through B or C. So if we now take the drawing to represent the four quadrants of the brain, and if we imagine that A is the Predominant Style, we can see how Associate Style D is the one that A will have to make the most effort to communicate with. And, just as it is with neighbors, we usually get chummy with the ones who share property lines with us, and we may even forget about the ones we seldom see. The picture can also be used to reinforce the idea that if your home were A, it would be a bit strange to spend most of your time in B or C (or especially D!); yet this is in essence what we do when we keep "living in" a Style that isn't our Predominant one.

Two of the four Styles are used in the outer world, while two function in our inner world. The Style located in the quadrant that is diagonal to the Predominant Style will function in the opposite direction; that is, if your Predominant Style is used in the outer world, the one diagonal to it will be used inwardly. This diagonal pairing means that one of them will reside in one of the rational brain quadrants and the other in one of the experiential-emotional brain quadrants. For example, if your Leader (outward focus) is your Predominant Style, your Artist (inward focus) will be on your Squad as the opposite; if your Predominant Style is the Stabilizer (inward focus), your Performer (outward focus) will be on your Squad as its opposite, and so on. These pairings are intended to work in a balancing fashion, in the same way other systems in our bodies do (for example, the autonomic nervous system, which comprises two systems; the sympathetic system, which stimulates and moves us to action; and the parasympathetic system, which is responsible for rest and relaxation). Each brain quadrant is paired in this manner, which means that your other two Associate Styles, located adjacent to your Predominant Style, will also be used in opposite directions to each other and will balance each other in terms of their functionality.

The Predominant and Associate Styles together are called the Striving Style Squad. The Predominant Style plus three Associate Styles make up what we call the Striving Style Squad. Becoming aware of the attributes and strengths of each of these Styles and using them all is like having the energy of four different "people" at our disposal. When we learn to use our Striving Style Squad in an integrated fashion, we achieve greater choice and flexibility in our interactions with others and the world.

If you have watched the TV show *Survivor*, you have an idea of how the members of the Squad work together. On the show, a group of strangers comes together and has to cooperate as a team in order to survive in a challenging physical environment with little but the shirts on their backs. Each individual has his or her own strengths, and typically one leader emerges early to hold it all together. Some members have great skills of physical strength, some possess mental ingenuity, some excel at caring and compassion, and some are best at practical survival skills. Each individual approaches the situation according to his or her natural strengths. They work together to ensure that their team functions, becomes cohesive, and can surmount each challenge. In this environment, as in our amazing brains, things go best when all the different energies work together, each contributing its natural talents and allowing the others to compensate for any weaknesses.

The remaining four Styles are called Auxiliary Styles. There are also four Striving Styles that will not be part of our Striving Style Squad. We call these Auxiliary Styles. These Styles will be used in the opposite orientation (external or internal) to those in our Squad relative to the brain quadrant they reside in. The needs of our Auxiliary Styles are less acute and therefore mostly out of our awareness. We tend to be aware of them only when we have to do something that requires their unique abilities, so it's important to understand the deficit that exists when you don't have them on your Squad. Attempting to access the energies and abilities of our Auxiliary Styles is difficult without focused effort, and tends to push us far out of our emotional comfort zone. Think of Lady Gaga taking a vow of silence, or Chef (Gordon) Ramsay being sensitive and empathetic, and you'll get an idea of the type of focused energy it requires.

Overusing our Predominant Style gets in the way of our development. Because our Predominant Style is where we experience the greatest comfort and ease of use, we tend to overuse it or to apply it in situations that don't naturally suit it. This limits our options and our ability to live our life fully. As the saying goes, "If the only tool you had was a hammer, you'd treat every problem as though it were a nail." Using all of your Styles gives you greater flexibility and versatility to deal with life's opportunities and challenges.

To become who we are meant to be, we need to learn how

to use our whole brain. In order to self-actualize and achieve our potential, we must learn to use our brain as a whole, with each quadrant and its corresponding Striving Style from our Squad contributing to our overall functioning. The four Styles that make up our Striving Style Squad are designed to be used together. One Style does not fit all situations, and when we try to use just one, we make ourselves one-dimensional. Each of the quadrants of the brain is balanced by the talents and abilities of one of the other corresponding quadrants, and each one has a specific role to play. By using all four striving energies found in our Striving Style Squad, we emerge as stronger, more capable human beings.

The SSPS also shows us how we can play to all of our strengths. Knowing our Predominant Striving Style and each member of our Squad enables us to consciously and enthusiastically gain self-awareness and build a foundation for solid psychological growth and development. Living from our whole brain, with our predominant need fulfilled, we can see life more optimistically and understand our purpose more clearly.

Why Focus on Our Needs?

You have to know what your highest priorities are and have the courage—pleasantly, smilingly, non-apologetically—to say "no" to other things. And the way to do that is by having a bigger "yes" burning inside.

—*Stephen Covey*

Our psychological needs are our highest priority after we have satisfied our physical ones. Although most of our psychological needs operate below the radar of our awareness and we don't talk much about them, they play a major role in our personality and behavior. Well-known theorists like Sigmund Freud, Carl Rogers, Karl Marx, and Abraham Maslow spent decades trying to understand how needs are related to humans' mental health and potential. Although their theories are different, they all agreed that human needs are the source of motivation for all behavior and social interaction. They believed that while some needs are temporary and changing, others are fundamental to our nature and even regulate emotional and psychological balance.

Psychological needs are a physical reality and are experienced in the same way other human appetites are. Take hunger, for example: we can't see or measure it, but we can sure feel it when it goes unsatisfied. Observe the emotional reactions that occur when the body is starved for a while. When we meet our needs, we are strong, confident, curious, living our lives in the pursuit of happiness. When our needs aren't met, we are more emotional and feel anxious, angry, or irritable. We try to have everything our way and get upset when we can't do so. We pick fights and blame others for our emotional distress. We live our lives in survival mode.

Our needs themselves aren't bad; they cause us to take action toward a goal, thereby giving purpose and direction to our behavior. Unfortunately, the word "need" has such a negative connotation that most people cringe at the idea of admitting they have them for fear they'll appear "needy." We are so determined as a society to be self-sufficient that admitting we have a need is like saying that we are deeply flawed. Apparently, we seem to believe that people who admit to their needs are weak, desperate, unstable, and undesirable, among other things.

It is actually quite the opposite. When we say, "I have a need to be recognized," we can put together a plan to do just that and organize activities that put us center stage. It doesn't make us vulnerable; it makes us strong and in charge of our life. And the best news is that we are more likely to get a need met when we know what it is and then do something about it.

What Happens When Our Needs Aren't Met?

Frustrated, because I can't tell if it's real.
Mad, because I don't know how you feel.
Upset, because we can't make this right.
Sad, because I need you day and night.
Angry, because you won't take my hand.
Aggravated, because you don't understand.
Disappointed, because we can't be together.
But I want you to know that I will love you forever.

—Unknown

Frustrated needs are the inspiration of the poets, songwriters, and authors of every generation. The poem above conveys the full range of emotions experienced by the author because his need to have the love of his woman has been thwarted. Much of the time we think that what we need is for someone else to change their behavior so that we can feel satisfied—"I need you to help more around the house" or "I need you to communicate more" instead of "I need to feel connected and love to do things with you—even chores," or "I need to understand what's going on and need more information." This is a direct result of looking outside of ourselves, blaming others when our needs are frustrated.

When we don't allow for or acknowledge our needs, we end up living in a frustrated, unfulfilled, and dissatisfied state. Frustrated needs create emotions, and emotions ignite our engines in an attempt to move us into tactics to get our needs met. Consider the young father with a need to be in control. He has a tendency to micro-manage his world, and everyone in it, to satisfy his need. However, his two-year-old son, simply by being himself, frustrates the young father's need. The father comes home and there are toys everywhere.

He ignores his smiling child and starts screaming about the mess. His harried wife scurries to put things back in order. The father has successfully used his emotions to satisfy his need, at the expense of his wife and child's feelings.

If he were aware that he had a need to be in control, he would be able to negotiate to get his needs met and manage his emotions more effectively. For example, knowing that he was feeling over-wrought because of work, he might have called ahead to his wife and asked if she could make sure the environment was ordered and if he could have some quiet time before dinner. When we are conscious of our needs, it's easy for us to recognize when they aren't being satisfied, particularly when a situation or a goal has no intrinsic way of satisfying them. We also have to learn to bear the frustration we feel when we can't have instant gratification.

Human needs are like the furnace in the basement—out of sight and out of mind. We could almost forget that they exist. But when the house turns bitterly cold, we have to be willing to go down and investigate, because we realize that the furnace is essential to our comfort and security. As everything we do is an attempt to meet our needs, these needs give form to our personalities and the ways we interact with the world. The SSPS takes into account the complexity and diversity of personalities and the unrelenting biological nature of human need, as well as the impact that need satisfaction or dissatisfaction has on the way we experience our life.

Chapter Three
STRIVING STYLE SQUAD AND THE FOUR QUADRANTS OF THE BRAIN

Coming together is a beginning; keeping together is progress; working together is success.

—*Henry Ford*

The four quadrants of the brain are home to our Striving Style Squad. Although each member of the Squad has a different need and set of behaviors it uses to meet that need, the Squad is meant to function as an alliance to create a solid and enduring foundation for the personality. Our brain has all of the hardware it needs to ensure that this happens; it just needs us to consciously engage in our development.

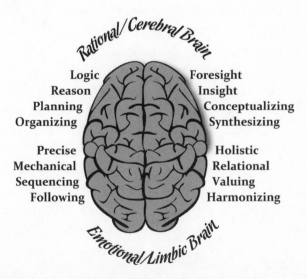

Once we develop awareness of what the brain quadrants do, we can learn to direct our conscious mind to perform the tasks and behaviors using the right Style from our Squad. For example, the right emotional quadrant is home base for Socializers and Artists, and is largely responsible for processing information according to its subjective values and feelings. This is the part of the brain that is tapped for making connections with others, for example by reading cues from body language, tone of voice, and facial expression. It's an area that is weak for many people, especially when they are in situations that call for small talk.

Nancy's friend Kate convinced her to go to the opening of a neighborhood art gallery. While getting a drink from the bar, Nancy found herself face-to-face with a popular neighbor from across the street. Thinking she should at least try to make conversation, she cautiously ventured a few obscure comments on the ways in which a nearby painting is reminiscent of devotional art in Holland during the fourteenth century (one of Nancy's favorite topics). She failed to notice that her neighbor is looking restlessly around the room, tapping her fingers on the bar, taking frequent sips of her drink, and only occasionally responding to her remarks by mumbling things like, "Uh, right…"

If Nancy could develop her right emotional quadrant a bit, she wouldn't necessarily become a social butterfly and the darling of the neighborhood party circuit, but she would be able to recognize how others are responding to her behavior, and she would learn to make moment-to-moment shifts in the behavior to ensure more enjoyable conversations. Because she is not outgoing by nature, she might focus on her ability to listen and to encourage others to talk, and in that way she might find she has to expend less effort actually thinking of things to say. She could also perform some other activities at this type of event that she might find more enjoyable, such as giving tours of the gallery to guests who are interested in the stories behind the art, or volunteering to help with refreshments. This would allow her to interact with others from a more secure position, reducing her anxiety about having to make small talk.

The following discussion provides more detail about each of the quadrants. Knowing more about the quadrants' functions helps you understand why the Striving Styles behave the way they do and helps you determine which Style you need to use during certain activities. It can also help you confirm which of the quadrants or Styles you tend to use most of the time.

Left Rational Brain (Leader, Intellectual)

Knowledge will forever govern ignorance; and a people who mean to be their own governors must arm themselves with the power which knowledge gives.

—*James Madison*

The goal or purpose of the left rational brain is to decide what something is, where it belongs, what its relative usefulness is, and what the priorities for attention are. It is objective, logical, and principled, seeing the world in data points. It creates a complete ideology of how the world should operate by developing principles, laws, and structures, then sorting things accordingly. It helps us to consider objectively and dispassionately what needs to be done, how soon it needs to be done, and who must do it. It processes information in a reasoned and logical fashion, allowing us to decide things pragmatically. It decides where we need to place our effort in order to achieve goals.

The left rational brain plans and organizes information. It has an impersonal, systematic basis for focusing attention. It notices the parts of objects that are similar and different. This part of the brain is not holistic; instead, it breaks things into their component parts, measures and sorts objects and experiences, and then decides how to respond accordingly. It is able to organize numerous objects and to establish logical relationships between them. If the left rational brain could talk, it would say things like, "Hey, nothing personal, but I'm sorting you into the 'Plumbers' category and also into the 'People Who Live on My Street' category," or, "You wear crystals, long skirts, and sandals like my Aunt Betty, and you drive a Honda Prius like my sister Wanda. It's likely, therefore, that you are an environmentally conscious, New Age sort of person." The left rational brain doesn't "feel" any particular way about all this information; it just goes about its tidy, analytical way, keeping track of what's what.

The left rational brain is responsible for the formation of our self-concept, or the idea of who we are. Our self-concept is the collection of ideas and beliefs that we have about our self. For example, it might include "I am an intelligent and clever individual," "I am decisive person who can think on my feet," or "I am talkative and entertaining." This might not be how other people experience us, but it is what we have decided we are like, on the basis of on our behavior. For example, even if we give money to a home-less person on the street only once a year, we add "generous" to our self-concept.

When functioning from this part of the brain, we decide what is right and wrong according to our own personal charter of rights and are willing to go to battle when others don't want to do things the way we know they should be done. "I think, therefore I am" is the credo for this part of the brain, and it happily rationalizes our experiences so that those messy emotions don't interfere with its logical processing.

Unlike the two quadrants of the emotional brain, the left rational brain is not affected by moment-to-moment feelings and experiences. It observes them from a distance and focuses more on what it thinks about people and situations than what it feels or experiences. This brain can dominate, disavow, or detach us from our emotions and experiences by causing us to think about instead of being involved with what is going on. For example, it can observe the behavior of a crying child in a restaurant and contemplate why the child has to be so noisy. From there, it can go on to think that children should not be allowed in public places because they are disruptive and consider what might be done to make this happen.

The following are the activities that the left rational brain is most efficient and least efficient at. The activities describe the function of the brain and what this looks like in the outer world, being acted out by the Leader, and in the inner world, by the Intellectual.

Leader

Most Efficient	Least Efficient
Leading and managing	Meeting emotional needs of others
Managing emotions and impulses	Recognizing and trusting emotions
Understanding and deciding	Asking for help
Direct communication	Empathizing
Being objective and purposeful	Being original and authentic
Ordering, planning, and organizing	Letting things happen
Setting objectives and goals	Creating for pleasure
Being objective and purposeful	Creating harmony
Being self-assured and confident	Bonding with others
Establishing authority and responsibility	Cooperating and trusting others

Intellectual

Most Efficient	Least Efficient
Researching, investigating, compiling data	Developing/maintaining relationships
Focusing attention on ideas, interests	Making small talk
Critiquing and analyzing	Recognizing emotions, empathizing
Ordering and accumulating information	Adhering to social rules
Acting on own authority	Doing what is expected of them
Independent thinking and decision making	Collaborative decision making
Measuring, qualifying, or quantifying	Socializing
Applying logic and reason	Reflecting on others' motivations
Managing impulses, emotions	Dealing with emotions or conflict
Problem solving	Creating harmony

Right Rational Brain (Performer, Visionary)

Imagination is more important than knowledge. For knowledge is limited to all we now know and understand, while imagination embraces the entire world, and all there ever will be to know and understand.

—Albert Einstein

The goal or purpose of the right rational brain is to imagine, conceptualize, and synthesize information and experiences. It produces awareness of what is possible by processing and integrating information and experiences, and then synthesizing them into a clear and cohesive concept or a vision for the future. It is with this part of the brain that we develop foresight and the ability to imagine a future different from our present. Our right rational brain envisions the world the way we desire it to be and formulates ideas about how to bring the vision to life. This part of the brain processes things as a whole and can leap from point A to conclusion D without feeling the need to collect any facts, or even to visit point B or C along the way. It is strongly intuitive and perceptive; it knows without knowing why. It sees the big picture and gets excited about the possibility of making it real.

The right rational brain is optimistic and hopeful, so it can help us to see our way out of difficult situations and to approach new activities with a fresh, open-minded attitude. It helps us create mental order out of seemingly random thoughts, impressions, and experiences. Using indiscriminate pieces of information, it intuitively knows how to create a cohesive whole. It provides us with the ability to see the potential in things and to view the world as rich with endless possibilities.

While the left rational brain oversees our self-concept, or idea of who we are in the objective sense (e.g., "My name is Tom Hanks; I make my living as an actor; I starred in *Big*, *Philadelphia Story*, *Apollo 13*, and many other movies; I went to high school in Oakland, California…"), the right rational brain maintains self-image—the subjective vision of who we are or who we want to be. This self-image is based on the integration of interactions with others over the years and on impressions gathered through reading, the arts, cinema, and so forth. You'll know the right rational brain is talking when someone says, "I'm the kind of person who…" A well-known actor who shall remain nameless was drawing on her right rational brain when she declared that she was "not the sort of person who slops around in sweatpants." The image that we have of ourselves determines how we behave, dress, act, and respond to others. A positive self-image leads us to move toward becoming all that we can be. A negative self-image will cause us to stay where we are or move in the opposite direction. Brian Tracy, author and motivational speaker, frequently said in his training sessions that, "Our self image, strongly held, essentially determines what we become."

Self-image is often affected by how we feel or how others feel about us. When country music singer Shania Twain was honored with a star on the Hollywood Walk of Fame, her reaction suggested that her right rational brain was at odds with that honor. She expressed it this way: "I mean why is a girl from Timmins, Ontario, standing here, getting a star on the Hollywood Walk of Fame? I really don't know." The right rational brain clearly had not, until that time, built a self-image for Twain that was anything like that of the legendary stars whose names line the Walk of Fame, so the honor didn't seem to align with her self-image. With time and congratulations from many fans and other celebrities, which reinforce their agreement with the honor, she likely has learned to accept it as well.

The more consistent our self-image is with how we actually are, the less we will be affected by negative or corrective feedback from others. So if Lance Armstrong was right about his tendency to learn from difficult experiences, then the next time he is beaten in a race, he will be able to resist becoming demoralized by criticisms that he's no longer at the top of his career; instead, he will rest assured in his conviction that the loss is an opportunity for some kind of growth.

The following are the activities that the right rational brain is most efficient and least efficient at. They illustrate the function of the brain and what this looks like in the outer world, being acted out by the Performer, and in the inner world, by the Visionary.

Performer

Most Efficient	Least Efficient
Inventing and reinventing themselves	Doing things in a prescribed order
Playing to win	Playing by the rules
Envisioning a desired future state	Following traditions
Inspiring or impressing others	Being one of the crowd
Having an optimistic outlook	Meeting emotional needs of others
Achieving results	Having a disciplined approach to self-care
Getting recognition	Taking constructive feedback
Speaking in front of an audience	Doing solitary activities
Inspiring others to achieve their potential	Enforcing rules and giving boundaries
Seeing the big picture	Maintaining the status quo

Visionary

Most Efficient	Least Efficient
Foresight, anticipating what might be	Living in the present moment
Creating a positive self-image	Respecting authority
Using intuition	Staying connected to physical experience
Playing with possibilities	Conforming to rules
Perceiving the big picture	Sequencing and planning
Attuning to others	Focusing on facts and details
Reflecting	Being guided by experience

Most Efficient	Least Efficient
Imagining and brainstorming	Making things real
Making connections and systems	Making small talk
Helping others see their potential	Having a disciplined approach to self-care

Right Emotional Brain (Socializer, Artist)

I've learned that people will forget what you said, people will forget what you did, but people will never forget how you made them feel.

—*Maya Angelou*

The goal or purpose of the right emotional brain is to have emotional experiences. It can produce emotions about the present as well as retrieve stored emotionally charged memories from the past. This quadrant decides what value something has or what the intrinsic attractiveness or aversiveness of an event, object, or situation is. In other words, it figures out whether we like something or not. It compares and judges what is being experienced and generates feelings about those experiences on the basis of those judgments. Because we are all attracted to and repelled by different things, this subjective valuing is unique to each person. For one person, hearing the song "White Christmas" can activate happy feelings of nostalgia, while for another, it can bring tears of remembered pain and sadness. The right emotional brain doesn't know why the song makes us happy or sad (although this information may be held elsewhere); it knows only what it feels.

The right emotional brain focuses on present moment experiences as they relate to past emotional memories. For example, if you do something to make me sad, I will connect with myriad memories that have made me sad, which will cause me to accuse you of being just like my mother. This part of the brain seeks to create harmony and is easily pulled off center by emotional conflict. It will focus on restoring harmony by adapting behavior or emotions or by expecting others to adapt theirs during disagreements or in emotional climates. This means that if I'm feeling happy and in my right emotional brain and then I come home to a partner who is angry, I will do what I can to make my partner feel happy or get angry at my partner for wrecking my mood. Whatever the behavior, we will both end up feeling the same.

The holistic nature of this part of the brain doesn't allow it to separate what is felt from itself, or feeling from fact. Feelings rule; in fact, they are experienced as more important than anything else that is going on. The right emotional brain can use imagination to create scenarios that produce certain feelings so that we can experience those feelings on demand. The actor who can cry on cue, the rebellious teenager who flies into a rage when a younger sibling picks up her diary, and the elderly grandparent who frequently chuckles when talking about old memories are all summoning past experiences or imagined ones to produce a feeling in the present. This quadrant tends to believe something is true because it *feels* that it is true, despite fact-based evidence to the contrary. It fulfills its mandate by re-creating feelings that were experienced in the past. If the past was fulfilling and desirable, this can be a tremendous asset. If it was not, the right emotional brain can continue to create negative emotional experience despite situations being different.

The following are the activities that the right emotional brain is most efficient and least efficient at. They illustrate the function of the brain and what this looks like in the outer world, being acted out by the Socializer, and in the inner world, by the Artist.

Socializer

Most Efficient	Least Efficient
Developing relationships	Doing solitary activities
Conforming to social norms	Technical or mechanical problem solving
Helping and supporting others	Establishing own authority
Networking and socializing	Accepting help
Achieving social status	Focusing attention or self-reflecting
Assigning value to people, things, activities	Tolerating conflict
Collaborative decision making	Applying logic or reason
Subjective, interpersonal reasoning	Independent thinking
Creating harmony	Using facts to support decisions
Doing cooperative activities	Asserting opinions and ideas

Artist

Most Efficient	Least Efficient
Seeking to create perfection	Scheduling and organizing
Holistic, authentic living	Creating structure and limits
Assigning value	Practical or logical analysis
Doing solitary activities	Maintaining confidence
Alignment with personal values	Supporting decisions with facts
Attuning empathetically	Following rules
Creating emotional experiences	Directing and organizing others
Authentic self-expression	Communicating directly and assertively
Subjective decision-making	Impersonal decision making
Meaningful bonding experiences with others	Setting goals, planning

Left Emotional Brain
(Adventurer, Stabilizer)

The only source of knowledge is experience.

—*Albert Einstein*

The left emotional brain is the most mechanistic of the four brain quadrants. This means that it does things in a fashion that is both impersonal and automatic. Its primary purpose is to experience physical sensations. It doesn't mind doing the same thing over and over again, if the action produces the desired sensations. It is oriented to the present, focusing on what has to be done now and following instructions to the letter. Precise and procedural, it doesn't reflect on the "why" of things, only on the "how."

This quadrant is connected to the processing of positive emotions and relatively complex emotions. It is more objective in its emotional processing than the right emotional brain is because its goal is to produce sensations, not feelings. It is more black-and-white when deliberating and tends to quickly filter out experiences that it labels "bad." It seeks to determine how an object or person we encounter might create the type of sensations we want to feel. It wants to experience what is known or has been experienced before so it can cause us to keep repeating or tolerating unpleasant sensations when we have experienced them in the past. For example, a hockey player will skate despite having a sprained ankle because he has been experiencing pain from the time he was young. Experiencing sensations in the moment is the goal of this quadrant, and it doesn't consider the emotional consequences of the chosen activity. It seeks to re-create experiences, often with increased or prolonged intensity.

This quadrant also sequences activities so that things are done in a specific fashion. Like the athlete who practices the same activity over and over again to achieve a predictable result, the left emotional brain strives to re-create conditions that will bring familiar sensations. It is planful, linear, and deliberate, and it can follow activity to the letter with no need to know the final outcome. Like the soldier following orders, it is comfortable with its role in performing the specific task without knowing the big picture.

The following are the activities that the left emotional brain is most efficient and least efficient at. They illustrate the function of the brain and what this looks like in the outer world, being acted out by the Adventurer, and in the inner world, by the Stabilizer.

Adventurer

Most Efficient	Least Efficient
Having active, physical experiences	Theorizing and conceptualizing
Thinking on their feet	Seeing the big picture
Promoting, selling	Reflecting on the meaning of things
Living in the present moment	Envisioning the future
Negotiating	Perceiving the emotional needs of others
Handling crisis, troubleshooting, and firefighting	Believing in what can't be experienced
Making activities fun	Exploring psychology
Storytelling and entertaining	Doing solitary activities
Playing games, sports	Honoring personal commitments

Stabilizer

Most Efficient	Least Efficient
Planning	Acknowledging their emotions
Sequencing and ordering activities	Guessing or estimating
Following rules, authority	Envisioning a desired future state
Doing solitary activities	Speculating on motivations of others
Maintaining traditions	Being adaptable, flexible
Saving for the future	Maintaining optimism
Disciplined approach, practice and routine	Empathizing with others
Taking care of physical needs	Emotional self-expression
Enforcing rules	Making activities fun
Respectful compliance	Inspiring, persuading others

How the Four Quadrants Work Together

The power of one, if fearless and focused, is formidable, but the power of many working together is better.

—*Gloria Macapagal Arroyo*

The information on the quadrants of the brain can help us think about our development and ourselves in a new way. In the past, some brain theorists referred to the quadrants as thinking styles, which has helped make them more objective and therefore more palatable to those who automatically reject or discount emotions as important. By thinking about the four quadrants as a Squad made up of individual avatars, each with its own need, behavior, and way of approaching the world, we can immediately see how we can put our Squad to good use in our personality.

After we learn about our Predominant Style, we need to also understand the function of the three other Squad members and whether or not we are using them on a regular basis. While it's easier to use our Predominant Style, we have to start thinking about it in the context of our Squad. It needs to learn how to be a team player rather than a one person show and to delegate the activities that are not it's unique ability or role to perform because of the quadrant it resides in. Using all four Styles on your Squad in an integrated fashion requires that you consciously focus your attention on the activities and behaviors of the Style you wish to use. It will take more energy and effort to do so, but over time new neural pathways will form, giving you more automatic access to all quadrants of your brain.

The brain is on a physiological mission to function as a whole, but it needs attention and focus to use the four Styles on the Squad together. Living our life as the person we are meant to be becomes a reality when we use more than just one quadrant of our brain. Our potential for dealing with the demands of any situation becomes unlimited. Once we begin integrating all four of our Striving Styles, we are no longer limited to seeing ourselves and our world through a single lens.

Now that you know about the functions of each of the quadrants of the brain, let's move on to another important component of the SSPS and the biology of becoming our best self.

CHAPTER FOUR
THE BIOLOGY OF BECOMING OUR BEST SELVES

At birth, the brain is the most undifferentiated organ in the body—with a plasticity that enables it to create new circuitry throughout life.

—*Dr. Daniel J. Siegel*

THE MYSTERIES OF THE mind are no longer as mysterious as they were twenty years ago, thanks to brain-scanning technologies. We are now able to see what is going on in our brain instead of just theorizing about it. Similarly, understanding how the personality works is no longer a speculative activity, as we can view it functioning in real time. We can see how different areas of the brain light up when we are performing activities, how our emotions and behavior interact with our thoughts, and where these activities reside in the brain.

This chapter is about the how the brain has evolved and how it develops. In a simple and useful fashion, it describes the functions of the different brain areas and the ways they affect the personality. You will learn about neuroplasticity, the brain's natural ability for growth and change that lets us keep growing and developing despite negative conditioning and habits of mind. You will see that the brain can change long-standing patterns of behavior that impede our fulfillment as human beings. You will be able to understand how pathways of communication between the different brain areas develop, which makes it possible to use your whole brain to achieve your potential.

This chapter is organized in two sections: the first is about how the brain has evolved and how it develops, and the second provides the theory behind the Self-Protective and Self-Actualizing Systems of the brain, a key component of the Striving Styles Personality System (SSPS), and how these systems affect our emotions and behavior.

Our Evolutionary Brain

We are the product of 4.5 billion years of fortuitous, slow biological evolution. There is no reason to think that the evolutionary process has stopped. Man is a transitional animal. He is not the climax of creation.

—*Carl Sagan*

Until the middle of the last century, it was widely believed that we had one unitary brain. During the 1960s, following years of research, American physician and neuroscientist Paul MacLean proposed that we have three brains: the reptilian (instinctual), the limbic (emotional), and the neocortical (rational). He determined that each of the three brains has its own purpose, function, and intelligence. He called this three-brain system the triune brain. MacLean reported that the reptilian brain developed first, and each subsequently developing brain represented a new evolutionary layer that formed over the previous one. He demonstrated how each of the brains is connected to the layer above and/or below via neural pathways, and how they communicate with each other in computer-like fashion.

The following are descriptions of the three brains and the role they play in our thinking, feeling, and behavior.

Instinctual Brain

The instinctual or reptilian brain, located in the brain stem, was the first to evolve. This brain is concerned primarily with ensuring our physical survival and has the most primitive level of awareness. It reacts, in an automatic, knee-jerk fashion, to whatever is going on in the present moment with no concern for the past or future. It doesn't have the ability to think about itself, nor does it have any memory. This means that it doesn't learn from its mistakes and will react to a situation in the same way it did before, despite a negative outcome. For example, a primitive person who came upon a snake might have ventured close enough to be bitten because of the animal's small size and lack of obvious threat. The next time a snake appeared—provided the first one hadn't delivered a fatal bite—the person would probably approach it again.

The instinctual brain reacts directly to what it encounters in the environment on the basis of four simple questions that relate to the most basic animal instincts: Can I kill it, or can it kill me (instinct to live)? Can I eat it (instinct to use, hoard, and store)? Can I mate with it (instinct to ensure survival of the species)? Can I have dominance over it (instinct to compete and beat, which helps ensure survival of the fittest)? In other words, the instinctual brain contains primitive processes that cause us to explore and gain mastery over the world around us, to seek food, to display aggression for the purpose of dominance, and to reproduce and use our sexuality to attract a mate. It is responsible for all of our basic instinctual reactions and behaviors related to primitive survival concerns.

At various times, each of us is affected by impulses from our instinctual brain, although some people seem more beholden to them than others do!

Emotional Brain

The limbic or emotional brain evolved next, as humans realized that safety and survival were best accomplished in groups. This brain contains the mechanism to form bonds with others, providing us with a sense of psychological security and belonging. It has a regulatory system to mediate emotions that arise from our bonds to others, such as pleasure arising from being with friends and loved ones, separation distress when someone leaves us or we leave them, playfulness and touch, and the desire to nurture and care for others (i.e., maternal nurturance).

As its name suggests, the emotional brain is concerned with producing emotions—pleasure, rage, fear, and joy—that we feel and experience physically. This brain produces the desire to relate to others as well as to recognize the positive or negative quality of emotions (also known as "emotional valence"). The emotional brain makes a value judgment about the emotions that we have with an experience and then categorizes them as positive or negative, pleasurable or uncomfortable. It then stores negative emotional memories for future reference, using them to judge new situations and decide whether to enter them or avoid them. This means that our primitive person, if bitten by the snake, would have stored the experience of the bite as "bad." Should our friend come upon that snake a second time, the recall of negative emotions (pain and fear) produced by the first bite would lead to evasive action, which most of us would consider a more intelligent response! He would then go and tell all his friends.

But it's not only physical threats like snakes that cause our emotional brain to send us messages that a situation is likely to create unpleasant feelings. Here is another example of how this part of the brain works: *Dennis's wife Kate recently took a new job. Her employer is holding a holiday party to which spouses are invited. Dennis hears the words "office party" and feels immediately uneasy. His heart beats faster and his mouth feels a little dry. A shy man who hates small talk, he would much rather stay at home while Kate goes to the party. However, Kate insists that he go, and Dennis gives in. At the party, he tries to be pleasant but quickly becomes embarrassed when his attempts at conversations with strangers turn to awkward silences, just before the partygoers abandon him to find someone more interesting to talk to. For Dennis, the evening can't end soon enough.*

The reactions of discomfort that Dennis feels when the party is mentioned come from his emotional brain dredging up a negative association it had made in the past between office parties and unpleasantness. Although Dennis may believe that he just doesn't enjoy office parties, his emotional brain knows something deeper than this: Dennis has suffered embarrassment in this situation before, and he is now afraid of feeling embarrassment again; he therefore attempts to avoid the situation rather than face his fear. Because he is afraid that he is going to be socially awkward, he ends up working himself into a tizzy and ultimately creating exactly the experience he dreads.

Rational Brain

The instinctual and emotional brains are by nature, reactive. They have automatic responses that occur via the nervous and hormonal systems outside of our conscious awareness. By contrast, the neo-cortical or rational brain makes possible our organizing and planning abilities so that we can consider first and then respond, rather than just react. It enables us to decide what type of response to use when we are upset, overwhelmed, or hurt, and to learn how to deal with recurring challenges. Using the example of the primitive person and the snake, the rational brain would enable our friend to learn something about snakes so that he would know which ones are harmful. He could try to plan and order his surroundings so he doesn't ever have to be around a snake!

The rational brain also enables us to decipher the meaning of our experiences (for example, in Dennis's case, why he hates office parties). By using the rational brain effectively, we can develop self-awareness. It gives us the capacity to reflect objectively on what we are feeling and to decide the best way to respond. It is the center for learning and using self-management skills. The rational brain allows us to name our experiences and objectively determine which information about these experiences is useful, so we are not subject to the automatic survival reactions of our emotional or instinctual brain.

The rational brain's skill of self-management allows us to take the time to decide what is actually going on so that we are not constantly reacting to thoughts, feelings, and situations as they arise. It helps us tolerate our feelings until we have had time to think things through, and to bear frustration and delay gratification. It is able to selectively override impulses that are valuable at certain times but inappropriate at others.

For example, in Dennis's case, the same fear response (e.g., increased heart rate, dry mouth) is activated when he attends the office party as would be activated if he were confronted by physical danger, such as a house fire. In the case of fire, running away (flight) might be the best response; in the office party situation, it's probably not wise. If he can apply his rational brain to the situation of the party, he can learn to manage the impulses created in his emotional brain, that is, to tolerate some fear or embarrassment while he learns how to talk to people he doesn't know.

The rational brain is also responsible for overriding impulses that would lead to immediate gratification at the expense of long-term goals. Suppose that Dennis, a slave to his emotional brain, enters the office party and sees two choices: a well-stocked buffet table that no one seems to have approached yet and a bar area where all the guests are making conversation. His impulses scream, "Buffet table!" but his rational brain, however reluctantly, decides that it's not in his or his wife's long-term interest to bypass the social niceties and storm the buffet. If it's functioning at a high level, Dennis's rational brain can help him bear his discomfort so that he can get through the small talk. And once the time is right to move on to food, his rational brain can also help him manage the instinct to eat too much, because it recognizes that food is not scarce and that good manners call for restraint. If necessary, the rational brain can also recite for Dennis the likely consequences of giving in to his emotion-driven impulses.

How the Brain Develops

Every man can, if he so desires, become the sculptor of his own brain.
—*Santiago Ramon y Cajal*

To achieve our potential as human beings, we must also know a little about the biology behind our development. It is now widely recognized that our brain continues to grow and develop until our mid-twenties. Most of the developmental activity that occurs after adolescence is in the prefrontal cortex or the rational brain, which undergoes the longest period of development. This development does not happen in all young people, as their environment, social circumstances, and choices can get in the way. For example, teen pregnancy that leads to dropping out of school, a lack of higher education, and the use of drugs or alcohol to excess all tend to interfere with the brain's full capacity for development.

Our three brains don't all develop at the same time. To ensure our survival, our brains develop from the brain stem up, with the rational brain developing last. Although the brain stem is almost fully functional at birth, the emotional brain is slower to develop and mature, in part because development of the emotional brain is activity dependent. How many or how few experiences we have dictates how neural pathways form and interconnect, and how strong or weak the links are. As neuroscientists often say, "Cells that fire together, wire together." Every experience that a child has causes certain neural pathways to strengthen and others to fall away, a process called pruning. The brain does not discriminate as to whether the pathway is helpful or harmful to us; it simply fortifies *what it experiences the most*. So there's actually a neurological basis for the saying "good habits last a lifetime." Unfortunately, the same can be said for dysfunctional and maladaptive patterns.

When we're born, the rational brain has limited neural pathways connecting it to the emotional and instinctual brains. It is wired to be the last to develop and the last to receive communications via neurons from other parts of the brain. And just as our brains develop from the instinctual brain upward, neural pathways process information and experiences from the instinctual brain upward as well. This means that if you put your hand too close to a hot stove, you will have moved your hand away from the burner before your rational brain has registered that it felt hot. It doesn't take a brain scientist to see that the instinctual and emotional brains do the lion's share of decision making and have a greater influence on the rational brain than vice versa. They also have more control over our behavior.

When the brain develops along its ideal trajectory, connections from our emotional to our rational brain strengthen, reinforcing the communication between the two. This increases the ability of the rational brain to influence our decisions and behavior. In this way, we continue to develop self-awareness and self-management as we learn from our experiences. If something gets in the way of our brain's development, its natural plasticity allows it—when given the chance—to take care of that unfinished business the second time around.

The Striving Styles Model for Brain Development

You can't imagine how much detail we know about brains. There were 28,000 people who went to the neuroscience conference this year, and every one of them is doing research in brains. A lot of data. But there's no theory.

—*Jeff Hawkins*

Within the SSPS, we have developed several theories and applications for what we now know about the brain. We use MacLean's triune brain theory and the neuroscience behind brain development to help us to understand how our brain develops and what our brain is capable of doing when we decide to take our development into our own hands as adults. Our emotional and instinctual brains are wired to communicate to each other at birth, to ensure our survival. Because of their survival orientation, we named these two brains and their neural connections the Self-Protective (SP) System. Its primary goal is to protect us from physical and emotional experiences that cause us pain and suffering.

The brain's biological mandate is to build connections between the SP System and the rational brain. The result of connecting the three brains is what we have named the Self-Actualizing (SA) System. This system allows us to direct our energy toward meeting our needs, our goals, and our potential rather than just ensuring our survival. Development is complete when enough neural networks have been laid down from the rational brain to the emotional and instinctual brains to consistently and habitually manage, plan, direct, and organize our experiences. Without a developed SA System, we are left with a disconnect between what we know (think) and what we do (experience). This might explain why many people behave in less than admirable ways despite their considerable investment in self-help books.

Self-Protective System™
of the Brain

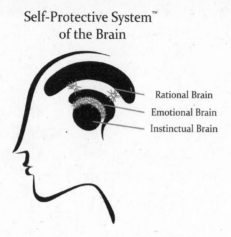

The SP System, with its hardwired brain circuitry, ensures our survival as human beings. During our formative years, the pathways between the instinctual and emotional brains are used almost exclusively. (If you've ever tried to win an argument with a two-year-old, you already know that the rational brains of toddlers cannot be accessed!) The instinctual brain alerts us to danger, and the emotional brain gets our physical and psychological needs met. So while we are operating from this system, we are acutely aware of our emotions and reacting to them as though our lives depended on it.

The SP System is wired to protect us from real or perceived threats to our survival and is activated by fear and other associated emotions. Threats may be external or internal, real or imagined. The system's reactions are automatic in nature and give rise to freezing, withdrawal, avoidance, or flight reactions without any attempt to understand or question; the only goal is to survive. Because this brain system does not learn from mistakes, it keeps doing the same things without really understanding why. Think of poor Dennis, his SP System working overtime at every office party he's ever attended, telling him to freeze, withdraw, avoid, or flee—although there's no real danger at all. Not surprisingly, the behaviors prompted by our

SP Systems are often mystifyingly self-destructive. Like Dennis, we may find ourselves tempted to do things that only compound our problem, like getting drunk at the office party, grazing the buffet table all night, or making inappropriate comments in an attempt to be funny.

Self-Actualizing System™ of the Brain

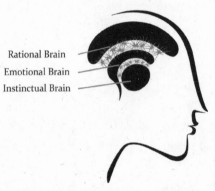

Rational Brain
Emotional Brain
Instinctual Brain

Our SA System regulates impulses from the instinctual brain the way a good leader deals with competing priorities. When this system is fully functional, we are able to set goals, dream our dreams, imagine, delay gratification, manage our impulses, and make decisions in the interest of self-care. We respond to situations instead of reacting to them, trying to solve problems rather than focusing on our emotions. In the SA System, we don't experience our emotions in the same way as we do in the SP System. We might notice that we are afraid, upset, or anxious, but we don't allow our emotions to dictate our behavior. Instead, we decide what our best course of action is. Most important, we develop the capacity to use our whole brains, becoming flexible and resilient, able to manage our lives, adapt to change, and become who we are meant to be.

When we're successfully using our three-brain system, we spend more time seeking pleasurable and self-promoting experiences than avoiding perceived threats. We are curious about the world and embrace our lives with joy and vigor. This system promotes behavior that is likely to bring us a variety of pleasurable outcomes (including fulfillment of our physical and psychological needs). It is an energizing system that moves us outward to explore and experience our environment.

When we get angry, anxious, afraid, or otherwise upset, the entire brain is activated, and it is up to our rational brain to slow down the process between activation and reaction so that we are able to consider the best way to deal with the situation. The rational brain tries to decode or understand impulses from the emotional brain before responding. It attempts to figure out where things fit in the bigger picture rather than reacting to the situation as a stand-alone event. For example, if my best friend has just been stood up by her boyfriend for the umpteenth time, I may be tempted to say, "That guy is a loser. Why don't you break up with him?" My rational brain allows me to pause before speaking, to consider how my words might affect her feelings and our relationship. This reasoning process takes much longer than automatic reactions of instinctual and emotional brains, which explains why sometimes we do blurt out things that we later wish we'd never said. However, the more we use our SA System, the stronger and faster it becomes.

The rational brain is also the only brain that has insight into itself and learns from experience. In the example here, my rational brain will ask, "Is that really the most helpful thing you could say? She might need support more than advice right now." As a result of repeated use of the SA System, of the rational brain with the instinctual and emotional brains, the neural networks strengthen, so that the next time a similar situation arises we can respond with greater ease. The rational brain can also take dysfunctional patterns of reactions and revise them so that we can exercise greater skill in dealing with challenging or emotionally charged situations.

When we aren't aware of these two systems in our brain, we don't really know what we are capable of nor do we fully understand how self-protective we are in our daily lives. When we are able to identify when we are afraid of expressing ourselves or when we are saying no to ourselves without really thinking something through, we can make different choices. Because we aren't familiar with our self-actualizing behaviors, we are at the mercy of acting from automatic self-protective behaviors that limit our capacity to become who we are meant to be. By knowing our self-actualizing behaviors, we make the decision about what behaviors we are going to use to help us achieve our goals.

What Happens When Brain Development Is Stalled

Be not afraid of growing slowly; be afraid only of standing still.

—Chinese proverb

As we have mentioned previously, the development of the SA System is not automatic. We know that children need significant social, emotional, perceptual, and cognitive experiences during the first several years of life to develop normally. If this doesn't happen, or if the environment is somehow chronically threatening or neglectful, neurons and neural pathways will connect in an abnormal fashion, or they will "prune" themselves, dropping out at an accelerated rate. Other factors, such as nutrition, frequency and consistency of care, and touch can affect brain development as well.

At a certain age, during the normal development process, the rational brain takes over from the instinctual brain the responsibility for deciding which situations are threatening and how threats should be handled. Primitive impulses occur less frequently because the brain has learned that they aren't necessary in an environment that is consistently safe and secure. However, if a child still senses a threat to her survival, the takeover by the rational brain does not develop normally and the impulses keep firing from the instinctual brain. This means that the rational brain has to "police" these impulses (to stop us from throwing something when we are angry or from eating buckets of ice cream when we are upset). The policing effort can stall the rational brain's own development, and we can experience extremes of in-control or out-of-control behavior. Addictions, dieting, road rage, compulsive shopping—our society unfortunately offers many examples of situations in which behavior swings in and out of our control.

Helen met with three of her girlfriends every other week for lunch. They had known one another since high school and kept up with what was going on in one another's lives this way. Lately Helen found herself getting irritated with the ever-present conversation about what new diet her friends were on and their comments about being "bad" for not sticking to the diet. She noticed that two of her friends had lost the same fifteen pounds at least three times since high school.

In these situations, it can seem like the brain is fighting with itself instead of integrating its various abilities. The rational brain wants to get to bed early to be ready for a big day of job hunting, and the instinctual brain wants to stay up late and play poker online. The rational brain wants to find a compatible woman and settle down, while the instinctual brain is still hooking up with multiple women and counting them like trophies. The two brains are working to satisfy very different needs. Behaviors that go against our best interests and our own common sense are a result of an SA System that is severely in need of repair.

A Lifetime of Brain Development

Twenty years from now you will be more disappointed by the things that you didn't do than by the ones you did do. So throw off the bowlines. Sail away from the safe harbor. Catch the trade winds in your sails. Explore. Dream. Discover.

—*Mark Twain*

Neuroscience confirms our brain's phenomenal capacity for development over our life span. This means that it is never too late to develop your brain, to change dysfunctional habits of mind, to free yourself from addiction, or to have the relationship you desire. Unlike any other organ in the body, the brain, with its neuroplasticity, can create new neural pathways and even learn to use its cells in different ways.

The good news is, if we missed out on some of that natural development the first time around, we can always re-create developmental opportunities for ourselves. In fact, in chapters 14 and 15, the SSPS Roadmap for Development takes you through the process of planning for and completing the developmental experiences you need to become who you are meant to be. Then, when primitive reflexes are in check and we have integrated the three brains into a healthy functioning SA System, we are poised to fulfill our potential.

CHAPTER FIVE
STRIVING STYLES
SELF-ASSESSMENT

He who knows others is wise. He who knows himself is enlightened.

—*Lao Tzu*

THE STRIVING STYLES SELF-ASSESSMENT allows you to narrow down your Predominant Striving Style in a matter of five to ten minutes. It lets you see what area of your brain you are using the most as well as the other areas you draw on frequently. It serves as a kind of mirror that shows all the facets of your true self, and it gives you the opportunity to think about how you operate in the world on a regular basis. It deepens your understanding of yourself by providing insight into the most basic need that you have to meet in order to feel psychologically secure.

The Striving Styles Self-Assessment asks you to consider attitudes and behaviors that reflect the use of the four quadrants of the brain and the mental functions that are associated with those quadrants. It also allows you to discover whether you tend to apply those functions in your inner world or the outer world.

Once you have determined your Predominant Striving Style, read through the descriptions to see how well they seem to fit you. You may find that more than one Style describes you, and if that is the case, refer to the instructions that follow the assessment. Remember, this assessment is like a mirror: it can only reflect whatever is shown to it. It is not a diagnosis but a tool for self-understanding. After reading the following chapters on each of the Striving Styles, you will probably settle comfortably into one of the Styles, seeing your-self in the descriptions and examples.

This Self-Assessment is for you to determine how your brain is organized and to discover your Predominant Striving Style. It is not to pigeonhole you, judge you, or limit you in any way. As you will see, every Style has its admirable qualities and its vulner-abilities, so don't worry if you read some things about your Style that seem negative or undesirable. Rather than judging yourself or rejecting the Style, just notice your reactions to reading about it. You might feel pleased, excited, embarrassed, or irritated when learning about yourself; all of these reactions are perfectly normal. Knowing how your brain is organized is like knowing whether you are left or right handed, and I'm sure you'll agree that having this knowledge has never hurt you. You can only benefit from gaining awareness about yourself and your Predominant and Associate Striving Styles.

As you read, you may start to get some clarity about certain aspects of yourself or others. You might even have an aha moment, in which you suddenly understand why you bristle every time your brother-in-law starts to tell a joke, or why you have a million Facebook friends (or none at all). Whatever initial thoughts you have when you read about your Style, remember that observing your reactions to this new information is the first step in a learning and development process.

Here are some important tips for taking the Self-Assessment:

Take your time. Don't rush through it. It should take about five to ten minutes to read and complete. Choose a time and place where you won't be disturbed or interrupted.

Go with your first reaction. Try not to second-guess yourself. When you are waffling between "Occasionally" and "Frequently," think about what you prefer or what is most like you. Avoid analyz-ing the statements or your responses in detail.

There are no right or wrong answers. For each statement, just think about how much time you spend behaving in this fashion. Ask yourself whether this is because you prefer to behave this way or because your work, social circumstances, or conditioning requires that you do so. The best answer to choose is the one that reflects your preference, not the pressure of external forces.

Answer honestly. Avoid the temptation to choose answers simply because they seem like the most desirable way to respond. This approach will diminish the accuracy of your results.

Instructions

The Self-Assessment has four main sections (labeled A, B, C, and D). Each section has two parts (labeled 1 and 2), and within each part there is a list of statements. You will read each statement and decide how often the statement applies to you or describes you. The scale that you will use for making your decisions is: Rarely = 0; Occasionally = 2; Frequently = 4; Always = 6. For example, if you read the statement "I tend to be self-critical" and you feel that this is only occasionally true for you, you should enter 2 as your response. After you have read all the statements for part 1 and responded to them, add up your score for part 1 and enter it in the space provided, then go on to part 2. When you finish part 2, check to see whether your score is higher for part 1 or part 2, and enter that information at the bottom of each page in the space provided. At the end of the Self-Assessment, you will be asked to transfer the results from each page to determine your Predominant and Associate Striving Styles.

Sections A1 and A2 (Leader, Intellectual)

The following two sets of statements will determine which Striving Style of your **left rational brain** you prefer to use.

Use the following choices to rate each statement: Rarely = 0; Occasionally = 2; Frequently = 4; Always = 6	
I prefer being in management or leadership roles so I can define how things are done.	4
Others depend on me to tell them what to do and ensure it gets done.	2
I get impatient with others who take a long time to make up their mind	2
I usually know what is best for others and expect them to heed my advice.	0
I communicate directly to others (i.e., I don't mince my words).	4
I like to have plans for myself even when I am not working.	0
The time I spend working interferes with my relationships and social life.	2
I like to be the one who makes final decisions for everyone.	0
Leader - Section A1 Total	14

Use the following choices to rate each statement: Rarely = 0; Occasionally = 2; Frequently = 4; Always = 6	
I can get absorbed in my interests and can focus on them for hours.	6
I enjoy gathering information and consider myself an expert in several areas.	4
I think of a deadline as something easily moved.	6
I am an individualist and a nonconformist.	6
I prefer working on my own rather than collaborating with others.	4
I often make plans in my mind and forget to communicate them to others.	4
I tend to forget dates that are important to others (e.g., birthdays, anniversaries).	0
I prefer to process information on my own before discussing with others.	6
Intellectual — Section A2 Total	36
Higher score of A1 or A2 **(Leader, Intellectual)**	~~36~~

50

Sections B1 and B2 (Performer, Visionary)

The following two sets of statements will determine which Striving Style of your **right rational brain** you prefer to use.

Use the following choices to rate each statement: Rarely = 0; Occasionally = 2; Frequently = 4; Always = 6	
I enjoy being the center of attention and seek opportunities to be there.	0
I am optimistic and enthusiastic about what I can achieve and what the future holds.	2
I am very conscious of my image and work hard to ensure I appear successful.	0
I tend to try to be what I believe others want me to be and seek approval for it.	2
I am self-assured, goal oriented, and ambitious.	0
I tend to avoid situations in which I cannot win or be the best at something.	2
I can work so much that I lose track of the effect it is having on my health, relationships, and behavior.	0
Others look to me as a source of motivation and inspiration.	0
Performer — Section B1 Total	6

Use the following choices to rate each statement: Rarely = 0; Occasionally = 2; Frequently = 4; Always = 6	
I tend to listen more than I talk.	4
I enjoy work in which I can independently research, innovate, investigate, or invent.	6
I try to understand the deeper meaning of things.	6
I prefer to figure out how something works rather than read directions.	4
I place great importance on my inner sense of knowing or intuition.	4
I have a unique talent for seeing how things are connected.	4
I can focus excessively on little, unimportant things when avoiding what I really need to do.	0
When I am fatigued or stressed, I tend to withdraw and go off on my own.	6
Visionary — Section B2 Total	34
Higher score of B1 or B2 (Performer, Visionary)	40

Sections C1 and C2 (Socializer, Artist)

The following two sets of statements will determine which Striving Style of your **right emotional brain** you prefer to use.

Use the following choices to rate each statement: Rarely = 0; Occasionally = 2; Frequently = 4; Always = 6	
I am a "people person" and easily develop relationships with others.	2
I enjoy socializing with others and making connections between the people I know.	0
I think it's important that people are polite and mannerly.	4
I tend to overextend myself socially, having too many commitments in my calendar.	0
It upsets me when people don't welcome or value the advice I give them.	0
I like to help others and prefer not to let anyone help me.	0
I enjoy giving compliments to others and letting people know how special they are.	6
I tend to make friends easily at work.	2
Socializer — Section C1 Total	14

Use the following choices to rate each statement: Rarely = 0; Occasionally = 2; Frequently = 4; Always = 6	
I like to understand the deeper meaning of how people behave.	6
I tend to be self-critical.	6
I seek authenticity and depth in relationships with others.	6
I try to live my life according to my own values.	6
I tend to listen more than talk.	6
I feel that most people do not understand me.	6
I look composed to others even though I am feeling something intensely.	2
Having to do something because of duty or obligation does not motivate me.	4
Artist — Section C2 Total	42
Higher score of C1 or C2 (Socializer, Artist)	56

Sections D1 and D2 (Adventurer, Stabilizer)

The following two sets of statements will determine which Striving Style of your **left emotional brain** you prefer to use.

Use the following choices to rate each statement: Rarely = 0; Occasionally = 2; Frequently = 4; Always = 6	
I tend to talk more than listen.	0
I have a strong need for adventure, excitement, and new experiences.	10
I dislike having to do the same thing the same way twice.	2
I tend to be outgoing, friendly, and sociable, with many friends and acquaintances.	2
I like to be where the action is.	0
I work well under pressure. I enjoy and am good in a crisis.	0
I am generally unaware of the impact of my behavior and actions on others.	0
I prefer work that lets me interact and socialize with people.	0
Adventurer — Section D1 Total	4

Use the following choices to rate each statement:	
Rarely = 0; Occasionally = 2; Frequently = 4; Always = 6	
I am loyal, hardworking, and predictable.	4
I enjoy the comfort and security of things staying the same.	4
I strive to do what is expected of me and am respectful of authority.	⊘ 4
I tend to say no when asked to try new things, preferring to stay with the tried and true.	4
I am more likely to take on too much responsibility than shy away from it.	2
I prefer to stay in the same job or line of work rather than look for something different.	2
I am prone to worrying and usually imagine the worst-case scenario when something happens.	2
I tend to focus more on tasks and less on relationships.	0
Stabilizer — Section D2 Total	22
Higher score of D1 or D2 (Adventurer, Stabilizer)	26

Your Results

For each section (A, B, C, and D), enter the name of the Style that received the higher score, then enter the score.

Section	Style That Received the Higher Score	Score
A	*Intellectual*	*50*
B	*Visionary*	*40*
C	*Artist*	*56*
D	*Stabilizer*	*26*

The highest of the four scores you entered in the table represents your Predominant Striving Style. The other three scores are likely your Associate Styles. Remember, two of the Styles on your Squad must be focused in the outer world (Leader, Performer, Socializer, Adventurer), and two must be focused in the inner world (Intellectual, Visionary, Artist, Stabilizer). If your Predominant Style is externally focused, it's possible that you picked externally focused Styles in each of the other three quadrants. The same is true if your Predominant Style is inwardly focused; you may find you have picked all internally oriented Styles.

Check your results, and if you need to, go back through the assessment and identify which two quadrants you use externally and which two you use internally to ensure you have identified the right Associate Styles. Modify the chart above as necessary. Keep in mind that the assessment in the book serves primarily to help you to identify your Predominate Striving Style and, as a result, helps you only to narrow down your Associate Styles.

Brief Descriptions of the Eight Striving Styles

Leader: I Need to Be in Control

As a Leader, I achieve control through understanding and deciding what has to be done; who has to do it; and how and when they should do it. I focus externally. I use reason and logic to make decisions. I plan so that things are done according to what I believe is important. I maintain control over people and activities. I direct and oversee others to ensure they do things right.

Intellectual: I Need to Be Knowledgeable

As an Intellectual, I achieve knowledge through understanding and deciding how something works, what something is, and where it fits with an inner worldview. I focus internally. I use logic and reason to guide my decisions. I plan according to what I believe is important. I categorize, inspect, and analyze in my mind. I build information data banks that lead to expertise. I order and accumulate information.

Performer: I Need to Be Recognized

As a Performer, I produce awareness of what is possible, then set goals and seek recognition for achieving them. I like to win and try to be the best at all I do. I have a quick mind that synthesizes information and experiences. I use insight and intuition to help me conceptualize solutions to problems. I focus externally. I see the potential in others and inspire them to go for it.

Visionary: I Need to Be Perceptive

As a Visionary, I produce awareness by perceiving how things will be, how they connect, what they mean. I foresee implications. I have images of the future and intuitive knowledge of what to do next. I focus internally—on my concept of a whole plan, a theory, and/or a pattern. I demand action. I have insight into people and their potential. I gather and synthesize information.

Socializer: I Need to Be Connected

As a Socializer, I produce relationships by connecting with others. I respond to the expressed or unexpressed wants and needs of others. I am socially astute and demand adherence to social norms. I disconnect from relationships when others don't act "right." I focus externally. I value others by comparing and contrasting them with myself. I express feelings with exuberance. I see harmony in relationships.

Artist: I Need to Be Creative

As an Artist, I produce relationships by creating a perfect, deep, meaningful bond with another person. I seek authentic expression of myself in life, work, and relationships. I destroy relationships that fail to meet their perfect image. I idealize others. I focus internally. I value myself by comparing and contrasting myself with others. My expression is self-focused; I think my feelings.

Adventurer: I Need to Be Spontaneous

As an Adventurer, I achieve spontaneity by producing and reproducing new experiences. I seek any variation of experience that will intensely excite my sense. I observe, notice, and live what is real and immediate. I discriminate against the quality of experiences. I focus externally. I experience in the now, and I am at one with that experience. I follow the natural order by adapting to the experience.

Stabilizer: I Need to Be Secure

As a Stabilizer, I achieve security by producing and reproducing the same experiences. I build continuity of experience by doing the same thing over again. I qualify, evaluate, and measure. I compare, link, and decide what is proper. I contrast the present to past to ensure continuity. I focus internally. I connect to the idea of the way it "should be" based on how it has been.

#4

Understanding Your Results

Sometimes we live our lives like puzzle pieces turned upside down—only showing the world our gray sides. Then along comes life, and it starts flipping them over, showing to us and the world more than just the outline of who we are—it shows us the colors. If we can start to turn more over and put them together, we can see the picture of who we really are emerge.

—Manifest

The results of your Self-Assessment provide you with a starting place to understand how your brain is organized. However, the results might not be what you expected or fit with how you think of yourself. While everyone has four quadrants in their brain and is a mix of four Striving Styles, one Style is our main base of action. Not everything in the description of your Predominant Striving Style will apply to you all the time, because in various situations, you will use your Associate Styles. If you feel that your results don't match how you see yourself, you can redo the assessment, but first consider a few things that may have influenced your responses.

When you were completing the self-assessment, did you do the following?

- Respond on the basis of how you have to behave at work, or how you are expected to behave because of your role in your family, rather than how you naturally prefer to behave?
- Think about what you wish to be like versus how you currently are?
- Respond according to your first impulse, or override it after a lot of thought?
- Answer on the basis of what comes most naturally, or what you

have learned to do to override your natural instincts? For example, did you rate yourself as being self-critical "Occasionally" but think to yourself, "Well, I do criticize myself a lot, but most of the time I catch myself and stop"?

Your results may not reflect who you think you should be, or similarly, they may not reflect the attributes you most value. Reflect on the way you are thinking about your results:

- Are you interpreting the results in terms of what is desirable versus undesirable, judging them good or bad, right or wrong? Have you thought to yourself, "I don't want to be that kind of person"?
- Were you thinking about which responses would be most desirable to others, or how others might perceive your results?
- What would have been your desired results? Which Style(s) do you think describes you better?

When we respond authentically, it takes much less effort and energy because we don't have to think it through or take the time to evaluate how we respond. Take a minute to go back through the section(s) you are unsure about, review your responses, and reflect on the amount of effort it took to answer the questions and whether your first instinct was overridden. If any of the above scenarios apply, reflect on your answers to see whether you might respond differently with a second look. Ask someone you trust to offer an opinion about whether the results seem to fit how he or she experiences you based on observations of your behavior. Read the description of the Predominant Style that your scores indicated, and of those that you scored strongly on, to see whether another Style is a better fit—not one you like better, but one that is a more accurate description of who you are.

If your score was tied between two Styles, read the chapters on both of the Styles to see which one sounds more like you. Often we will use two of our Styles together and with greater frequency because they are near each other in the brain. They may be in the same brain hemisphere, which causes us to use one side of our brain almost exclusively—a situation commonly referred to as being left brained or right brained. When we often use two Styles together, it can be difficult to figure out which is our Predominant Style with the Self-Assessment.

You can also ask someone you trust to answer the Assessment on your behalf. It is certainly an interesting exercise to see how someone else answers about you. (My husband and I did this.) The viewpoint of a trusted partner or friend can be a valuable part of self-understanding and can give you some insight into what Style you use when interacting with others as compared to how you tend to see yourself.

Most important, read the chapters on the eight Striving Styles. This will give you more detailed knowledge of the characteristics, behaviors, and tendencies of each of the Styles. After you have finished reading the chapters, review your responses to the Self-Assessment statements to decide which Styles are most like you. Remember, none of the Striving Styles is better or worse than any other. They all have their own value and function in your personality. Some tend to be more valued for one gender or circumstance or a particular type of society or family arrangement than others, but each has its unique abilities and potential when applied within the Self-Actualizing (SA) System, and each works to our detriment when we live from our Self-Protective (SP) System.

Remember that you are not your Striving Style. This means that you don't have to identify yourself as a Leader or an Artist. Instead, you can learn to recognize when you are using your Leader or Artist function so that you can shift easily from one function to the other when necessary.

This Self-Assessment gives you a general idea of your Predominant and Associate Styles and is meant only to introduce you to what your Striving Style might be. For a more accurate result, or to validate the results you came up with, you can complete the Striving Styles Personality System Assessment available at www.whoareyoumeanttobe.com.

The online SSPS Assessment is a more comprehensive assessment, with a greater number of statements. It therefore collects more detailed information about your preferences and is better able to distinguish the finer points of each of the Striving Styles. It will tally your scores and compute how your brain is organized on the basis of your Predominant Style, and it will identify the Associate Styles that go along with that Predominant Style. The results of the online SSPS Assessment will also reflect the degree to which you are using your Predominant and Associate Styles, so you can see whether you are using all of the quadrants of your brain optimally, over- or under-utilizing your Predominant Style, or relying too heavily on your Associate Styles.

Beyond identifying your Predominant Striving Style, the online SSPS Assessment provides you with a foundation for understanding how your brain works as a whole, as well as the information you need to proceed on your path to becoming who you are meant to be.

PART II
THE EIGHT
STRIVING STYLES

All the evidence that we have indicates that it is reasonable to assume in practically every human being, and certainly in almost every newborn baby, that there is an active will toward health, an impulse towards growth, or towards the actualization.

—Abraham Maslow

EACH OF THE EIGHT Striving Styles has its own unique attributes based on the quadrant of the brain it resides in. These attributes are recognizable by the way a Style behaves, communicates, and relates to others. (It may sound odd to talk about the Styles as if they are people, but often that's the best way to understand the concept.) The distinct talents, abilities, and behaviors of each of the Styles ensure that they get their predominant need met. Understanding the function of the part of the brain each Style originates from, and what its predominant need is, enables us to identify how each Style will behave at its best, how it will behave when it feels threatened, and what its blind spots are. Looking at the Styles in terms of the brain quadrants also shows us which situations will satisfy the Style's need and which will thwart it. Having this information about your Striving Style gives you the ability to identify behaviors that will ensure you stay on the path to achieving your potential.

The following chapters provide descriptions of each of the eight Striving Styles. For each Style you will find the following:

- An overview and highlights of the Striving Style, which provides its general characteristics
- What makes each Style tick, including information on the part of the brain the Style is located in, and what types of activities it is therefore oriented toward
- Its relationship style, which includes aspects of its communication style, and its social and emotional orientation
- Its need satisfiers, which includes the "must-have" activities that satisfy the Style's predominant need, how it is likely to behave if it is self-protective, and how it behaves if it is self-actualizing
- A list of the types of situations and activities that activate the Style's Self-Protective System
- What the Style's blind spots are likely to be—the things it is often most unaware of and how these can affect other people
- Recommendations for the types of activities and behaviors that will enable the Style to upshift to its Self-Actualizing System in order for you to become who you are meant to be

CHAPTER SIX
THE LEADER—STRIVING TO BE IN CONTROL

I planned each charted course, each careful step along the byway
And more, much more than this, I did it my way.

—*"My Way," Paul Anka*

WE ARE ALL FAMILIAR with Leaders, those take-charge individuals who seem like they were born to lead and who expect others to follow. They need to be in control, they know what they want, and they go after it. Leaders are perhaps the most self-confident of the Striving Styles. They enjoy taking the helm, and the ease with which they do so makes them seem like naturals for the role. Undaunted by the challenges of responsibilities that others shy away from, they often end up in leadership positions at work and in their communities.

Leaders are outgoing, gregarious, direct, and upbeat people. Working and being productive gives them a sense of their own power and authority. Their goals energize them and they have a passion to turn ideas into reality. Their need is satisfied by introducing order to people, activities, or the environment. As they need to be in charge of their own destiny, they seek careers in which they have the authority to create and implement whatever they think is appropriate to get the job done. Goal oriented and ambitious, they want to climb the ladder to the top, where they are "king or queen of the castle." They look for ongoing challenges that provide a feeling of personal mastery. The following quote from *Elle* magazine describes the Leader Style that's predominant in the young actress Emma Watson:

There's something efficient about her, as though life is a big to-do list that needs to be addressed...Being Emma Watson is serious business.

Leaders are compelled to be the authors of their own lives. They tend to live by the motto "I think, therefore I am." This is a tremendous boost to their confidence, because all it takes to instill a great self-concept is to think of oneself as great. Leaders are the people who believe they can't fail, who channel all of their energy and determination into making things happen. These strong-willed individuals are compelled to fashion the world the way they believe it should be. When this doesn't work, they can resort to more aggressive tactics to force their will on the environment and everyone in it.

Giving advice comes easy for Leaders. They automatically seem to know the right thing to do in any situation. Free with both solicited and unsolicited advice and opinions, Leaders let people know their thoughts on which direction to take in life. If you're not careful, the Leader will sit right down in the driver's seat of your life and speed away. This is the way Leaders show their love and affection—by taking charge of the planning and activities of their family, friends, neighbors, and colleagues. They don't just help people get started; once Leaders are involved, they stay in control to ensure that everyone stays on track.

The character Monica Geller on the TV show *Friends* is a prime example of the Leader Style:

Well known for her need to be in control, Monica was often described as "freakishly strong." Not one to give up this control easily, she was always more careful with dating than her female friends were, ultimately choosing Chandler as her mate—a man she could certainly dominate!

Monica's need to control her environment and everyone in it was acted out frequently in her obsession with cleaning. In the pilot episode of Friends, roommate Phoebe had just moved out because she was concerned that their friend-ship would not survive Monica's maniacal tidiness. In the episode "The One with the Stain," Monica arrives home to find that the apartment has been cleaned. She asks Chandler, "Oh, no, was I cleaning in my sleep again?" Sheepishly, Chandler replies that he hired a maid to clean. Monica replies anxiously, "I hope that by maid, you mean mistress, 'cause if some other woman was here cleaning, then…!" Chandler tries to soothe her by saying, "Honey, I know you don't like to relinquish control…" but it doesn't work. Monica blurts, "Relinquish *is just a fancy word for lose!*"

What Makes Leaders Tick?

The Leader Style operates from the left rational brain and therefore tends to focus more on thoughts about people and situations than on any personal experience of the situations themselves. Recall that the left rational brain is responsible for the formation of our self-concept or our idea about who we are and is unaffected by moment-to-moment changes in our feelings. This makes Leaders confident and self-assured as long as they think they are right. "Sometimes in error, but never in doubt" captures the essence of the Leader's self-concept. While other Styles feel they have to earn the right to take charge, Leaders believe they are born with it.

The left rational brain is strong on self-regulation, or the manage-ment of impulses and emotions. Leaders are able to dispassionately consider facts and situations and use reason to decide on the appro-priate course of action relative to their desired results. However, they also have the tendency to control rather than manage. Should they have an impulse to see a friend or to do something special for their partner, they can easily override it in favor of finishing whatever task they were doing.

Generally, Leaders have a powerful presence and need to stay in control of any situation they are in by exercising this power. Leaders enjoy feeling powerful—to achieve, to produce, and to control outcomes—both their own and others'. They desire to be the person implementing their agenda and influencing others to follow it. They don't like having to depend on others to get things done.

Leaders have the ability to be intensely involved in many things but not personally invested in anything. They will discuss all subjects with vigor and not be personally hurt or affected by what is said. Their conversations often involve them thinking out loud and using the other person as a sounding board. They put all ideas forward, even the ones that don't make sense. Leaders need to say things aloud so they can "see" what they are thinking more clearly.

Terry is the chief operating officer of a global manufacturing company that has recently become unionized. He is taking the unionization of the workforce very personally, as he believes it reflects negatively on him as a leader. Terry now has to follow new procedures and can no longer operate with full control and impunity in managing his employees. In classic Leader style, Terry is growing increasingly frustrated with the situation, feeling his power and control slipping away from him.

At home, he has started being hypercritical of his wife, Lara, and their children, insisting that they do everything his way. He lost his temper twice in a single week and almost got into a fight with a driver who cut him off on the way to work. He blamed his behavior on the people who led the unionization movement at the company, and his rants against them have become legendary.

Lara finally put her foot down, telling him that he couldn't keep acting the way he was. She suggested they go to counseling to improve the situation. When Terry and Lara came to see me, it was clear in the first session that the issues were not between them, but with Terry's loss of control at work. We agreed that Terry would continue with counseling but that Lara didn't need to return unless Terry's behavior escalated at home.

During the ensuing sessions, Terry began to see how his need to be in control was being frustrated by the unionization at work and that he was trying—unsuccessfully—to meet that need by becoming more controlling at home. I presented Terry with the choice he had to make: he could either reflect on his leadership style and work to change his approach, or he could leave his employer and find another position in a nonunion environment. Either way, he could not bring his frustrated need home.

Terry decided that after working so hard to get where he was in his job, he was not willing to leave, and we began working on developing his emotional self-awareness. I gave him feedback on the emotional impact of his behavior on others and how frightening he could be. This was a shock to him, as his idea of himself was very different from the reality of his behavior. He couldn't believe that people didn't see how much he cared about them and how hard he was working for them. Through many sessions and a lot of hard work on Terry's part, he shifted to a more synergistic and collaborative approach to managing people. Just talking about his behavior and recognizing he could do something about the situation helped him feel more in control. His home life returned to normal as he practiced new ways of dealing with issues at work.

Relationship Style of the Leader

Leaders' relationships tend to be open, honest, and stimulating. Leaders like to do things with others and often have a large circle of friends and acquaintances. They are entertaining, engaging, and social people who easily attract people to them. Both at work and in their personal lives, Leaders form relationships based on what they are doing or producing. They tend to get involved with people in organizations that have a purpose—serving on the board of organizations associated with music, art, and literature, or managing fund-raising projects. They may become the coach of their children's soccer team or head of the board for the local homeless shelter. This is the way they show their caring to others. They take an active part in their relationships and express their thoughts and ideas with enthusiasm.

Though not overtly tender and empathetic, Leaders are often loyal and committed partners and friends. They make sure the lives of their partner and children are well organized and directed, and they provide equal praise for success and criticism should they stray off course. They want their partner to participate in their social world and often have rituals with other family members to make sure they stay in touch. While they enjoy being active and doing things for fun, their need to critique what they are doing instead of just having fun can be a source of puzzlement for others.

For twenty years, Blake (Stabilizer) has golfed with his brother-in-law Steve (Leader) three or four times a year. Steve had the habit of recounting exactly what he had done wrong after every missed shot. Blake would listen to his self-critiques and would agree with Steve; however, he couldn't understand why, if Steve knew what he was doing wrong, he wasn't fixing his own mistakes.

Some Leaders try to run their relationships as they would run their real estate firms or widget factories. They believe there is a place for everything and that nothing should be out of place. They are constantly intervening to do things for others and easily take over from people who can't keep up with their pace. At some point, when Leaders takes stock of their relationships, they realize that they are the ones who do everything and that without their nagging or cajoling others, nothing would get accomplished. When their take-charge behavior unconsciously becomes a taking-over behavior, others just step back, afraid to get swept up in the Leader's warp-speed productivity. Leaders have a tendency to foster dependency in others because they think they know how to do things faster and better than others can, and often they're right!

Although they deeply care about their loved ones, Leaders can be so focused on work that it interferes with their personal relationships. If it's your birthday, you can bet that your Leader partner has that information tucked away somewhere, neatly organized, but you can't assume that this knowledge will translate into anything like a romantic weekend, or anything with a heart or a flower on it, although sometimes it might if he or she scheduled it into a planner. Although Leaders are armed with the best intentions and enjoy time spent with family, doing so often takes second place to work. When at home, they may even go as far as to sneak their iPhone to the washroom with them after you think you've won the "turn your iPhone off when you get home" battle.

How Leaders Satisfy Their Need to Be in Control

If I allowed these tragic letters to affect me, I'd be a wreck, because I get many heartbreakers, and I just have to separate myself from the problems of these readers. Otherwise, I wouldn't be able to help them.

—*Ann Landers*

Giving Advice

It often seems that Leaders have a finger in every possible pie. Their talents for organizing and advising in a variety of situations are both useful and beneficial to others. Leaders will take on the role of adviser with friends, family members, and others in their community. Their unique ability to be objective and detached lets them delve deeply into someone's personal problems without being emotionally affected themselves. They can then move on to something totally unrelated in the next moment, cool and collected. They aren't bogged down in the emotions of others, so they can stay with the issues long enough to give advice that is substantial and undiluted by their own feelings.

Self-Protective Leaders overpower others. In their SP System, Leaders are tougher, more aggressive, and domineering. No longer objective in their advisory capacity, they become impatient with others, lose their temper, and become emotionally and physically intimidating. They behave like dictators, pushing or browbeating others to take their advice. They can go from zero to ballistic in seconds, leaving the witnesses to their behavior in shock. Leaders amp up their criticism of others to get others to do things according to the advice they have given. When it comes to being critical, Leaders are in a class by themselves. Their critical thoughts are almost palpable before they are unleashed. Self-protective Leaders can be so intimidating that they cause a domino effect of activating others' SP Systems. When the SP Leaders convention comes to your town, it's a good time to take a vacation somewhere else!

I have sometimes...forgotten...to pat the back of someone or say "thank you"...I wish I were just the nicest person [but] I am a business person.

—*Martha Stewart*

Self-Actualizing Leaders let others be. Leaders often know the best course of action for people to take, but need to develop influence skills. Their command and control tactics are fine when situations warrant them, but taking over someone else's life is generally not a good use of these skills. Although not being attached to whether people take their advice initially causes them to feel anxious, SA Leaders let go. They learn to let people find their own way and make their own mistakes. They also cultivate an appropriate amount of patience and wait for others to take the initiative. Leaders show their caring for others by helping them without giving into the impulse to take control. They can tolerate their own feelings of helplessness while they watch a loved one struggle with problems, and they trust that everything will work out. They have learned that people are not objects to be fixed but feeling beings to be understood, cared for, and nurtured.

Being Productive

Leaders are much more motivated when their activities have a purpose, when they can feel a sense of their physical power and mastery, and when their efforts produce a tangible result. Having goals and achieving them provides opportunities for Leaders to increase their sense of mastery and power. Because there must be a component of usefulness and productivity to their activities, Leaders don't make a point of satisfying their social or personal needs. They prefer to do things with others rather than alone while at the same time either calling the shots or giving input into the rules of the game. Leaders radiate a cool, calm, and collected attitude while doing whatever they must do to reach their goals.

Kyle was a highly successful business manager in a brokerage firm. He worked fourteen-hour days and usually weekends, sending emails to his subordinates at all hours. His work ethic and management style made everyone around him feel both anxious and inadequate. Although most of the time Kyle was pleasant enough, he never engaged in small talk or inquired about the lives of his staff. If someone got sick and couldn't meet a deadline, or made a mistake, Kyle would blow up and rant, then storm into his office and slam the door. He would later reappear as though nothing had happened. He was surprised when his managers told him that several staff members had threatened to quit if he didn't change his behavior.

Self-Protective Leaders work, work, work. SP Leaders can dehumanize themselves when they work as hard as they do without taking into account the impact this has on their well-being, their behavior, and their relationships. These Leaders end up working so much that they are absent from their personal lives. They usually love their work, so they have difficulty setting boundaries around the amount of time they spend there. Work is probably the most common addiction for Leaders and is a way of avoiding their relationships, emotions, and interpersonal conflict. They risk being perceived by others as machinelike sticks in the mud or "married to their work."

Donald Trump once said: "Deals are my art form. Other people paint beautifully on canvas or write wonderful poetry. I like making deals, preferably big deals. That's how I get my kicks."

He made no bones about being a workaholic or about wanting those types of people in his employ. In 2007, Trump told the *New York Post*, "They [workaholics] don't want to miss what's going on. Although vacations are supposed to be about de-stressing, some people admitted it would be more stressful not knowing what was going on at work while they were away. And those are the kind of people I want working for me."

Self-Actualizing Leaders take time to be. They have learned the value of doing things for sheer pleasure, including spending time with others. They are no longer willing to sacrifice their personal lives and relationships for work. They have learned to tolerate feeling helpless, practice acceptance, and just go with the flow in those moments when they can't control what's going on. They know it's futile to demand that life remain within their control. Self-Actualizing Leaders have learned to reflect on what they are feeling and how they are affected when they disconnect from feeling. They know how important it is to build bridges between their thoughts and feelings and how it ultimately makes them more effective at leading and interacting with others. They see the value of getting to know their needs and feelings, and they know that this takes time and should not be postponed.

Being Logical and Rational

Leaders view human behavior from a principled, logical, and objective position. They are comfortable with who they are and are transparent in their dealings with others. If someone isn't playing by the rules, a Leader will make sure to correct that person to get things back in control. If there are no rules, Leaders make them up. When you lay out the word "pronk" in a game of Scrabble with a Leader, she'll be the one to consult the dictionary before allowing you to collect your points. (A Leader will also want to choose the dictionary.)

Self-Protective Leaders deny or repress their feelings and

those of others. They insist that everything be done and conflicts resolved according to their criteria, which they consider fair and equitable. Their position is simple: "I am right and you are wrong, and no matter how condescending and arrogant I am being, you should change your position." They fail to see how dehumanizing it is when they disallow others' freedom to express their feelings or challenge their ideas. They use logic like a sledgehammer, bludgeoning the other person with it as though force would change that person's mind. In the drive to win, they end up beating people down instead of listening to them. Self-Protective Leaders will make the same arguments again and again, as if repetition alone could alter someone's view.

The following is an excerpt from a counseling session with Jerry, a Leader who shares his thinking process when he is in his Self-Protective System.

I was so tired of having the same fight with my wife, Donna. She was always going on and on about how unhappy she was because I was working all the time. She was driving me crazy. I told her a hundred times that she had to just get over it, as I had a very important job and couldn't just leave work at five o'clock like everyone else. She said she needed help with the kids, as though I should come home and help her! I told her to hire someone to babysit and go out with the girls. She told me that she was going to throw me out if something didn't change, and I thought she was just blowing smoke. Well, I couldn't believe it when I came home from work at nine o'clock one night and my suitcases were on the sidewalk and the locks on the door [had been] changed. Can you believe that she would do this after how hard I have worked for her and my children? I do it for them.

Self-Actualizing Leaders listen to the needs and feelings of others. They no longer argue other people into submission. They listen to how others feel and remind themselves often that their own and others' emotions are important and useful and should be considered. Self-Actualizing Leaders understand that discussions needn't be competitions and have come to terms with how their inner "warrior" can overpower and alienate others, thereby undoing all of the hard work they have done to build trust in relationships. They consistently work to break the habit of dismissing or criticizing other people. They listen to what others actually need instead of assuming they know.

Planning and Organizing Their Lives

Leaders are naturals at scheduling, planning, and organizing. Their daily plan will include a prioritized list of things to do. Their long-term plan will be more detailed, setting out their financial, physical, and material goals, to be completed in order of priority. If for any reason the Leader's plans are derailed, all activity will cease until he or she can design another plan to get back in control. Leaders' plans form a vital part of their security because they serve to confirm that all of the elements they are responsible for are progressing in a prescribed way, toward the desired outcome. Their plan is like a GPS device with carefully designed waypoints for charting the course of their life.

Self-Protective Leaders react. Armed with their to-do lists, they are intolerant of interruptions or obstacles. Self-Protective Leaders adopt a quick-fix, "get out of my way" approach to their problems, including those in relationships. They want to keep things moving, and they become increasingly reactive when things aren't going as they planned. They make decisions so quickly that they create chaos and confusion for themselves and for people around them. This makes them even more impatient with others, whom they blame for the chaos. They are quick to anger, complain about relatively small matters, and get annoyed with others' slow pace—all driven by their urgency to conquer their to-do lists. They are frustrated when others don't do what they tell them to do and can create waves, rather than smooth sailing, when they become too intent on keeping things moving.

Phyllis, Stanley, I want you to switch desks. I am going to reorganize and restructure the physical layout of the office to maximize everything! I think we are getting a lot done, don't you? On paper, at least, and we are, after all, a paper company, are we not? Are we not? Are you with me? Are you with me? Thank you very much.

—*Michael Scott (Steve Carrell)*, The Office

Self-Actualizing Leaders respond. Self-Actualizing Leaders notice that things aren't going as they would like and are able to stay focused on identifying the problem. They understand the pressure that they put on themselves to check everything off their to-do lists and are more realistic about what they can and can't do. They plan for interruptions and contingencies. They manage their own impatience and frustration and are tolerant and patient with those who are having difficulty or don't see it their way. Doing right by people is as important to them as completing tasks in their time line. Self-Actualizing Leaders gain insight into the impact of overplanning and scheduling their lives and give themselves time to get things done in a more realistic time frame.

Activators of the Self-Protective System

The Self-Protective System in Leaders is activated by people and situations that cause Leaders to feel weak, helpless, or powerless. Leaders fear not being able to rein things in and become ferocious in an attempt to get their power back. Feeling powerless frustrates their need to be in control and therefore is what they fear most. They will do whatever they can to protect themselves from those feelings.

Absence of Influence

Any situation in which Leaders can't influence a person or situation will frustrate their need to be in control and activate their SP System. For example, say a Leader wants to go to a concert and her partner doesn't want to. The partner doesn't like the artist and won't be persuaded. This angers the Leader, who doesn't want to go alone. Feeling helpless, the Leader quickly shifts to aggressive behavior to help gain control over what is happening. The more helpless or trapped the Leader feels, the angrier she becomes.

People Who Don't Listen

Leaders feel in control when people listen to them and do what they want. Their SP System is activated when others clearly need help but don't heed their advice. Although their intention is to be helpful, people sometimes just want the chance to vent rather than being told what they should do. Leaders can feel powerless when their children ignore or rebel against them. Leaders need others to defer to their wisdom and authority to avoid feeling helpless or out of control.

Overcontrolling Emotions

Leaders like to feel in control of their emotions and often neglect, deny, or repress them instead of paying attention to them. This absence of emotions makes them feel powerful; however, in reality, they are constantly living on the edge of a blowup. Their SP System is activated by prolonged overcontrolling of their emotions. Others can feel the volcano that is on the verge of erupting and will steer clear of the Leader as a result. No one wants to be the spark that unleashes the fury, and the Leader's SP System can be triggered by just about anything.

Emotional and Irrational Behavior

Leaders have little tolerance for the emotions of others as they see them as something to be fixed rather than expressed. They don't see the point of getting upset or acting irrationally, or otherwise losing control of emotions. They rule their relationships by making sure that everyone conforms to their code of conduct. Leaders treat others' emotions like problems to be solved, and once they come up with a solution for them, they expect people to stop emoting. When accused of being cold or unfeeling, they believe they are being treated unjustly or don't really care.

Are you crying? Are you crying? ARE YOU CRYING? There's no crying! THERE'S NO CRYING IN BASEBALL!
—*Coach Jimmy Dugan (Tom Hanks),* A League of Their Own

Being Blindsided

Nothing causes Leaders to feel out of control faster than being blindsided, for example by unexpected news or by being told that they have to redo something a different way. You can almost see the power draining from the Leader's body and the fury rising up. Something as simple as a friend canceling a dinner date can throw a Leader into an emotional storm.

Depending on Others

It is very difficult for a Leader to trust that other people are capable of running their own lives for themselves. When Leaders are forced to spend too much time in situations in which they cannot control or influence their environment or the people in it, they start to feel helpless and powerless. To battle these feelings, they start finding fault with those who do have the authority over the situation. Leaders easily feel out of control when they have to let go and trust that others will do what they have promised.

Blind Spots
Creating Power Struggles

It's difficult to give feedback to Leaders because of the force of their personalities. When challenged or opposed, Leaders are adamant that they are right. They can dismiss the input of others as irrelevant. Because they think they are being logical, they refuse to see themselves through the eyes of others. Leaders have a tendency to create power struggles by insisting that they're right. Many people don't even bother to contradict Leaders because they are afraid to.

Blaming Others

Leaders blame others when they lose control. "If they would do what I say, I wouldn't have to get mad," a frustrated Leader mother laments about her children. Rather than examining what they are feeling, they attack others and may deliver threats or ultimatums, giving in to the feeling of power and control that anger temporarily gives them. This external outburst masks the quieter inner implosion of helpless feelings.

Acting from Emotions

Leaders don't believe that they are motivated by their emotions. Because they don't think of themselves as emotional, they belittle those who express more vulnerable and tender feelings. They can get angry when someone cries, as they can't see a reason for it. They don't consider emotions such as anger, frustration, or impatience—which they express without hesitation—to be in the same category as feelings of sadness or despair.

Steve (Leader) hosts his family's annual picnic at his home, and for the last two years it has rained—not enough to call the picnic off but enough to put a damper on the event. This year, relatives who had not come to the picnic before were going to attend. Steve wanted everything to be perfect, and he started getting anxious when he first heard the long-range forecast calling for rain on the day of the picnic. Not being able to be in control of knowing whether it would rain or not activated his SP System, causing him to act like a hungry bear coming out of hibernation. His family avoided interacting with him because he had become so easy to anger, lashing out at anyone and anything that got in the way. Fortunately, the storm system passed without as much as a drop of rain on the happy picnickers. Steve later lamented that he had worried so much over something he couldn't control.

Criticizing Others

Leaders don't recognize when they need to turn off the criticism. Although they may have the best of intentions, the way they express themselves can seem hypercritical. They believe that their criticism will be welcomed because, in their view, it is only the truth. For example, a Leader husband may say to his wife, "I thought I told you that dress didn't look good on you. Why are you wearing it?" To the Leader it seems like a simple question, but it can have devastating results. Leaders don't always consider how their message may affect the other person before they ask it. As a result, Leaders are frequently accused of being hurtful, insensitive, and critical.

I never give them hell. I just tell the truth and they think it's hell.

—*Harry Truman*

Controlling Others

Leaders don't see how controlling they are of others. They can be so afraid to lose control that they insist everything be done their way—the "right" way. An impromptu jaunt to the beach can become an overly orchestrated execution of plans, rules, and schedules that removes every shred of spontaneity (not to mention fun). Leaders don't see that they are treating friends and loved ones like employees.

Upshifting to Their Self-Actualizing System

For Leaders to upshift to their SA System, they need to become more self-aware and to redirect their striving energy by doing the following.

Talking Less and Listening More

Building awareness of cues that they are talking over or down to someone can cause Leaders to upshift and take in what is being said to them. When Leaders notice that others have stopped talking or are becoming increasingly emotional, they can pause to consider why this might be happening.

Releasing the Pressure

Leaders upshift by recognizing when they need to release their emotions safely in order to restore balance. Barking out orders and yelling at people only leads to resentment and power struggles in relationships. Recognizing that they are feeling frustrated and that they may just need to vent allows Leaders to relieve the tension they feel inside so they can get calm enough to stand on the sidelines or to talk through what they are feeling with others.

Tolerating Feelings

Leaders need to recognize when they are feeling helpless and are trying to get back in control. An awareness of how their behavior changes when they feel helpless (not being able to influence or control others) allows Leaders to intervene on their own behalf and upshift to a place of reasoned response. They learn to identify the warning signals that they are about to lose control of their emotions.

Taking Time Away

Most Leaders can upshift by taking time away from anything goal oriented. The pressure they put themselves under is alleviated, rather than elevated, when SA Leaders play and have some fun. Getting familiar with their "tipping point" allows them to go out and replenish themselves. But if it's not on the day planner, they may never do it!

Counting to Ten

To upshift, Leaders have to recognize when they are escalating and consciously de-escalate themselves. Focusing on their breathing for a couple of minutes or counting to ten can quickly help them step back into a more objective position where they name what is happening, identify the issue, and shift to problem solving.

In the Wilson family, the first Sunday of every month is Kids' Day. On that day, the three Wilson children, ages thirteen, ten, and eight, are allowed to decide and organize the family's activities. This tradition has helped their Leader mom Yvonne take a breather from being the orchestrator of all family events. At first, Yvonne was reluctant to give up her power to set the family's agenda, but after implementing the idea for a few months and realizing that she could still be a great parent without always being "the boss," she began to look forward to Kids' Day. She found that by taking on the task of organizing activities for the family, her kids were actually learning some skills of collaboration and leadership that would serve them well in other life situations.

Achieving Their Full Potential

Leaders are "masters of their universe," taking control of their destiny and everything in it. Responsible, authoritarian, and conscientious, they show us the way and expect us to follow. They believe they know what is right for everyone and will tell us the way it ought to be. They have the potential for tremendous achievements in business, in their community and with their family. With their strong organizational skills, assertiveness, decisiveness, objectivity, and can-do attitude, Leaders who are also able to exert measured, respectful control—over themselves and others—while staying well connected to their emotional life and that of others can fulfill their own potential and lead others to do so as well.

CHAPTER SEVEN
THE INTELLECTUAL— STRIVING TO BE KNOWLEDGEABLE

In this head my thoughts are deep…
I'm off again in my World!

—*"My World," Avril Lavigne*

AVRIL LAVIGNE'S WORDS PERFECTLY characterize the Intellectual Style. The thinkers appear to be doing nothing; however, they are always busy thinking, living their lives from the inside out. They have an aura of detachment and are more interested in observing what's happening than in participating. Quiet, reserved, and distant, they are often perceived as aloof and uninterested. In extraverted North America, others can mistakenly (and negatively) judge that nothing much is going on with them. However, Intellectuals are often "lost in thought" because so much is going on inside them. They have an extremely active inner world, where they enjoy analyzing, learning, understanding ideas, and gathering information.

Fiercely independent, focused, and self-sufficient, they are compelled to live their lives according to their own inner ideology or belief system. They aren't concerned with how others live their lives and don't seek to influence others to follow them. They need the freedom to decide what to do and how to do it on their own time line. Although their outer world may be chaotic, in their inner world everything runs exactly the way they believe it should. They can seem like rebellious nonconformists, yet they conform perfectly to the principles and values of their own inner system of self-government.

Intellectuals have a distracted, "absent-minded professor" quality about them—arriving at the last minute for work or social events, looking disheveled or mismatched. When it comes to what they consider unimportant, superficial, and insignificant, they "live and let live." Intellectuals won't impose their views on how people "should" be living. While they may have advice to give, as they can see what's going on with objectivity and clarity, their nonjudgmental approach to people's life choices gets in the way of them offering advice freely. They don't want others telling them how to live their lives and so refrain from doing so to others, even when it would be useful and appropriate. Should you ask them, however, they will happily offer their opinion.

The character Gregory House, on the TV series *House*, shows how Intellectuals focus singularly on solving problems and demonstrating their expertise. House takes only the patient cases that interest him, pursuing neither fame nor wealth. He solely seeks intellectual stimulation and engagement. He is more interested in the disease than the patient. For him to be interested in taking on a new patient, the case must be incredibly challenging or already considered unsolvable by others.

Intellectuals get excited about learning, and they approach new subject matter with excitement. They collect information the way others might collect stamps; however, no one really gets to see the vast database of information and knowledge they have accumulated. Their passion about learning drives them to spend countless hours in quest of mastery over the desired subject. Intellectuals' love affair with knowledge often gets in the way of staying connected in their relationships. Even when they pull themselves away to be with people, it often looks like they are present in body only. They seem to go somewhere else when caught up in thinking. One minute the Intellectual is talking to you, and the next it's as if his or her mind has floated off elsewhere. Once Intellectuals seize upon a puzzling problem, they pursue it until they understand its complexity completely, to the dismay of those left out of this inner event. The following quote describes the impact this can have on others:

For my own part, I would rather be in company with a dead man than with an absent one; for if the dead man gives me no pleasure, at least he shows me no contempt; whereas the absent one, silently indeed, but very plainly, tells me that he does not think me worth his attention.

—*Lord Chesterfield*

What Makes Intellectuals Tick?

Intellectuals live out of their left rational brain, which focuses more on what they think about people and situations and less on their own personal experiences of those people or situations. Objective and logical, Intellectuals see their own personalities and those of others as a conglomeration of tendencies, strengths, weaknesses, and abilities, which they don't judge but simply accept as the way people (including themselves) are. Intellectuals dispassionately consider facts, people, and situations, and create a complete inner ideology of how the world should operate, much the way others create principles, structures, and forms in the outer world.

The left rational brain is not holistic: it breaks things into their component parts, measures and sorts objects and experiences, and then decides how to respond. It decides what it needs to focus on when multiple objects are competing for attention. This enables Intellectuals to mentally organize numerous objects and to establish logical relationships between them. Their mental lives revolve around thoughts ("What is it?"), decisions ("What should I do with it?"), and systems ("What's the process for doing that?"). It's a great system for assembling a child's playhouse but not for building intimate relationships.

While they do not need to have control over others, Intellectuals need to have control over themselves and over how others may touch their lives or affect their behavior. They fashion their lives in such a way that they have the ability to do this. Intellectuals apply reason to decide on actions; impulses and emotions have no place in their ideological world, so they are easily managed. Their self-regulatory system often rejects emotional information, and they can easily thwart their own desires and physical needs. Should they feel something strongly, they cut off from the impulse or the person or situation that causes it. This leads to controlling their impulses and emotions rather than managing them.

Eric is a fifty-year-old motorcycle mechanic whose wife, Layla, came to me for help with their marriage. Because of Eric's knowledge and expertise, people in the motorcycle community across Canada seek him out. He spends most of his time in his garage or workshop, working on a hybrid engine he has designed. Layla, angry at the amount of time he spends in the garage, has embarrassed him a few times by bursting into his workshop and yelling at him in front of customers. Usually Eric handles these situations by withdrawing until his wife cools down. The last time she did this, he felt she had gone too far and he yelled back at her. Instead of sounding clever and articulate, he came across like a rebellious teen, which only humiliated him more.

Eric stubbornly believed that if Layla would just stop being so emotional, they could get back to normal. He expected her to apologize to him, which she did do, after a few sessions with me. However, she also explained that she felt hurt and ashamed by his lack of interest in her, and masked these feelings by staying angry with him. She asked him whether it was more important to be right than it was to be married. Although it was a risk, she told him that if he didn't put more time into their relationship, she would have no choice but to leave.

Her calmness unnerved Eric because he was used to her temper. When they came to see me together, Eric clearly believed he'd easily convince me that he was not the cause of their problems. Instead, Eric came to understand that his need to be knowledgeable had stopped him from developing relationship skills, and consequently, he was in a constant state of retreat or self-protection.

Intellectuals generally have little curiosity about what they are experiencing emotionally or how things affect them personally. It is as though there is no "I" with personal needs and feelings. They are more aware of their existence as observers, viewing how pieces of data and information converge into a form that is meaningful to them. In a sense, they are whatever happens to emerge in the moment. If they are researchers, they become cogs in the machine that is creating the research. If they are automobile engineers, they become integral parts of the teams that design cars. Because they ignore any personal reactions they may have in the process—whether offensive, irrational, pleasant, or painful—Intellectuals stay impersonal. They experience themselves as the vehicle for actualizing their ideas, with no significant personal connection to them.

Relationship Style of the Intellectual

Intellectuals are usually faithful and devoted mates who take their relationships seriously. They love deeply but don't feel the need to demonstrate their love in traditional ways. They can believe they are showing how much they care just by being there. As mates, they are easy to live with, although they can be somewhat forgetful and preoccupied. Operating from their own inner schedules, they are known to forget appointments, anniversaries, and daily schedules, even when written in their calendars. They are both devoted spouses and parents, and tend to be well informed about the best child-rearing practices.

Family and friends are very important to Intellectuals as they enjoy having people around them, although they don't actually have to interact directly with people to experience this enjoyment. They are passionate observers rather than actual participants: the Intellectual father who watches his children swimming in the waves may feel that he has spent quality time with them (although they may feel otherwise). Intellectuals often prefer to observe or figure out people rather than engage with them. Relationships are frequently based on common interests and scholarly pursuits rather than the sharing of feelings.

In social situations, Intellectuals act as if they are invisible, blending in like wallflowers. They will observe or find something to do so they don't have to interact with others. At parties, the Intellectual will keep score during games, coordinate the teams, or deliver a diatribe about the logic of the game itself—anything to escape actual involvement, especially if it involves sharing feelings or perhaps not knowing the right answer. For Intellectuals, emotions "do not compute."

Mr. Spock, a mixed human-Vulcan, and Data, an android, are two of the most well-known fictional characters from the Star Trek *franchise. Data has a "positronic" brain that allows him to store, categorize, and compute impressive amounts of information in little time. Data and Mr. Spock both experienced similar difficulties with understanding various aspects of human behavior— unable to feel emotion or understand certain human idiosyncrasies. Data's dilemma was addressed by the addition of an "emotion chip" to his positronic net. Spock had to find his own way.*

Like the Intellectual, both of these characters were able to offer an "outsider's" perspective on whatever situation they were in. Leonard Nimoy, who played the role of Spock, observed that Spock was "struggling to maintain a Vulcan attitude, a Vulcan philosophical posture, and Vulcan logic, opposing what was fighting him internally, which was human emotion" (Asherman, Alan. The Star Trek Compendium*).*

With all of the curiosity they have about how things work, Intellectuals have little curiosity about what they and others are experiencing emotionally. They have a very low orientation to sharing themselves with others and are unaware that people want and need to know what is actually happening in their lives. When Intellectuals share information, ideas, and expertise, they are giving others their most treasured possessions. However, this is not generally valued in relationships. If you are sick, don't expect warm, fuzzy comfort from your Intellectual partner or friend—you are more likely to get a carefully generated list of medical articles related to your condition. Intellectuals are more likely to work through their problems privately, keeping even the most important issues to themselves. This leaves those closest to them in the dark about what might be happening with them.

How Intellectuals Satisfy Their Need to Be Knowledgeable
Creating Their Own Worldview

Intellectuals are autonomous thinkers whose unshakable faith in their own ideas and beliefs drives them to keep doing their own thing. With an intense focus on their inner world, they don't just live their lives; their lives emerge from their ideas, experiences, and the results of their thought processes. They are self-governing, with their own personal "constitutions," and their behavior reflects these guiding principles and values. Intellectuals allow their reality to unfold, because they see reality as the culmination of ideas. If their ideology is aligned with that of their culture and community, they do extremely well. If not, they can seem out of step with mainstream society or even their own families.

I don't know about you, but I'm getting sick of pretending to be excited every time it's somebody's birthday, you know what I mean? What is the big deal? How many times do we have to celebrate that someone was born? Every year, over and over…All you did was not die for twelve months. That's all you've done, as far as I can tell.

—*Jerry Seinfeld*

Self-Protective Intellectuals do and say what they want, despite the consequences. If they don't value what family and friends value, they can put themselves at odds with the family culture. They don't mind being the "black sheep" and don't think that anything they do is weird as long as it aligns with their own internal playbook.

They make their own decisions, independent of the requirements or needs of others, or a sense of obligation to traditional commitments. When they feel cornered or pressured to do what others want them to do, they will make a show of compliance and then continue with what they were doing. They use passive resistance to avoid yielding to others' will; failing that, they retreat into their inner world, doing their own thing, even when this behavior may have negative results.

In the film A Beautiful Mind, *the math genius John Nash (played by Russell Crowe) inhabited an inner world in which he was a black-suited FBI agent (played by Ed Harris). Notably a brilliant but somewhat arrogant and antisocial man, Nash spent most of his time with his thoughts rather than with people, letting only a couple of people get near enough to connect with him. Gradually, Nash was able to observe his "inner FBI agent" and the mental world it represented with some distance and objectivity, rather than believing his imaginings.*

Self-Actualizing Intellectuals stay connected with others. They come to terms with the ways their "lone wolf" nature must be balanced so it doesn't prevent them from maintaining connections with people and other aspects of external reality. They consistently work to break the habit of setting themselves apart as dispassionate observers, on the fringe of society and unable to find their place in the world. They look to others for advice and feedback. They are aware of their tendency to reject anything that doesn't agree with their carefully crafted reality, and they work toward breaking that pattern. They enlarge their worldview rather than shrinking it to contain only those things that support their ideas. They don't just think about their view of reality; they work to make it real. They assert their authority, finding their voice during conflict and expressing their needs so that they don't feel overpowered by others' demands.

Being the Expert

To the Intellectual, knowledge is power. Intellectuals meet their predominant need by learning about and experimenting with things until they become the "expert," striving to be the knowledge leader in their careers and their personal lives. In their mind, they always know better or more than others. Never satisfied with a little knowledge, they keep themselves well informed about any subject that interests them. They are able to focus their attention exclusively and intensely on one area of interest, if necessary, letting everything else fall to the wayside as if nothing else exists while working toward becoming the authority. They keep themselves informed so they are never blindsided by new information or made to feel less than the person who knows the most. They communicate logically and directly, regardless of the impact it has on others. The logical and factual communication style of the Intellectual is demonstrated in this short dialogue between Special Agent Sealy Booth (Adventurer) and Dr. "Bones" Brennan (Intellectual) from the TV show *Bones*:

> Bones: You enjoy it [being an FBI agent] because you're a superb agent.
> Booth: You think?
> Bones: Of course, since I'm the best in my field. It would be self-destructive for me to work with someone who was beneath me.
> Booth: Okay, that's good, because I have to be honest, here. Sometimes I think you feel you're better than me.
> Bones: Well objectively, I'm more intelligent…
> Booth: See? There you go!
> Bones: In certain areas. And in others, I understand my limitations, and I admire your expertise.

Self-Protective Intellectuals hoard information. They hide behind an air of indifference and superiority. They may withhold information that others share freely, which adds to the impression of smugness and arrogance they create. They may also withhold from others information about their whereabouts or activities. Should their SP System be triggered at a party, the Intellectual may simply leave the scene without telling her date she is going. If Intellectuals can't flee awkward social situations, they may comfort themselves by luring others into intellectual battles over trivial details, where they can demonstrate their mental superiority. If you detect that a party conversation has been steered deliberately toward an obscure topic, you may be with an SP Intellectual who's challenging you to a mental joust. Intellectuals' reliance on being the most knowledgeable person in the room can become vulnerability: the more they win, the harder they must fight to maintain their position. You can't tell them anything they don't already know, and they may argue that you're wrong just to keep you in your place.

[I don't give] enough information so that [people]…absolutely know who they're dealing with.

—*Harrison Ford*

Self-Actualizing Intellectuals share their knowledge with others. They become who they are meant to be when they share their intimate and exhaustive knowledge with others—in words, deeds, and relationships—without feeling depleted by the experience. They allow themselves to experience their lives differently, understanding how they are connected to others and how their knowledge can serve the greater good. They are able to notice when they are staying in control by keeping information to themselves, even practicing sharing information when they really don't want to. No longer threatened by the thought of having to do something with their information, they complete things they have started and actually finish books, training programs, and college degrees. They also restrict their mental jousting to situations in which others show an interest.

Engaging in Lifelong Learning

With a hunger for learning, Intellectuals use their minds to experience the world. The intense interest they have in learning may not be readily apparent to others; however, they are lifelong learners, relentless in their pursuit of knowledge in areas of interest. Intellectuals enjoy the learning process, whether in a formal educational setting or on their own. Some Intellectuals are perpetual students with multiple degrees who are so enamored of learning that they never actually apply what they've learned. Some will consider returning to school later in life but will resist because they find learning in traditional settings restrictive. They are happiest when they can totally submerge themselves in the world of the mind. The following describes some of Intellectual and Facebook founder Mark Zuckerberg's pursuits:

Mark Zuckerberg pursued the subjects he was interested in voraciously. He excelled in the classics during high school, and in college he was known for reciting lines from epic poems such as The Iliad. *In his junior year at college, he won prizes in science (math, astronomy, and physics) and classical studies. He studied languages and could read and write French, Hebrew, Latin, and ancient Greek. His father taught him Atari BASIC programming in the 1990s, and by the time he began classes at Harvard, where he studied psychology and computer science, he was known as a programming prodigy.*

Self-Protective Intellectuals live in pursuit of perfect knowledge. With their compulsive need to know everything before doing anything, SP Intellectuals get caught up with seeking additional information or further educational credentials with no goal other than to know. They focus voraciously on one area until they know every possible thing about it, and only then will they stop their research. Regardless of being only one credit shy of a degree, for them knowledge is the goal, not its application. They then move on to their next topic of interest. While immersed in their pursuit of knowledge, they live solely in their heads, disconnected from the physical world, neglecting to take care of themselves and their environment. If they have children, their homes are chaotic and timetables are optional. In relationships they are present in body only, going through the motions of being with others, impatient to get back to what is most important to them.

Self-Actualizing Intellectuals try to live in the real world. This is a lifelong challenge, because it is easier and more comfortable for them to stay in their heads. They know the result of disconnecting from themselves, and they take the time to check in and see how they are feeling. Realizing that they cannot ignore their bodies without consequences, they devote energy to self-care, perhaps even becoming experts at it. Self-Actualizing Intellectuals recognize when their bodies need rest, reflection, cuddling, and connection, and they realize that they can get these things without negative consequences. They can observe their own behavior and see when they are disconnecting their minds from their bodies. They trust that others are giving them feedback to help them, not to make them feel stupid or inferior. They communicate to others when they are going away for alone time, also letting others know when to expect them back.

Being Accepted for Who They Are

With few social needs, Intellectuals don't spend a lot of time developing relationships or interpersonal skills and, consequently, can appear to be socially awkward. They don't mind this because they are generally content with their small circle of friends and family. Intellectuals use the Internet to connect with others, as it falls within their comfort zone to engage in data bytes of information rather than interpersonal dialogue. Secure in their intellectual endeavors, they do not require social validation, nor does it affect them when they don't get it. They have difficulty relating to others who need that kind of validation. They do, however, need people to understand them rather constantly misunderstanding or personalizing their behavior and berating them for it. Intellectuals are amazed at how people can distort their behavior and may have to go off and be by themselves to try to figure the other person out.

You seldom listen to me, and when you do, you don't hear, and when you do hear you hear wrong, and even when you hear right you change it so fast that it's never the same.

—*Marjorie Kellogg*

Self-Protective Intellectuals are there in body only. Because Intellectuals fail to communicate and stay connected to those around them, they often end up on the receiving end of someone's frustration with them. They feel misunderstood and don't see how their behavior has contributed to the problem. They don't tolerate interpersonal tension or emotional expression well, despite how often their lack of communication triggers it. They will listen to the other person while at the same time planning their escape. Getting angry with SP Intellectuals can cause them to immediately shut down and flee inside themselves. The words "we need to talk" can strike terror in the mind of the SP Intellectual, and their avoidance of emotional issues can create an undercurrent of unresolved tension in relationships. If the tension becomes great enough, Intellectuals will find ways to avoid the person who represents the conflict, such as being at home less often or escaping into books or television.

Self-Actualizing Intellectuals negotiate to get their needs met. They have learned to communicate and don't disappear when others are frustrated with them. They no longer segregate themselves in order to feel safe and are able to share information without being afraid of losing their power. When they feel hurt, they talk about it rather than pretending their feelings don't exist. Self-Actualizing Intellectuals make sure they have people around them who accept and appreciate them for who they are. They are able to tolerate their emotions and those of others, especially in close personal relationships. They stop demanding that others be as objective as they are. They learn to be aware of their partners' needs and feelings, and they invest in becoming reasonably knowledgeable about their own emotional needs, perhaps even turning their love of learning to emotions and how to use them to build healthier relationships. They offer to help others who also have difficulty understanding their own feelings. Over time, they learn what to expect at an emotional level in various circumstances.

Activators of the Self-Protective System

With their quest for the knowledge that ultimately gives them power, authority, and mastery over information, Intellectuals are activated by people and situations that cause them to feel incompetent, irrelevant, or dominated. They fear the loss of power and authority that comes from not being the expert. It makes them feel insignificant, and they will go to great lengths to get back "in the know." Feeling incompetent frustrates their need to be knowledgeable and therefore is what they fear most. Intellectuals do whatever they can to protect themselves from those feelings.

Demands of Others

Having to conform to social norms or others' rules makes Intellectuals feel dominated. They "march to the beat of their own drum" so that they can be self-determined and in charge of their own world. Their behavior aligns with their own set of rules; they are activated by people who tell them they have to do things a different way. Being forced to do things in prescribed fashion for long periods also feels threatening to them.

Having Expertise Unacknowledged

Intellectuals feel irrelevant, useless, and frustrated when others don't treat them as the expert or don't defer to their superior knowledge. Information is power, and if someone else has it, they easily feel dominated and out of control. They especially feel this way when someone they are with knows more than they do in their area of expertise. Without their standing as the foremost authority, they feel naked and defenseless against a world that threatens to overwhelm them.

Spending Too Much Time Alone

As much as Intellectuals love time alone, they can have too much of a good thing. As they seek more solitude, they become increasingly aloof, cold, and indifferent, causing problems in their relationships. The more time spent in pursuit of knowledge, the more challenging it is for them to function well in society. Their sense of themselves is distorted because it doesn't take into account how well (or poorly) they are getting along with others. They retreat inside the comfort of their inner sanctum and become intolerant of intrusions.

Others' Emotionality

Intellectuals can easily feel overpowered in an emotional climate because they don't understand why people have to get upset. Being yelled at, or simply being in the presence of someone expressing strong emotions, frightens them. If their attempts to reason with the other person fail, they withdraw into the safety of their inner world, fearful of coming back out. Any demands for them to express emotions or conform to the norms of romance and intimacy may result in stubborn defiance, as they make them feel incompetent.

I never found the companion so companionable as solitude.

—*Henry David Thoreau*

Unimportant, Mundane Details

Nothing fatigues the Intellectual faster than having to deal with details in the physical world. Intellectuals can spend countless hours sorting through details of interesting information, but when they have to do things like make a grocery list, sign up their children for music lessons, or decide on the best vacation spot, they feel incompetent and overwhelmed. This leads them to spend an inordinate amount of time taking care of unimportant details to increase their competence while leaving the important things undone.

Mary (Intellectual) and Earl (Stabilizer) had seen a vacation promotion in the weekend paper with several deals to the Mayan Riviera. Earl told Mary that it really didn't matter which of the resorts they went to, provided it was a four-star establishment within their budget. Mary began gathering information on resorts and was having trouble deciding from the descriptions. As she was researching, she noticed an article on the rate of tourists' illness in Mexico. Mary created a spreadsheet outlining the number of cases of illness at each of the resorts during the past ten years, along with the severity of the illness and availability of medical staff at the resort. She also included the rate of crime in the area. Her information was thorough and accurate, but it took so long to assemble that she missed the deadline for taking advantage of the promotion.

Confrontation

Intellectuals don't confront others and don't expect others to confront them, especially about the difficulty they have with practical matters. According to their self-governing system, they are playing by their own rules; unfortunately, this doesn't mean that they are playing nicely with others. They meet their own time lines and don't feel bound by externally generated deadlines. This doesn't sit well with others and leads to confrontation about what the Intellectual has done wrong—again. They feel incompetent and misunderstood when others repeatedly remind them of these perceived failings.

Blind Spots
Impact on Others

Most of the time, SP Intellectuals don't really care whether their behavior is embarrassing or rude according to others' definitions. It's their friends and family members who suffer the consequences of their behavior. An Intellectual who strongly believes that it is wrong to waste food may conclude that eating the leftovers from the plates of fellow diners in a restaurant is a morally upright act. The restaurant manager and the Intellectual's dining partner may beg to differ.

Adversarial Nature

Conversation with Intellectuals often feels like a battle of words. They act as if they know everything, so even the simplest comment, like "You have mustard on your cheek," is met with "I know." Contradiction is common: if you say, "I understand it's going to rain today," the Intellectual is likely to shoot back, "No, it's not!" without even checking the facts first. This habit is irritating to others, who lack the appetite for verbal sparring that SP Intellectuals crave.

Absence of Empathy

Although physically present at family events or other social gatherings, Intellectuals may still be in their heads and not engage with anyone. They appear disinterested and don't realize that their disengaged and detached manner can hurt others. Their straightforward comments and criticisms of people's behavior or beliefs can be offensive and inflammatory.

I became "the obnoxious one," "the opinionated one," or "the brutal one." Well, in my mind, I'm the honest one.

—*Simon Cowell*

Perfectionism

Intellectuals refuse to settle for less than being the expert, setting themselves up with unrealistically high standards. Others' standards are relatively unimportant, if Intellectuals notice them at all; their only concern is measuring up to their own. They ignore others' opinions that things are sufficiently done, insisting that they keep going despite how it is affecting their health, relationships, and environment.

Obsessive Thinking

Intellectuals can engage in unproductive thinking and obsession over details. They often feel driven to prove the accuracy of their ideas even as they notice flaws in their thinking. If a problem comes up that they can't resolve, they continue to work at it even if it's unsolvable.

Upshifting to Their Self-Actualizing System

For Intellectuals to upshift to their SA System, they need to become more self-aware and to redirect their striving energy by doing the following.

Developing an Observing Self

Intellectuals must be aware of the difference between the real world and their inner world. The practice of mindfulness is critical to their developing an observing self so that they are able to distinguish between their inner and outer worlds.

*As the mathematician John Nash became aware and able to separate his life as a professor and as a secret agent, he was able to function in his life. The world still existed inside of him, but he was able to live his extreme beliefs and emotions without being enslaved by them (*A Beautiful Mind*).*

Letting Others In

Intellectuals need to recognize when they are distancing others by withdrawing into their own world. They upshift by naming what they are doing ("Look at me. I'm withdrawing.") and letting others know who they are, not just what they know. Becoming aware of how secrecy and an attitude of superiority separate them from others can also help. Feedback from a trusted friend can be beneficial in this process.

Seeking Help from Others

It is critical for Intellectuals to let themselves take in information and advice from others in order to upshift to their SA System. This type of activity allows them to build tolerance to lowering their barriers to connections and intimacy with others. To shift to the SA System, Intellectuals need others to draw them out. In the film *How the Grinch Stole Christmas*, the cantankerous curmudgeon the Grinch mulls over an invitation from the kindly Whos of Whoville to attend the town's Christmas celebration:

The nerve of those Whos, inviting me down there—on such short notice! Even if I wanted to go, my schedule wouldn't allow it. 4:00, wallow in self pity; 4:30, stare into the abyss; 5:00, solve world hunger, tell no one; 5:30, Jazzercise; 6:30, dinner with me—I can't cancel that again; 7:00, wrestle with my self-loathing…I'm booked. Of course, if I bump the loathing to 9, I could still be done in time to lay in bed, stare at the ceiling, and slip slowly into madness. But what would I wear?
—*The Grinch (Jim Carrey),* How the Grinch Stole Christmas

Whether grinches or not, Intellectuals need to be drawn out of their neatly compartmentalized inner worlds, but this must be done in a loving fashion by someone who recognizes how interdependent the Intellectual's quest for knowledge and need for security are. Intellectuals must learn to notice when they are detaching from their family and friends and burying themselves in their learning. Just as Cindy Lou Who helped the Grinch nurture his heart that was "two sizes too small," a trusted friend can help usher the Intellectual back into the circle of living, feeling human beings.

Resisting the Impulse to Be Contrary

To upshift, Intellectuals must restrain their contrary behavior. They need to understand how focusing on people's errors or arguing and disagreeing can wear people down and destroy their relationships, and they must take responsibility for doing this. In particular, they need to know when they are agreeing to do something with no intention to do it. As they upshift, they get to know the signs that they are shutting down or feigning compliance and instead negotiate for what they need.

Deciding How Much Knowledge Is Enough

Intellectuals can shift to their SA System by setting limits in advance as to how much time they will spend becoming an expert or how much knowledge is enough. This prevents the perpetual student syndrome. Asking a friend or colleague to define an appropriate amount of time to research or investigate before moving to action can prevent the pressure that will come from others when Intellectuals fail to meet their commitments. When they don't set limits, Intellectuals can live their lives in the pursuit of knowledge for its own sake without ever completing anything.

Growing through Relationships

Relationships are the Intellectuals' anchor to the outer world. They need to become curious about their emotional experiences so that they no longer fear them. They must learn to tolerate the discomfort of difficult emotions. When they feel frustrated by the demands of others, they need to notice their desire to disappear into themselves. They also need to notice how the fear of emotions gets in the way of feeling safe and secure in their relationships. For them, emotions are indeed the "final frontier," and they do well when they explore this realm with a therapist, coach, or counselor. They need a safe place to practice emotional expression and to feel what they feel without the judgment of others.

Achieving Their Full Potential

Intellectuals are content to live their lives in pursuit of knowledge and a holistic ideology. They create an inner reality for themselves consisting of information, ideas, and conclusions, much like others do in the outer world. Independent and self-sufficient, they "march to the beat of their own drum." When they can tune in to the syncopated rhythms of emotion—theirs and others'—and can march in life's parade rather than only observing it, they can make harmonious music that resonates not only with themselves but also with others. They are deeply and profoundly concerned with the inner workings of things and bring us the gift of knowledge when they share themselves with others. Their individuality and alignment with their own inner ideals challenges us to question things that we do rather than accepting the status quo. When these people stay connected to the people around them, they are able to make manifest the wonderful world within them so that others can understand their call to go within.

CHAPTER EIGHT
THE PERFORMER—STRIVING TO BE RECOGNIZED

Remember my name (Fame)
I'm gonna…Light up the sky like a flame (Fame).

—*"Fame," Irene Cara*

YOU KNOW PERFORMERS THE minute one walks into the room. Whether it's through their wardrobe, their grand entrance, or their effusive greeting, Performers stand out. They capture attention easily and demand attention constantly. They don't just "do" things; they perform them and then look for the recognition they need for having done such an outstanding job! They are easily the most energetic of the Striving Styles, seemingly ready to take on the world at a moment's notice. They explode into life in the pursuit of their latest ambitious goal. It's obvious from the time you meet them that they enjoy being center stage, and they do it in a delightful and entertaining fashion. Performers love to be the "star" wherever they find themselves.

Goals excite and stimulate Performers, and they are energized by the process of doing whatever it takes to achieve them. Their appetite for success and recognition fuels their motivation to go for more. No sooner have they achieved their goal that they create another to strive toward, bigger and better than the last. A manager must become a director; a singer must become a diva; a homemaker must be the head of the parent-teacher association. Performers achieve more than most others of the same age do through focus, hard work, and their need to win. Singularly directed, they push themselves beyond what others may consider reasonable for a human being to accomplish or even aspire to.

Heather's story is a good example. She grew her consulting business from five employees to fifteen in just three years and was recognized as one of British Columbia's fastest-growing businesses three years in a row. As the company's tenth anniversary approached, she found herself avoiding the office, instead keeping busy with client meetings and new business prospects. She had reached her limit with employees who were constantly complaining about how she was never at the office and blaming her when they didn't do their work properly. Heather was frustrated because she had hired them so she wouldn't have to deal with the routine aspects of client work. They weren't doing their work in a way that supported her continuing to grow the business.

Heather loved the "wins" of selling client projects and working with senior leaders. She couldn't believe her staff needed her as much as they did and was shocked by their complaints about her and the expectation that she should be more available to them when they needed help.

Through discussions with me (Anne), it soon became apparent to Heather that she needed a bigger challenge. The reality was that she didn't like having to lead the business; she just liked growing it. Her staff couldn't do what she needed them to do to keep meeting her need to be recognized. She decided to close down her business instead and take on a new challenge that would more consistently meet her need: working with me to take the Striving Styles to market.

Performers dislike the mundane and routine, and they approach everything they do with an idea of how to make it more fun. They instinctively know how to enliven activities and are uniquely talented in the way they manage to make so many things exciting, including work. Their youthful energy is attractive to others, and they like to be around people who are similarly buoyant in personality. They take on social and familial activities in the home, extended family, and community that provide further opportunities for time in the spotlight. Performers do not do anything at half measure; they prefer to throw themselves into everything they do. A party becomes an event, a family gathering an opportunity to dress up and entertain.

Performers have a talent for seeing life as pregnant with exciting possibilities. They can be anyone they imagine they can be, and the sky is the limit when it comes to inventing and reinventing themselves. Their lives are likely to be like a book containing a number of different yet equally exciting chapters. They do not always finish everything they start, but all their ideas are exciting at the outset. Their motto could easily be "keep your options open" or "leave no stone unturned." Their life path is often the road less travelled. Performers live with childlike optimism and naïveté, going from one goal to the next with faith that things will work out and that everyone will be supportive of their undertakings. Whatever they do, they do it to win, or to be first. They get such pleasure from competing and winning that they don't always realize that no one else has noticed the race. Not that it matters—their enjoyment and pleasure come from winning and knowing that they are out in front of others who must be admiring them, even though they may not be giving any indication of it.

What Makes Performers Tick?

The Performer Style lives out of the right rational brain, the area that imagines and envisions what is possible. This part of the brain processes things in a holistic fashion and leaps to conclusions rather than troubling itself to sort out the facts. It knows without knowing why and is strongly intuitive and perceptive. It sees the big picture and gets excited about the possibility of making it real. Driven by a vision of their desired future state, Performers launch into an all-out effort to make it happen, and they gain recognition as a result.

Because they use this part of the brain to imagine what they can be, Performers tend to reinvent themselves continually. They are caught up in what they think is possible for them to do or be.

They create their self-image—their vision of who they want to be—and then strive to be that person. For them, the phrase "you can be anything you want to be" isn't just a cliché; it is an organizing principle for life. Acting like who they are trying to become helps Performers determine their behavior, their wardrobe, and what they show of themselves to the world. They behave according to the current image they have of themselves. They don't really worry about whether how they're behaving is different from what they said they were like last month. To them, it's all authentic. "Fake it till you make it" is the approach to becoming who they want to be that Performers tend to take. Performers are driven to become who they imagine themselves to be.

No matter who you are, no matter what you did, no matter where you've come from, you can always change, become a better version of yourself.

—*Madonna*

Because they set their goals so high, Performers work hard to be the best at whatever is important to them—money, social status, sports, good looks, or intelligence. Performers believe in themselves and their ability to make their glittering image come alive through hard work and dedication to their goals. They will work tirelessly to achieve recognition in their particular social environment. Being average is an insult to them, and if they can't be the life of the party, they'd rather not be invited at all.

Performers have great difficulty staying with any one thing for long because they become bored easily, especially when they are not getting enough attention. Because of this, they run the risk of working or doing things in an unfocused fashion and wasting time and energy in the pursuit of ways to alleviate their boredom. They are not as stimulated by obstacles as others are unless there is external approval and validation for doing this. Performers are easily discouraged and rarely do things they don't enjoy.

Relationship Style of the Performer

More than most of the other Styles, Performers are dependent on other people. They need others to be the audience for their performances and to mirror back to them how wonderful and amazing they are. Because of their natural charisma and charm, they usually have a large number and variety of friends and acquaintances to keep them energized. Charming and attractive to others, they delight in being the center of attention, entertaining and captivating others in conversations. They make both interesting and playful parents and mates. They consider activities in the home, extended family, and community as more stages on which they can play to their audience, accessing further opportunities to be in the spotlight.

It is not enough just to do something well. If I can't be recognized by others for having done so, why bother!

—*Blake Taylor (Performer)*

Performers love being with people. They both enjoy and need people to keep them energized, so they gravitate to situations that have the potential to meet their needs. Because their image of themselves is one of success, prominence, and attractiveness, they seek out people who have achieved these qualities. Being with socially prominent people who are doing things worthy of recognition—such as politicians, leaders of organizations, and celebrities—is extremely important to Performers. They will do whatever it takes to be among people they feel increase their feelings of self-worth. Because Performers need to be seen as successful, they work hard to make sure that everyone knows that their relationships are both ideal and enviable. Although they love their families and are usually deeply committed to them, they sometimes seem to use them as objects for enhancing their self-image.

Denise, a successful broadcaster and mother of two teenaged girls, is having drinks with a few female friends and recounting the wonderful weekend her family just had. She is excited because her girls are doing so well at school and one of them made the cheerleading team. One of her daughters turned down a date on Sunday night so that she could hang out with her mom, as they have an "amazing" relationship that includes a Sunday night "girls' ritual" of doing their nails and talking about what's going on. The accounts are detailed and entertaining, with carefully chosen bits of information added to support the notion of successful and admirable relationships. What is edited from the stories is the normal conflict and emotional ups and downs that are a part of daily life. The other women sit in silent envy, reflecting on their own kids' behavior and on their longing to have the kind of relationship the Performer describes, where they just "hang out" together.

Often extremely perceptive, Performers work hard at understanding people rather than judging them. They do not like to categorize people or to put them in boxes, as they intensely dislike when others do this to them. They are attuned to what is going on with other people, and they will adapt themselves to others' behavior to gain approval. When they focus on people, they often have remarkable insight into what motivates them. They have gut feelings about people and are usually right. They also notice when something is off, doesn't add up, or feels wrong. Although others accuse the Performer of talking more than listening, or of not paying attention, they can be shocked at how much the Performer has taken in and how well the Performer actually knows them.

Performers learn early in life how to perform in ways that get them the most recognition and attention. They learn to be very adaptable, using their intuition to inform them of what they need to do or say to get back in the game. When Performers sense that others want them to be entertaining, they can make serious errors in judgment about what they say. They may say something insensitive in an attempt to be funny, offending others without meaning to. Or they will say things that are illogical to sound smart when they actually miss the mark.

How Performers Satisfy Their Need to Be Recognized
Being the Center of Attention

Performers have a tendency to believe that the action gets going when they show up, and often they're right. Their charismatic and charming personality adds color and dimension to otherwise mundane events. They are confident talking, and once they have the floor, they don't easily give it up. Performers are the type of people whose behavior seems to say, "Enough about me. Tell me, what do you think about me?" They are masters at directing the conversation back to themselves, as they, and often others, believe that what Performers have to say is much more interesting than what others might. You won't often see Performers at a silent meditation retreat or alone in a mountain cabin. They want to be where the action is, hanging out with other exciting and interesting people—as long as those people are not so exciting and interesting that the Performer must take a backseat!

Self-Protective Performers act in a grandiose and entitled fashion. Self-Protective Performers' notion that they are special can cause them to act as though the rules of society don't apply to them. They are preoccupied with their own aspirations, needs, and appetites, as well as how others perceive them. They believe in their own preeminence and expect everyone to treat them accordingly. Self-Protective Performers think they are entitled to do what gives them pleasure and meets their need to be recognized without consideration for the needs of others. They can easily dismiss or disregard anyone who doesn't affirm their value.

Cathy loved to go to dinner parties where she would inevitably get attention from both her male and female friends for her good looks and her stories. She was fun to be with—smart, charming, and witty. Once Cathy arrived, the other women seemed to fade into the background. While her (mostly female) friends were together in the kitchen getting the food ready, Cathy would stay in the living room with the men, entertaining and being entertained. She didn't see anything wrong with this because she didn't enjoy cooking and preferred the attention from men. Once the party was winding down and others were cleaning up, Cathy would leave, usually for another social gathering. Her female friends kept vowing never to invite her again, but they couldn't deny that she made parties a lot more enjoyable, so they never kept their vow. Instead, they just complained about Cathy's behavior behind her back. They were afraid to confront her about it for fear she would fly into an ugly rant. Too many times, they had seen that criticizing Cathy only instigated a Jekyll-and-Hyde transformation, in which Cathy's sharp tongue would tear the offender to pieces.

Self-Actualizing Performers share the spotlight. Self-Actualizing Performers have developed the ability to know when they are using others to satisfy the need for recognition. They have a greater sense of others' needs and are willing to help meet them, even if it means putting their own needs on hold for a time. In addition, they take time to consider the impact of their actions and decisions on people's feelings. They no longer have difficulty when the spotlight shifts away from them in social situations, and they stop insisting on special treatment. They find comfort in being a part of a group that accepts them for who they actually are, and they are able to talk about their challenges and difficulties in a way that invites intimacy with others. The closeness that other people have always shared is present in the SA Performer's relationships as well.

Creating "Events"

Performers approach everything they do with an idea of how to make it more fun, as a way of being recognized. They look for or create opportunities to perform, intuitively knowing how to enliven situations and bring excitement to all they do. Performers don't do anything in half measure and are often considered "over the top" in the effort and energy they put into projects, relationships, and home. Whatever they place their attention tends to flourish and grow. They don't just have Christmas decorations in front of the house; they have an ostentatious Griswold family type of display, complete with an inflatable Santa Claus, sled, and reindeer; and an elaborate Kris Kringle Bavarian village—the whole extravaganza set off in blazing floodlights to make sure no one can miss the attraction. Generally, Performers are also on the lookout for new adventures and new venues in which to shine, and they discover what is "trendy" before others do. It was surely a Performer who developed the concept of a flash mob, if only for the sake of being the first one in the crowd to start belting out Handel's "Hallelujah" chorus or tipping the first top hat in a rendition of *A Chorus Line*. Good fun? No doubt! But for the Performer, it is fun with a serious purpose: to get (and stay) in the limelight.

Self-Protective Performers create drama. When they are bored or have no one to pay attention to them, SP Performers start to focus on every little thing about themselves. Because they spend so little time focusing on how their bodies usually feel, they have no measure for what is normal, and they start imagining, in their dramatic fashion, everything that could possibly be wrong. That little brown spot isn't a freckle; it's skin cancer. That bump on the skull is a brain tumor. Their panic about what is wrong with them quickly escalates. At the same time, a mental drama plays out in which our hero, devastated by the ravages of cruel disease, envisions his or her mourners at the funeral (and it's a funeral like no one has ever seen!), all of them wailing over the injustice of a brilliant life snuffed out too soon by a skin cancer or brain tumor tragedy. Good-bye, cruel world! Now that the Performer has something to talk about, he or she has to call someone immediately to get some attention!

Self-Actualizing Performers tolerate being alone. Self-Actualizing Performers are able to recognize their feelings and tolerate them. They recognize when someone has hurt and disappointed them, or when they are feeling bored and unstimulated. Instead of withdrawing and creating drama, they listen to what their feelings tell them they need in any given situation, and they negotiate with others to get their needs met. They learn to tolerate both disappointment and dissatisfaction as being a normal part of life. By acknowledging their true feelings, they can release the habit of creating drama to get attention and explore things they can do on their own to entertain themselves.

Winning at Everything

Second place is just the first place loser.

—*Dale Earnhardt*

Performers love to win, whether it's clients, awards, sales competitions, political races, or arguments. They seek opportunities to compete. Whatever they do, they aim to come in first. They also distinguish themselves by one-upmanship and spinning bigger and better "fish stories." Performers enjoy the process of debating and arguing and will do it just for fun. They can turn a casual conversation into an argument, and just when you think there is no way they will ever concede to your point, they'll start arguing your position for you. It's almost as if the Performer feels that there is one too many people in the argument and is saying, "Stand back and watch me argue both sides, brilliantly." Performers can even get pleasure from winning in situations where no one else has noticed there's a competition.

Self-Protective Performers become the "worst of the worst." One of the most amazing things about Performers is their inability to see when they have hijacked a conversation to talk about themselves. They are so focused on themselves that they neither understand nor care that they are using others. Most people are either intrigued enough by Performers to want to listen or are apprehensive about the consequences if they don't. Self-Protective Performers are expert spinners of yarns about how they are unloved and misunderstood. They become outraged at the horrible way others have treated them (after all the Performer has done for them!). This causes them to become divalike and volatile, lashing out at people close to them, accusing them of not offering enough love and support. They will recount the horrors of their lives to anyone who will listen. Self-Protective Performers (of either gender) can be the ultimate drama queens.

Psychotherapy is a profession with no immediate gratification and is often challenging to Performers who choose this field. Take Sheila, for example. She spent many years in training, enjoying the process and distinguishing herself from her peers by excelling in graduate school and building a practice quickly afterward. Although driven to pursue the best professors and advisers, and capable of impressing them with the mastery of her studies, once she was on her own, she could no longer get the recognition she needed. There was no one important to impress—only colleagues. She constantly took over discussions in her peer group, lamenting that she was an awful therapist and was messing up her patients' lives. She garnered a great deal of attention for doing this, because her peers were struggling to help her see that being a psychotherapist was not meeting her need to be recognized. While working with her during a session, I told her that if she really believed she was hurting her clients, she should perhaps consider a different kind of work. At this suggestion, she went ballistic, accusing me of not being supportive and helpful.

Self-Actualizing Performers inspire people rather than defeat them. Self-Actualizing Performers know when they are finding ways to feel superior to friends and family instead of just hanging out with them. They are more willing to offer to help them instead of spinning stories about how well they can do what the other person is struggling with. They take the role of mentor or coach, giving their time generously to help motivate others to move beyond self-imposed limits on personal achievement. Performers in self-actualizing mode seem to have magic stardust in their pockets, which they sprinkle on others to make them feel that anything is possible. Being in the orbit of the Performer gives others a vicarious feeling of "specialness," and they bask in the glow of the Performer's energy. The Performer inspires others to become who they are meant to be.

Pushing the Envelope

Good, better, best. Never let it rest. 'Til your good is better and your better is best.

—*St. Jerome*

Their talent for seeing life's many exciting possibilities makes Performers push themselves to attain higher and higher levels of success in all areas of life. They are very confident and rely almost exclusively on their gut instincts, which allows them to respond and react quickly to any given situation. Because they don't like feeling boredom, sadness, or any other difficult emotion, they are never content with the mundane or the status quo. "Why not try this instead?" they say. They have a fresh, open attitude toward everything they do. They don't accept the limitations that would hold others back. If someone tells them they won't make anything out of themselves because they didn't finish high school, don't be surprised if they are running a successful business within five years. Performers often hear from others that their ideas are too far-fetched and impossible to achieve. "Just watch me" is their inner response. And if they fall short? Well, the sun'll come out tomorrow. They simply change direction and are off again.

Oprah is a Performer who is constantly pushing the envelope, on both the personal and professional levels. She has made public the hardships she endured early in her personal life, and she is skilled at getting others to open up in the same way. She has gained tremendous recognition—both positive and negative—for revealing on television what was previously restricted to the privacy of the therapist's office, and in so doing she made "normal" many subjects that were previously considered too shameful to talk about. From sexual abuse to the death of her child, her abusive relationships, and her struggle with her weight, all have helped to meet her need for recognition while relaxing the societal taboo about these aspects of the human condition.

Self-Protective Performers do everything to excess. Self-Protective act as though they are invulnerable and invincible with little ability to set boundaries. They are magnanimous, saying yes to whatever people ask of them, whether they are able to accomplish those things or not. They may spend money they don't have on things they don't need, simply for the way it makes them feel. They will rationalize their behavior, saying that they are just enjoying life, and will dismiss anyone who tries to caution them about their excesses. They can easily end up overweight, overstimulated, and in debt. When the boss wonders aloud whether Performer Patty can take on three new clients, fly to Kalamazoo for a conference presentation, and deliver a companywide address on imminent downsizing, the words "Of course I can!" may slip from Patty's lips without any consideration of her calendar, her skills, or her current workload.

Self-Actualizing Performers honor their commitments. With Performers, opportunities abound. Self-Actualizing Performers have learned to say, "Let me get back to you" before they say yes. They learn how to reflect prior to jumping in and doing something new and interesting. They develop the capacity for discernment, using cause-and-effect thinking in their decision making. They develop a conscience about the harm they cause when they are not taking care of themselves and giving themselves enough time to rest and rejuvenate. They become very careful not to invest so much in meeting their need for recognition by trying to be all things to all people. They learn to say no without fearing that others will disapprove or think less of them. This allows them to decline requests to do things they don't want to do or shouldn't do.

Activators of the Self-Protective System

With their need to achieve and be recognized, Performers are activated by situations in which they are unable to maintain center stage or when they have to share the spotlight with someone else. Their need to be in the "winner's circle" causes them to fear feeling humiliated, worthless, or disappointed when they can't. Feeling this way frustrates their need to be recognized and therefore is what they fear most. The will do whatever they can to protect themselves from these feelings.

Intolerance for Losing

Performers want to win and have little tolerance for the disappointment they experience when they lose. They want their place in the winner's circle and feel ashamed of being anything less than the first-place winner. Everything Performers do is another opportunity to win or best someone else. For example, if a Performer would like to learn to play golf but realizes his friends already golf well, he would opt to not learn rather than be less than the best at the game.

Disapproval of Others

Performers are sensitive to the reactions of their audience and feel embarrassed when they are not holding the attention of the group or when they get a hint of disapproval. Even though Performer Paul has told you the spellbinding story about the seven-foot carp and the jelly doughnut a hundred times, you'd better look lively when he launches into it again, because his whole image of himself depends on his audience's rapt attention. If Performers feel that they are losing their audience, they try harder and become increasingly concerned that people are seeing them as superficial or without substance. "You don't love this story?" Paul's bemused expression says.

"Well, wait until you hear me tell it like *this!*" The harder Performers try, the more outrageous their behavior can become. Although they may not go to the lengths of Glenn Close's character in the movie *Fatal Attraction*, Performers share her conviction that they will *not* be ignored.

Being Alone

Spending too much time alone causes Performers to experience a loss of their own value. When nothing is going on or they aren't getting the recognition they need, Performers generally start feeling bored, sad, or depressed. Without people around to admire them, Performers have nowhere to go but inside themselves.

Listening to Others' Accomplishments

Performers don't like having to share the stage and feel devalued when others talk about their accomplishments. They will keep trying to snatch the conversation away from someone else, even if it takes lamenting the fact that they will never be able to do what the other person is claiming to have done. They can easily draw attention to themselves, making others soothe and support them. Once they have the floor again, they perk right up.

Not Knowing Their Limits

Performers' SP System is activated by overextending themselves. They want to be the best at all they do and push themselves to go beyond any perceived limitations, including physical ones. Pushing the envelope this way causes Performers to overdo physically and emotionally. They don't know when enough is enough. They have to play one more encore, have the last glass of wine, or eat the last piece of cake. They work until they are done and then some. They run out of energy and use stimulants like coffee, carbs, and chocolate to keep them going.

Criticism

The self-image of the Performer doesn't conceive of them doing anything wrong or contributing to problems they may be having. They are easily activated by anything that threatens their self-image and will attack those who criticize them. They take criticism very personally and believe someone else is to blame for what they are being criticized for and will rant about it to anyone who will listen.

Performer William Shatner complains about being mistaken for his Captain Kirk character from *Star Trek* in his parody of a Molson Canadian commercial.

> I am not a Starfleet commander, or T. J. Hooker. I don't live on Starship NCC-170, or own a phaser. And I don't know anybody named Bones, Sulu, or Spock. And no, I've never had green alien sex, though I'm sure it would be quite an evening. I speak English and French, not Klingon! I drink Labatt's, not Romulan ale! And when someone says to me "Live long and prosper," I seriously mean it when I say, "Get a life." My doctor's name is not McCoy, it's Ginsberg. And tribbles were puppets, not real animals. PUPPETS! And when I speak, I never, ever talk like every. Word. Is. Its. Own. Sentence. I live in California, but I was raised in Montreal…My name is William Shatner, and I am Canadian!

Blind Spots
Perception of Others

Performers don't always feel the need to cooperate with others, or to understand or empathize with them. They don't think about how their demands for special treatment impact friends and family. An extreme example is that of Leona Helmsley, the infamous "Queen of Mean." When a housekeeper remarked that the Helmsleys must pay a tremendous amount in taxes, she retorted, "We don't pay taxes; the little people do."

Creating Emotional Drama

Those who are privy to Performers in this state don't know how to react to their emotionality, moodiness, and behavioral swings. Performers don't consider the consequences of their self-centered behavior; they just expect others to be forgiving. Friends and family may walk on eggshells around them for fear of becoming a target for their emotions.

Seeing Themselves Realistically

If Performers aren't everything, they are nothing. If they aren't successful or a winner, they are an imposter or a loser. They don't realize how much they depend on winning to regulate their self-esteem. They are constantly measuring the achievements and status of others against their own, feeling envious and threatened by those they consider to be ahead of them. Performers are caught up in a web of feeling superior or inferior, inflating or deflating their value, using others or being used by them.

Behaving Self-Destructively

Some of the things Performers do to keep themselves from feeling low are detrimental to their own well-being. Habits such as workaholism, an inability to commit to one relationship, or jumping from one improbable scheme to another can wreak havoc on their existence as they attempt to keep themselves stimulated. In the long run, they can hit bottom and be unable to climb back up because they have not developed a strong enough inner structure.

Dependence on Others

Although they appear self-reliant and confident, their strong need to be validated causes Performers to be overly concerned with others' opinions of them. However, they have a blind spot because they believe they don't need anyone. Their tendency to be dependent on external approval can cause them to perform the way they believe others expect them to in order to be acknowledged and admired. They adopt the behaviors of an actor, becoming superficial and overly attentive to their image.

Upshifting to Their Self-Actualizing System

For Performers to upshift to their SA System, they need to refocus their striving energy by doing the following.

Sharing the Spotlight

Developing an awareness of when they aren't really paying attention to others helps them upshift and refocus their attention, making sure they aren't taking up all of the space. They remind themselves that they become stronger when they are not as dependent on the recognition and admiration of others. Once they get over the feeling that being an ordinary human being with needs and feelings somehow diminishes them, Performers find relief in being authentic, empathetic, and cooperative rather than just the headliner in an endless series of shows.

Letting Others Help

Having lost their ability to be rational and optimistic about themselves, Performers need others to reassure them that they are okay and to help them recognize that it's possible to accept criticism from someone without having to destroy that person. Others need to listen and empathize with the Performer's feelings before initiating a more rational, problem-solving conversation to help settle down the fear and anxiety he or she feels.

Establishing Discipline and Routine

Because it is so easy for Performers to disconnect from their bodies, they are able to stay in their SA System when they follow a discipline that keeps them grounded. Physical exercise—such as jogging, walking, and gardening—or grounding activities like meditation are critical for keeping their feet on the ground. But they need to take care not to use these activities as just another forum in which to compete. Commencing a program of weightlifting with an eye toward becoming Mr. Universe will probably defeat the purpose.

Staying the Course

Performers can get so focused on winning or being seen as the best that they don't realize when they have strayed from their own path or career track. They need to reflect before saying yes or get feedback from people when they are tempted to go off in another direction because something sounds good. In addition, learning to experience pleasure while achieving goals helps them resist the temptation to take on more.

Sharing Therapy or Counseling

Performers have the habit of depending on others to support their self-image, which gets in the way of the development of their authentic self. If they continue their constant quest for recognition, their authentic self remains fragile and vulnerable to perceived slights and criticisms from others. They can be seen by others as narcissistic and self-serving. They can be riddled with feelings of being a "fraud" and will work very hard to make sure no one sees this side of them. Performers gain security and personal strength when they seek counseling or therapy to help them connect their image of who they are trying to be with who they actually are.

Achieving Their Full Potential

Charismatic and charming, Performers live their lives for their audiences. For them, "all the world's a stage," and they explode into life with color and a flair for the dramatic. Achieving goals that others dare not dream of, they live inspired lives and in turn inspire others to reach for the stars. The Performer is a Striving Style with the potential for tremendous interpersonal strengths and resources, from strong communication skills and charisma to diplomacy and intuition. When Performers are able to turn down the spotlight on themselves and engage genuinely with others—both socially and professionally—their stars can rise high without undue risk of falling.

Chapter Nine
THE VISIONARY—STRIVING TO BE PERCEPTIVE

Climb to tranquility, finding its real worth
Conceiving the heavens flourishing on earth.
— "Higher and Higher," Moody Blues

THE VISIONARY'S WORLD IS a magical realm where everything is connected and all is possible. Delighting in building their utopian ideals, Visionaries live with one foot in the heavens and the other as close to earth as they can tolerate. Their ability to see how things can be lets them quickly formulate everything that has to be done to make it happen. Visionaries operate at more abstract, theoretical, and symbolic levels than any other Style, always curious about things that happen outside of the concrete realms of our human existence.

Visionaries believe in what they perceive and strive to live their lives according to grander ideals than they might ever accomplish. With their high personal integrity and faith in their vision for what is possible, they work tenaciously toward manifesting it. Their trust in their vision rarely falters, even in the face of popular opinion or established authority. Imaginative and conceptual, Visionaries prefer to spend time thinking about what might be and how to make it so, and less time taking care of mundane matters like going grocery shopping or doing the laundry.

You need to be in conversation with a Visionary for only a short period to recognize this Style. Visionaries easily see how things can be better and more efficient, and they can't help but tell you. They might also provide a theory to explain human motivation or educate you on how your problem is connected to a greater human issue. You can count on them to offer a different or unusual perspective whose connection to what you were talking about isn't readily apparent. Frequently recognized for their profound, intuitive insight, Visionaries take whatever you are talking about, draw it inside, and then return with the deep, unseen meanings or an unexplored solution. It's as if they can see what's hidden to most people; they can blindside people with unexpected personal revelations.

Shelley (Visionary) was talking on the phone with her friend Angie. Angie, as usual, was complaining about her boyfriend and was looking for a sympathetic ear. Shelley wanted to help her friend, so she said that the reason Angie tolerated her boyfriend was that he monopolized her energy, which kept her from going after the things in her career that she really wanted to do but was afraid to try. Angie became defensive and accused Shelley of being insensitive. She felt Shelley was blaming her for the poor treatment she was getting from her boyfriend.

The truth was that Shelley was dead right, but Angie had never considered that her relationship might be a distraction that limited her career potential by draining her energy.

Visionaries might not remember who you are, but they will remember a conversation they had with you that connected to something they were thinking about. Their inner wisdom and knowledge are sometimes hard to express and can make them difficult to relate to personally. The world of ideas and concepts is their playground, and they can spend long stretches of time just dreaming and creating visions. They love to have the freedom to do this and always encourage others to do the same.

Imagination is more important than knowledge. Knowledge is limited. Imagination encircles the world.

—*Albert Einstein*

What Makes Visionaries Tick?

The Visionary Style leads from the right rational brain, which recognizes, interprets, and interconnects information, events, and situations, aggregating these into a whole. It "knows," without the necessity of working linearly to arrive at a conclusion. With great insight and understanding, Visionaries take what currently exists and envision the possibilities for transformation to an exalted future state. Driven by their need to be perceptive, they seek to understand and connect with the deeper meaning and significance of everything they encounter in their daily lives, including people. If you ever questioned where human beings fit in the web of life, find a Visionary, who will delight in exploring the question with you. If you want to talk about your gun collection, better look elsewhere.

Visionaries are able to create mental order out of seemingly random thoughts, impressions, and experiences. They enjoy working to understand themselves and others, and they intuitively recognize the complexities of human existence. They are optimistic and have the gift of seeing potential in a world of limitless possibilities. They freely offer others the benefit of their perceptions to help them move past their self-imposed limitations. Continuous improvement is a philosophy Visionaries live by. They work to achieve their potential and to help others do the same.

It can be challenging for Visionaries to know the difference between what is theoretically possible and what is realistic. Their intuition about most things tends to be sharp, quick, and often eerily correct. It is as though they have a direct line into the future that enables them to envision what is going to happen long before other people do. This talent has nothing to do with psychic ability; it is an internal sorting and processing of information against possibilities that allows them to come up with exact solutions to even the most complex problems. Their empathetic abilities are so strong that they will sense another's emotional state, illness, or distress before that person is aware of it.

Hillary Clinton demonstrates some of the natural capabilities of the Visionary Style. Perceptive and intuitive, she has great insight and vision. With a natural capacity to create systems (her work with health-care reform, for example), she is able to motivate others toward their desired outcomes. Perfectionistic, objective, and self-determined, she will likely be a vital force in Washington for many years.

One of the challenges for Visionaries like Hillary is that they tend to lack the interpersonal skills that characterize other Styles, such as the Performer and the Leader. Visionaries are farsighted leaders who are hindered by their discomfort with the limelight. Because they are aware of this limitation, they often choose to become second to someone who can elevate them to places they would never go on their own. Hillary did this with Bill Clinton. As a result, she was able to use her access to others in power to demonstrate her true talents. Her ability to show dignity in the face of public humiliation also reflects the Visionaries' knack for getting past what is going on in the present by staying focused on what could happen in the future.

Visionaries are strong individualists who can easily feel threatened and insecure when they are forced to conform or adapt to what is considered normal. The act of fitting in, which is a present-moment experience, is hard for them because the moment they are aware of the nature of something (or someone), they immediately think of how to improve or transform it. They have the tendency to think of themselves as above average while at the same time fearing that they are below. Often setting themselves apart from people around them, they prefer to lead or advise a team or group than to be a part of it. When unhindered, Visionaries enjoy their independence and are willing to live life on their own terms. They are willing to challenge the status quo in order to live life in alignment with their vision.

Relationship Style of the Visionary

With their inquisitiveness and interest in what makes people tick, Visionaries can seem more social than they actually are. They have a way of listening that can make you feel like you are the most important person in the universe—and for that moment, you are. They can be extremely empathetic and compassionate. Visionaries are keenly interested in information about people and improving how they live their lives. They will fully engage people in conversations, but they tend to listen more than talk, playing the role of the observer or the adviser in conversations. Very seldom are they unaware of other people's emotions or interests. Their complex personalities are both sensitive and intense, and although they are quite willing to share their inner selves with people they trust, they tend to hold themselves back and can seem difficult to get to know. Usually, they have a small circle of friends.

Visionaries are wonderful romantics in their own minds. They love to envision all of the romantic things they could say to impress their partners. However, they are generally uncomfortable with physical and emotional expression and tend to express warmth and caring through action rather than words. As much time as they spend contemplating the desired state of their relationships, too often it stays in the mental realm, never becoming a reality. Visionaries find that expressing their needs and romantic ideas makes them feel anxious. In addition, their discomfort with self-expression prevents them from communicating how deeply they feel toward their mates, children, and friends, and they end up with a gap between what they want to say or do and what actually transpires.

Family and friends are extremely important to Visionaries, and they spend as much time with them as they are able to. They tend to put themselves wholeheartedly into their relationships and then need to spend time on their own to restore their balance. Friends and family usually open up to the Visionary and allow him or her to help them. From the outside it can look like Visionaries choose to affiliate with people who need them, and to some extent this is true. They establish their place in a relationship by being the person others come to for guidance or information. They seem to find security in relationships by being useful to others. Because of the way their brains are wired, they don't always seek to connect first with their emotional needs. They are much more connected to their own inner images and ideas about people and relationships. You could say that more goes on in their heads about the relationship than in the relationship itself.

Will (Visionary) knew that his girlfriend Tracy had been under a lot of stress lately. She was working full-time and taking classes at a commuter college at night with the hope of getting a degree. Her mother had recently been diagnosed with breast cancer, and Tracy was stretched to the breaking point in her efforts to keep up with work, school, and family responsibilities, not to mention the emotional impact of her mother's illness. Will wanted to take Tracy in his arms and console her, to tell her that he would always be there for her, that he loved her, and that she would get through this tough time. He fantasized about taking her away to their favorite place in the mountains for a weekend of romance and relaxation, and even thought of a beautiful spot on a remote trail where he might propose marriage to Tracy.

In the end, though, he worried that she might be in such a fragile state that she could say no, and this would make him feel foolish for having picked the wrong time to propose. So instead he bought her a gift certificate to a day spa, which included a massage, sauna, and facial. He hoped that she would take away the same message from this gift as from his imagined vacation.

Visionaries are intensively introspective and probing in communication. The Visionary who sits next you at a community event may grill you with questions about seemingly unconnected aspects of your life—such as your pets, your diet, and your tendency to pepper your speech with phrases like "heavens to Betsy" and "holy smokes"—after which she may render a conclusion that you could realize more peaceful sleep by lowering your intake of gluten and spending more time walking barefoot each day. Without trying to do so, Visionaries can intimidate others with their intensity. Their desire to understand a subject or someone's intentions can cause others to feel that they are being interrogated. Their listening skills and uncanny sensitivity to the nuances and nonverbal aspects of communication can make people feel exposed and vulnerable without understanding why. At the end of a conversation, Visionaries may feel they have skillfully removed the pretenses that can clothe relationships, although the other person may simply feel naked.

How Visionaries Satisfy Their Need to Be Perceptive

Don't be afraid to go out on a limb. It's where all the fruit is.
—*Shirley MacLaine*

Helping Others Achieve Their Potential

This type of encouragement is frequently heard from Visionaries. They meet their need to be perceptive by seeing others' potential and encouraging, inspiring, and helping them to achieve it. They have a strong desire to use their intuition to contribute to the welfare of others, either in personal or impersonal ways. Their focus with friends, spouses, or children is on showing them how to achieve their personal best and offering regular feedback and correction. They love making connections for others and tend to give more than they get, as their needs are not always apparent to others.

Cathy (Visionary) shows her caring for her stepchildren by listening to their problems, allowing them to see the nature of their personalities, and helping them to avert potential pitfalls. When her stepdaughter Elisa (Artist) was fourteen, Cathy realized that if Elisa wasn't able to direct her energy toward something beyond "rescuing" boys who were lost souls, she would likely end up pregnant at an early age. In an attempt to illustrate the amount of energy a baby would take, Cathy and her husband gave Elisa a puppy for Christmas when she was sixteen, hoping that it would drive home the amount of attention and work that caring for another being requires. Although Elisa loved the puppy, she left the lion's share of the work for Cathy and her father, and ultimately gave the dog away when she got pregnant at seventeen.

Self-Protective Visionaries keep themselves at a distance in relationships. They adopt a detached approach with people, sometimes treating others as though they were specimens to be inspected and critiqued. This type of scrutinizing makes them seem arrogant and haughty. Even Visionaries themselves may not understand how their detached attitude affects others. Underlying this attitude is often a fear that others will in some way meddle with them and that they will have no way of protecting themselves. They can inadvertently intimidate others with their intellect and can be argumentative for no other reason than to push people away. If you hear a statement like, "I'm not going to discuss this with someone who can't even open their eyes enough to see they're being a doormat!" you've just been a victim of a Visionary brush-off.

Self-Actualizing Visionaries work at sharing themselves in relationships. When they are self-actualizing, they initiate opportunities to go out and play with their friends. They start to share their thoughts and feelings with people they trust, becoming less reserved and easier to know—although they are still more likely to share jokes, ideas, spontaneous thoughts, and their many inventive theories rather than their feelings. Self-Actualizing Visionaries let people know when they need distance rather than behaving in a way that pushes others away. They recognize that how another person reacts to their advice reflects that person's level of functioning, and they don't take it personally.

Connecting the Dots

And the day will come, when the mystical generation of Jesus, by the Supreme Being as His Father, in the womb of a virgin, will be classed with the fable of the generation of Minerva, in the brain of Jupiter.

—*Thomas Jefferson*

Jefferson, in true Visionary style, drew connections between two seemingly different mythical systems. By nature, Visionaries build wholeness out of chaos. They are the architects of dreams and visions—their own, or those of others. They are able to see both the big picture and the intricacies of its component parts. They are tenacious and often will not rest until they complete what they see in their mind's eye, although they do have a tendency to start more things than they can complete. If they are told they can't do something, they want to know why. Even when they are given a reason, they can believe so much in their own vision of what might be that they pursue it anyway.

In a bar in South Texas, two friends enjoy a cold beer while discussing the ranching business. Visionary Randy has had a brainstorm that he's convinced is pure genius. It came to him one day last summer as he enjoyed a plate of beef brisket. "Everybody in the south loves to barbecue," he began, as his friend Bill (Socializer) listened intently, his mouth beginning to water. "But cutting up raw meat for the grill is a health hazard. And when you have to cook the meat piece by piece, you can't feed everybody simultaneously. You forget which pieces you turned already, so some of 'em get burned. Why not just breed a mini-cow that could be split and sold in halves, ready for the barbecue?" Bill wanted to think that Randy was joking, except Randy was not the type to joke about his business schemes. "Just imagine pulling out a miniature side of beef, perfectly sized and ready to slap on the grill!" Randy was getting more excited by the minute. You could almost see the barbecue sauce dripping from his chin as he mentally tucked into his petite bovine brainstorm. Bill shuddered at the image of something the size of a dog on the family barbecue grill. With Randy, you never knew if he was a brainiac or just a crackpot. But he knew Randy well enough to resist the urge to tell him that. So he just nodded, toasted Randy with a swig of beer, and hoped he wasn't going to get hit up for an investment.

Self-Protective Visionaries are prone to creating intrigue laced with paranoia. They can come up with some far-fetched ideas they feel compelled to defend even when they have an inkling the other person is right. Their resistance to taking in what others tell them can give them tunnel vision, excluding all feedback that does not fit their vision. Instead of listening to how others are trying to help them, they discredit dissenting ideas by convincing themselves (and others) that the person who gave them the feedback was plotting against them, was envious, or just wants to see them fail. They are masters at creating conspiracy theories, supporting their rejection of others' feedback, because this gives them an excuse to do what they want.

Self-Actualizing Visionaries learn to tolerate feedback. Self-Actualizing Visionaries learn to gather all pertinent and factual data from different sources to ensure their ideas are workable. This includes going to others for constructive criticism, which can help them make necessary improvements before investing large amounts of time and energy in a project. They also learn to simplify their often theoretical and complicated ideas to make them comprehensible to others. In addition, they come to trust that others are giving them feedback in order to help them, not as part of any diabolical plot to bring them down.

Inventing, Envisioning, and Innovating

The perceptions that Visionaries have about the way things naturally relate and evolve, as well as their access to the resources of the unconscious, help them develop visions of what could be. They look for opportunities to approach new activities with a fresh, open-minded attitude. Because of their future orientation, they love to devise plans—for themselves, their children, and anyone else who cares to let them do it. Possibilities, which tend to be far grander than actualities, are much more interesting and pleasurable to them.

Kelly loves the idea of the holiday season. Every year she experiences excitement and joy as she imagines all of the presents she will either buy or make for her family. Around September, she decided she would make a poster board for each of her children, her grandchildren, and her husband—a memory collage with photos and mementoes representing their lives together. She felt that this was a great way of communicating to everyone how special they all were to her and that she treasured each of the shared moments that were reflected in the pictures. She was energized by imagining how delighted each of them would be when they received their individualized poster board.

Flash forward to December 20. Kelly is doing last-minute shopping. Her husband has bought most of the gifts for their family, so she only has to buy for a few people. But time is short and there are no poster boards to be found. Kelly is filled with regret and self-recriminations for not creating the vision she had back in September. She recognizes that she has done the same thing for years and doesn't know why. The trouble is, when Kelly finishes envisioning what she wants to do, her energy goes elsewhere. Her strength and pleasure are related to creating the vision, not the reality.

Self-Protective Visionaries disconnect from their bodies. They are not attuned to the emotional and physical cues that let them know when they are no longer grounded. It is as though some wiring gets crossed. When they are tired, they eat. If they are too full from overeating, they eat more. They know they need to exercise, so they sit in front of the television. Overeating or bingeing is very common for them, as are doing other things to excess—drinking, socializing, gambling, or shopping for things they don't really need. Although they observe themselves behaving this way, they feel helpless to stop, which leads to great guilt and remorse. They can become obsessed with controlling the impulses that triggered the unwanted behavior or fantasizing about how they will act tomorrow while in the midst of the impulsive behavior.

Self-Actualizing Visionaries take care of their physical, emotional, and spiritual well-being. They make sure they have physical activities in their agenda so that they stay connected with their body. They are willing to listen to and appreciate loved ones who express concern about their self-neglect rather than becoming self-protective and defensive. They know the result of disconnecting from their bodies and emotions and take the time to check in and see how they are feeling. Realizing that they cannot control their needs, they attend to them with self-care. They build tolerance to feeling human and vulnerable and are no longer enslaved by their impulses. They turn important personal visions and plans into realities.

Being Ahead of the Pack

I've never reacted well to other people telling me what to do.

—*Tom Selleck*

Visionaries meet their need to be perceptive by being independent and aligning their actions with their vision. As people who see themselves "on the cutting edge" or "ahead of their time," they like to show others the way, but they prefer to do it without getting personally involved. They don't like a lot of attention on themselves and so exert their influence by allowing their contributions to represent them. They are strong individualists with a breadth of interests and abilities. They tend to feel most powerful when they are not limited by the confines of a group, instead observing a group from the outside so that they are able to envision what the group needs to do to achieve its full potential. They stay at the head of the pack, inventing new ways of doing things and championing a more enlightened way of living life.

Benjamin Franklin was a leading author, printer, political theorist, politician, postmaster, scientist, musician, inventor, satirist, civic activist, statesman, and diplomat. He was a major figure in the American Enlightenment and in the history of physics for his discoveries and theories regarding electricity. He invented the lightning rod, bifocals, the Franklin stove, a carriage odometer, and the glass "armonica." He formed both the first public lending library in America and the first fire department in Pennsylvania.

Self-Protective Visionaries are like the Wizard of Oz. Like the Wizard of Oz, the Visionary wants to be held in the highest regard and seen as the only one who can solve problems—the all-knowing, all-perceiving one who others must obey and who never needs to be taught or told anything. Keenly aware of their own limitations, Visionaries try to show the world their brilliance without revealing their vulnerabilities or humanity. Self-Protective Visionaries feel that they must keep demonstrating how wise they are so they won't feel invisible. They feel compelled to show people how much they know and to hide the fact that they are not all-seeing and all-knowing.

Self-Actualizing Visionaries live in the real world. They are aware that real perception, understanding, and wisdom come from experience, participation, and involvement with people and situations as they are in the present moment. Instead of hiding out in the pursuit of deeper awareness, they strive to live authentically with both feet on the ground. Like the Wizard of Oz, once the curtain is pulled back to reveal their mere humanness, they see no more use for the pretense. They show the same type of empathy, understanding, and kindness that the Wizard extended to Dorothy and her companions. They exercise humility in place of grandiosity.

Activators of the Self-Protective System

Visionaries are activated by situations and people who can't, don't, or won't see things the way they do. When they can't be the perceptive one, they feel attacked, ridiculed, or diminished. This is what they fear most, and they will do whatever they can to protect themselves from these feelings.

Absence of Meaningful Relationships

Visionaries' SP System is activated when there is an absence of meaningful relationships. Because part of what makes relationships meaningful to them is finding the source of people's problems, in both personal and professional life, spending much time in environments where they can't fulfill this role makes them feel inconsequential and invisible. The SP System is also activated when people don't listen to them and they struggle to understand why people don't want to hear their insights or to seek deeper understanding through meaningful dialogue.

Feedback from Others

Visionaries fear being attacked or diminished by others. When they spend too much time on their own, their ideas can become quite far fetched, having little relationship to reality. When they actually talk to someone about an idea, believing they have perfected it, the other person may spot flaws. The very act of pointing out the flaws or telling the Visionary that the idea is too "out there" can activate the SP System. The Visionary feels she has been attacked or "shot down" by the other person.

When Visionary Terry's brother Phil was about to turn sixty, Terry decided that she was going to host a birthday party for him at her home. She sent an invitation to her four siblings and their children, suggesting a date and asking what they thought about extending the invitation to some of their cousins as well. She also asked everyone to let her know if they thought another venue might work better, and her sister Mariel suggested that it might be less of a hassle to have the party at the Legion Hall.

A few days later, Mariel checked the party evite to see who had responded. She was surprised to see that the birthday party was now shown as a "Tribute" and that a number of Phil's friends had been invited. Mariel (also a Visionary) emailed Terry because she was curious about the changes.

Terry, believing that her vision for the event was being attacked, sent Mariel a lengthy email telling her to "quit finding fault with everything I do." In a separate email that was addressed to another family member but ended up going to Mariel by mistake, Terry lashed out even more. "Does she think that my house isn't good enough? Or maybe she's just worried that she won't be able to hold court. She could be helping me, but instead she goes behind my back and trashes my plans." Mariel was deeply hurt by these comments and had no idea what she had done to provoke such an outburst.

Making It Real

The fear of being ridiculed by others when they have to convert their perceptions into reality activates the Visionaries' SP System. With visions of what might be, they have great difficulty translating what they see and would like to do into reality. They struggle to get out of their heads and into their lives. Having to move from their global, futuristic perspective to the factual, sequential steps required to build their visions makes them anxious because they can't always envision the specific course of action to get them there, or they feel insecure about what the first step is.

Making Minor Mistakes

Visionaries think that making simple mistakes proves that they really don't know what they are talking about. They think they are ridiculous and that everyone else probably thinks so too. Because their brains are wired to deal with a more wide-ranging global perspective, Visionaries are prone to making mistakes in things like spelling, grammar, or math. Realizing they have made these irritating minor mistakes, they become even more obsessed with doing things perfectly.

Thinking Small

Visionaries are normally adaptable and flexible in their thinking. It is like their minds are elastic, able to stretch and twist to accommodate all the random ideas inside. Their SP System is activated when others rein them in. Being told that their ideas are too far fetched, or that they can't do something the way they envision it but have to do it someone else's way instead is enough to raise their ire. For them, if their ideas are diminished, so are they.

For the past 33 years, I have looked in the mirror every morning and asked myself: "If today were the last day of my life, would I want to do what I am about to do today?" And whenever the answer has been "no" for too many days in a row, I [knew I needed] to change something.

—Steve Jobs

Details, Details, Details

Having to deal with details of ordinary activities, such as housework, mowing the lawn, or even balancing a checkbook, is both frustrating and boring to Visionaries. They can have difficulty controlling their impatience when forced to attend to such matters, so they often choose to procrastinate for as long as possible. When placed in a situation where they must address mundane tasks, they become irritable and cranky.

Blind Spots
Sharing in Relationships

Visionaries are known for approaching others as if looking at a puzzle that needs solving; they are ready to start giving advice on how the pieces should fit together. They forget that they have their own needs and that a healthy relationship means not just giving help but also receiving it. They can think that helping someone is the same thing as having a close relationship, only to have the other person walk away when help is no longer needed. Their super-radar for discerning other people's feelings doesn't seem to work when it comes to knowing what others really want from them, or how their harsh words make others feel. When they accuse their critics of having malicious motives, they can unwittingly damage and even destroy relationships.

Addiction to Connection

Visionaries run the risk of becoming addicted to their pursuit of proving how all things are connected. They seek understanding through perpetual study and the pursuit of knowledge. They then create a complex synthesis of everything they have learned.

Look again at that dot. That's here. That's home. That's us. On it everyone you love, everyone you know, everyone you ever heard of, every human being who ever was, lived out their lives. The aggregate of our joy and suffering, thousands of confident religions, ideologies, and economic doctrines, every hunter and forager, every hero and coward, every creator and destroyer of civilization, every king and peasant, every young couple in love, every mother and father, hopeful child, inventor and explorer, every teacher of morals, every corrupt politician, every "superstar," every "supreme leader," every saint and sinner in the history of our species lived there—on a mote of dust suspended in a sunbeam.

—*Carl Sagan*

Visionaries need to keep making connections to create relational systems about how the world works. Carl Sagan, unlike some less fortunate Visionaries, was able to let his mind soar in this way while keeping both feet on the ground.

Perfectionism

Visionaries have a blind spot around how perfectionistic they are. They usually expect too much from themselves and from others. They refuse to settle for an average understanding, an average relationship, or a mundane way of living, so they set themselves up with unrealistically high standards. The standards of others are relatively unimportant, if noticed at all; SP Visionaries only care about measuring up to their own self-image.

The thing that is really hard, and really amazing, is giving up on being perfect and beginning the work of becoming yourself.

—Anna Quindlen

Estimating How Long Things Take

Visionaries consistently underestimate how long things take. They can commit to doing things with or for others only to find that they have painted themselves into a corner. They leave things unfinished, keeping themselves in a constant state of frustration.

Upshifting to Their Self-Actualizing System

For Visionaries to upshift to their SA System, they need to become more self-aware and to redirect their striving energy by doing the following.

Learning to Share

Visionaries need to remind themselves that sharing involves both giving and taking. They become aware of when they are having one-sided conversations and are withholding information about themselves. They learn to make a habit of sharing something about themselves rather than jumping in and advising. They avoid alienating others with their impersonal approach and learn to express genuine intimacy.

Miguel thought he was a pleasant enough guy to be around, but he seemed to have a lot of first dates that didn't turn into second dates. He was a great listener and was always relieved when he met a woman who liked to talk about herself, because it was so easy to get to know her just by listening. But when several of the women he dated declined to go out with him again, he finally asked one of them what was wrong. She said that she didn't feel he was really interested in a relationship with her because when she tried to get to know him, he gave the shortest possible answers to every question she had asked. Miguel was stunned, because he thought that's what women wanted.

Visionaries need to learn that conversation is not an exchange in which one person listens and the other only talks but more of a shared experience.

Stopping the Paranoia

Visionaries have to keep reminding themselves that others are not out to get them, and that this mind-set is only an excuse for retreating from relationships and for pushing others away. In the birthday party fiasco, had Terry held the imagined insult up to the light of reality by taking the time to consider all of Mariel's possible motives for inquiring about her changes to the party plan, she could have saved both herself and Mariel a lot of suffering.

Being in the Present Moment

Visionaries need to remember to keep both feet on the ground, in the present moment. They need to stay connected with their physical bodies through meditation and exercise forms such as jogging, yoga, and dancing, which are grounding for them. The practice of mindful meditation can be particularly helpful for building present-moment awareness.

Stopping Their Dehumanization of Themselves

It helps Visionaries to remind themselves that they are human so they can recognize their limits and tolerate their feelings. It can be extremely helpful for them to explore their emotions and to gain self-awareness by seeing a therapist, coach, or counselor. Even talking to someone they trust about their insecurities can help.

Approaching Conflict Skillfully

Visionaries need to identify when they are afraid, and to accept and work through conflicts. Taking a course on conflict styles or alternate dispute resolution to learn an approach to conflict management that uses a logical system is very useful for them.

When introverts are in conflict with each other…it may require a map in order to follow all the silences, nonverbal cues, and passive-aggressive behaviors!

—Adam S. McHugh

Spending Time Alone

Visionaries must recognize when they are overloaded and need to get away from it all. It doesn't really matter what they choose to do—go to a movie or art gallery, or take a drive—as long as they are by themselves. A change of scenery or activity usually helps to break thinking patterns that are driven by fear. Effective activities could also include getting outside, exercising, or simply getting a good night's sleep.

Achieving Their Full Potential

It is their depth of insight and understanding that distinguish the Visionary from other Styles. They see the world from another perspective. Not just what it is, but what it could be. They live their lives envisioning how the future could unfold if everyone embraced their higher selves. To them, a utopia exists, as does the possibility of self-actualization. The Visionary is a Striving Style with the potential to understand things at a very profound level. Visionaries' caring and concern for humanity, their intellectual abilities, and their rich inner lives are only some of the gifts they bring to the world. When Visionaries are able to hold the tension between their perceptions and the existing reality long enough to deeply understand the true situation, their visions can change the world.

CHAPTER TEN
THE SOCIALIZER—STRIVING TO BE CONNECTED

I'll reach out my hand to you
Just call my name and I'll be there.

— *"I'll Be There," Hal Davis*

IF YOU WANT TO find a good hairdresser, need a plumber for that leaky faucet, or are looking for contacts to help your niece get a job, the Socializer is the person to talk to. Socializers go through life building their social network, making connection after connection, like a real-life Facebook with friends of all ages and walks of life whom they have touched through their many interests. Socializers have to meet and chat with someone only for a short while to make them feel like they've been "friended."

Because of their gregarious and outgoing nature, Socializers inject energy and enthusiasm into any social situation. Often lively and entertaining, they take great pleasure and personal satisfaction from generating good feelings in other people and in themselves. They are quick to give compliments and seek the positive in people, making others appreciate and enjoy having them around. They are enthusiastic, charming "people people," as well as social organizers in all settings. The effervescent head of the parent-teacher association who's friendly with nearly every parent in the school and uniquely inspires others to pitch in, the charismatic manager who seems to know intuitively how to connect with the sales team, the person who approaches that uncomfortable-looking soul at the party and puts him at ease—those are Socializers.

Often friendly and chatty whether you know them or not, Socializers communicate with ease and are seldom at a loss for something to say. They usually develop communication skills early in life as a means to connect to others. This early development translates into excellent interpersonal skills in adulthood. In fact, it sometimes seems like Socializers were born to help others. They are the older sibling who was always in the kitchen helping Mom while you were watching TV. Or the kid who volunteered to stay and help the teacher after school when everyone else had flown the coop. They love to help and to be seen as helpful. This lets them use their gift for seeing human potential, whether it is in their friends, children, coworkers, or a hapless stranger in a line at the movie theater. Intuitive and empathetic, they are typically patient listeners and always have a word of advice to offer someone in need of help.

Socializers focus on what's happening outside of them and don't spend a lot of time reflecting or doing things on their own. They are the women who get together every year for a "girls' weekend" or the men who arrange a weekly poker game. They have their lives organized so that they can be with someone most of the time, preferably in the context of being "in the know" about what is going on with everyone. The person who rounds up long-lost high school friends for a twenty-year reunion is likely a Socializer. Socializers love to talk about other people, and although they will try hard to keep a secret, it's a challenge for them to do so. In fact, it's not uncommon for Socializers to become reporters or writers, or to work in other media-related roles so they can dispense information about people. Consider Barbara Walters, for example:

Barbara worked her way up through the ranks of a male-dominated industry to be the queen of interviewers, achieving the coveted role of doing interviews with the stars before the Oscars. Using one of the Socializers' innate talents, she is able to establish connections with people quickly and to make them feel as though they were intimate friends.

With a vision for where she wanted the interview to go, Barbara established a reputation for getting people to lower their guard and reveal personal information they never intended to disclose. Barbara knows intuitively what will interest the public and how to get this information without alienating her interviewee. Her connection to people is as important as the information she coaxes from them.

What Makes Socializers Tick?

The part of the brain that Socializers live in is responsible for establishing and maintaining the social order of the group or society they belong to. Socializers therefore strive for harmony with others—in their beliefs, values, dress, and behavior. This means that they are constantly appraising how people look, act, and behave on the basis of their book of social norms. Many Socializers work hard to keep etiquette alive and dress according to convention even when it has gone out of fashion. This doesn't mean they are unfashionable. It means that even when the dress code at work allows casual clothing, they will still dress in a suit, according to their job and social status. They will remind others to keep their elbows off the table when eating and don't allow their children to wear sweatpants to school, even though all the other kids (and teachers) do.

In an age where civility and charm are often left by the wayside, Miss Manners reminds us that etiquette and grace never go out of style. She deftly answers…readers' questions about correspondence and guest lists, but also weighs in on such varied subjects as jealousy, mooching friends, dating fiascos, in-laws, loutish co-workers and dreaded invitations one seemingly can't get out of politely. From rude texters to pushy "helicopter parents," Miss Manners has the proper response for all of us who long for a return to common courtesy.

—*Miss Manners*

Socializers, by using their right emotional brains, are constantly judging and comparing themselves and others to what they have deemed the appropriate social behavior. To feel safe and to make everything right in their world, they need others to conform to the same social order that they believe in. For this reason, Socializers often take the lead in societal, familial, or political roles. They tend to focus more on their own judgments of events or of people's behavior in situations than on the events or situations themselves. For the Socializer, feelings are facts, and Socializers talk about feelings in a way that says, "You should believe this too." They will often believe something is true because they feel it is true, despite fact-based evidence to the contrary.

People often go along with what Socializers are saying because it can be difficult to reason with them. Theirs is a fuzzy logic that comes from an emotionally driven value system. Their manner of judging people quickly judges everyone's behavior and then pigeonholes them as good guys or bad guys. For example, if someone behaves rudely, that person is forever a "rude young man." If someone is doing work with the homeless, she'll be "that wonderful young woman with the heart of gold." Should Socializers have a disappointing dining experience, they will eternally refer to the restaurant as "that disgusting Italian dive." You get the picture. Socializers have a full repertoire of words they use to describe people, places, and things, and are free and easy in using them.

Because their right emotional brain is most active and focused outward, they often speak in stream-of-consciousness style, which can be little more than a monologue of critiques loosely strung together. A drive in the country might sound like this:

Look at that house! You'd think those people would fix it before the thing falls down on them! I don't understand some people—why they don't take better care of their homes? They probably spend all of their money on beer. Or maybe they're waiting for PBS to come and feature them on This Old Crappy

House. *Oh, there's the store. It was closed the last time we drove by here and the shopkeeper was really rude to me when I knocked on the door because I knew they were still there. What was the big deal, I ask you? People just aren't as helpful as they used to be, don't you think? Like my friend Sara, who I didn't find helpful at all last week. I was trying to get to my appointment on time and I couldn't get off the phone. You'd think I had nothing better to do that listen to her problems. And can you believe they still haven't fixed this section of the road? With all of the money we pay in taxes...*

They can go on indefinitely, and their monologues are often laced with humor and playfulness. You only need to stand there and listen. In spite of their critical streak, Socializers are often the life of the party because they're basically warmhearted, extraverted, relationship-oriented people who place great importance on getting together and socializing with others. Socializers work hard at making any occasion a lively one, even if it only involves two people. They are at their best when they can mix and mingle with their large network of friends, coworkers, and family.

Relationship Style of the Socializer

Socializers make excellent companions and mates because they are deeply devoted to their partners. They like spending time entertaining and being entertained, and their home is often the place where friends and family gather. They like to have their partner with them at the center of their social framework, participating and enjoying it as much as they do. Although Socializers don't really need to spend significant amounts of time exclusively with their mate, they take pleasure in getting to know their partner's likes and dislikes and making their partner feel special by remembering his or her favorite dessert or bottle of wine. There is no effort too great in this regard, as Socializers want to show their partners how much they care.

Socializers idealize their relationships and they will do whatever it takes to mold others into whoever they are capable of becoming—often on the Socializer's time line. They have insight into what others can do and will offer their advice, financial support, and energy toward helping them. They believe it is their job to help the other person, who is not living up to the Socializers' expectations. Because of this tendency, Socializers may unwittingly push their partners, family, and friends too hard by setting the bar too high with implied expectations that can't be met. A Socializer mother might say, with good intentions, "Why don't you take some of my lasagna home with you? I know you're a terrible cook." Or the well-meaning Socializer husband might say to his wife, "Why don't I run the kids to soccer practice? Your driving makes me nervous anyway." They seem to offer you a tasty carrot with one hand and use the other hand to smack you with a stick. In their hearts, they feel their actions are in the best interests of everyone involved.

Both Princess Diana and I were, in our ways, manipulative people, perceiving quickly the emotions of others and able instinctively to play with them, all in the cause, of course, of the greater good.

—*Tony Blair*

Socializers enjoy taking care of the needs of others, as though this were the paramount contribution one could make in a relationship. They may even believe that their partner and others love them because of their special, helpful qualities. Socializers will do everything for their partner if the partner allows it, taking over simple things that their partner could easily do but may not get around to. They may insist on cooking and cleaning up because they feel a sense of their own ability to "take care of things" when doing this. A partner can easily become dependent on the Socializer; this turns problematic when the partner stops doing anything at all. The Socializer will then start to complain about his or her long-suffering martyrdom. Should the partner offer to take over doing some of the work, the Socializer will refuse, melodramatically insisting, "Don't worry about me; I'll just take care of everything myself!" It's not just that the Socializer wants to suffer; it's that to accept help would mean giving up his or her power in the relationship.

These loving and caring individuals provide understanding, closeness, and emotional support to their partners, children, and friends. They place a high value on communication and try to keep the lines of communication open. They like to be the one who gets to define the social order in their relationships, advising others how they should behave, what they should wear, and whom they should talk to when they go out. They can be quite tyrannical when it comes to appearances. They want others to see what a perfect relationship they have or how perfect their children are, and they place a lot of importance on how this reflects on them. Should their children not behave appropriately, Socializers can become cold and punishing. It's as if a wall goes up inside of them, leaving the disappointing person out in the cold. They see whatever transgressions someone has made as motivated by a desire to hurt, embarrass, or get back at the Socializer for something, and the Socializer will make the person pay for those transgressions. No one plays the role of the long-suffering giver in a relationship like the Socializer does. "How could you have acted that way, after all I've done for you?" is a well-rehearsed line in their favorite melodrama, called *I Give So Much Better Than I Get.*

On a road trip, Susan (Socializer) and her partner Ted (Artist) stopped to get gas. There was a promotion offering a choice of popcorn, coffee, or a doughnut if you filled your tank with more than ten gallons of gas. As Susan was filling up, she told Ted to go in and get popcorn. When they were back on the road, Susan opened the popcorn and offered it to Ted, who declined. "What?" she said, unable to believe her ears. "But I got it for you because I know how much you like popcorn. You always eat popcorn, and I wanted to do something nice for you." Ted started feeling the deep freeze coming. Not wanting to have to bear the next four hours in silence, he ate the popcorn, but he was miffed at having to do something he really didn't want to do. Susan, however, was beaming. "I knew you'd like it," she said.

How Socializers Satisfy Their Need to Be Connected
Working and Playing with Others

Socializers are people who need people. Fortunately for them, others are automatically drawn to the warmth and friendliness that Socializers radiate. Their affable and uncomplicated nature makes them popular without really trying. They have an affinity for working with groups and a tendency to enhance and enliven any group they belong to. They interact well with all types of people, regardless of age or background, provided they aren't opposed or put down. Others want Socializers to be a part of whatever is going on because of their personality and energy; thus, they often attract opportunities for themselves. They see the world through rose-colored glasses and believe the world should be as they see it. They are optimistic and determined to live life in a positive fashion and to encourage others to feel the same way.

Self-Protective Socializers must have validation from others. It's not always apparent to others that Socializers need people to need them and that they are energized by the feedback and affirmation they get when they are needed. When SP Socializers don't receive this affirmation or are left to work on their own, they feel rejected or devalued. They can appear "flighty" in their relationships as they go from person to person, looking for a place where they can be helpful and appreciated. Socializers can spend excessive amounts of time helping strangers at the expense of friends and family when they don't get the appreciation they need from those relationships. Driven to gain this validation, SP Socializers are unable to say no to the demands of others. If they are forced to say no because they do not have time or energy, the guilt they feel is out of proportion to the reality of the situation.

Lucy: Do you think I'm a crabby person?
Charlie Brown: Yes, I think you're a very crabby person.
Lucy: WELL WHO CARES WHAT YOU THINK?

— *"Peanuts," Charles M. Schulz*

Self-Actualizing Socializers are helpful to others at work and to themselves at home. They stop trying to be all things to all people. They know that juggling many activities and people satisfies their craving for relatedness and their need to be energized through others; however, they also realize that this behavior is depleting when done to excess. This insight allows SA Socializers to take the time they need to recharge their batteries by being alone. They no longer fear a loss of connection if they say no to the demands of others. They also recognize that they, too, need help from time to time, and they are willing to ask for it.

Creating Harmony

Socializers have a great need for harmony in relationships, and they work hard to make sure people get along and join wholeheartedly in activities with family and friends. At the backyard barbecue, the Socializer will be sure to have every variety of food and drink to please the crowd, won't let anyone's glass go empty, and won't allow anyone to sit out of the festivities. "If you aren't into lawn bowling, how about croquet, or a game of Yahtzee? And by the way, have you met your neighbor Penelope, who's a flying trapeze artist? Did you know that she shares your love of bonsai gardening and steam loco-motives?" Socializers often feel that it is their personal responsibility to eliminate or resolve any type of conflict or disharmony around them, whether they are involved in it or not.

Self-Protective Socializers take everything personally. They are personally offended when people do not hold the same values or want the same things that they want. They take trends and fads seriously and can be furious when others don't value these choices. Appearance is extremely important to them, as they believe it should be to everyone. Liking the same television shows, reading Oprah's Book Club recommendations, even buying clothes from the same popular stores are all ways that SP Socializers affirm their connections to people. To SP Socializers, harmony means everyone is in agreement with them, and they feel personally rejected when others express tastes that are different from their own. They blame others for how they feel, rarely seeing that the problem has arisen because they have taken something personally, and they rarely apologize. They become upset and exaggerate the importance of minor breeches to social etiquette. The following scene from the TV program *Gilmore Girls* shows how Emily (Socializer) and Richard (Performer) react and take offense when someone in their neighborhood does not conform to the social norm. Their very confused daughter Lorelai (Adventurer) can't quite figure out what the issue is.

Emily: It's simply disgraceful.

Richard: For years, we've had peace in the neighborhood.

Emily: I knew the Richmonds were going to be trouble when they missed the block party last month.

Lorelai: I don't understand. They gave out full-size candy bars for Halloween. So what?

Emily: Not full-size candy bars, Lorelai—king-size candy bars.

Richard: We've been giving out full-size candy bars for years now.

Emily: And then those people move in and throw the

entire balance of the neighborhood off. They made everybody look ridiculous.

Richard: It's very embarrassing.

Emily: I think we have to do something about this—maybe go to the homeowners' association.

Self-Actualizing Socializers tolerate disharmony. Although they continue to seek harmony, they stop demanding that others conform to their likes and dislikes. Self-Actualizing Socializers can tolerate differences of opinion without feeling devalued. They are able to learn from others and stop insisting that things be "their way or the highway." They work at fostering independence in themselves and tolerating it in others. This is especially helpful when they need to move on in their work and relationships and when their children are maturing and getting on with their own lives.

Establishing Social Order

Socializers look outside of themselves—to their culture, their parents, their politicians, and educators—to tell them what their values are and how the world should operate. They then become champions of the "way things should be." Like Miss Manners, they become leaders in their own right. Socializers believe in a social order and want to know where they are in the ranks, what their role is, and how they are connected to others. In new situations, they evaluate others to see where they stand, and they adapt their behavior so that they don't offend or overstep their place. They do their best to rise to the top of the social hierarchy while maintaining their connections to others. Whether it is as a minister, the principal of a school, or the coach of the local skating team, the Socializer likes to be the queen bee or the king of the hill, with a busy hive of people following and swarming around him or her.

Self-Protective Socializers insist everyone do things their

way, or else. They want to be connected at all costs and have the attitude "you are either with me or against me." They can police friends and family members to make sure that they are doing things according to their advice. An SP Socializer might even call up a friend and say, "I've been thinking about your problem, and here's what you need to do." Needless to say, the advice can come as quite a surprise to a friend who hasn't asked for it. But SP Socializers are fiercely protective of their position as problem solvers, and when their advice isn't heeded, they can undermine people by making belittling, disparaging remarks. "Can you believe how Sara acted when…?" or "Who does Dave think he is, talking to me that way?" are the type of statements you will hear from rebuffed Socializers, along with some defaming evidence that they have created about poor Sara or Dave. Socializers are pros at laying guilt trips when others don't go along with their agendas.

> *Socializer hostess: I can't believe that George didn't come to my party. What an insult. He didn't come to your party last month either. How rude! Does he think he's too good for us? What a snob, blowing us off like that!*

> *Friend: Actually, George had to go visit his dad in the hospital. He had surgery yesterday, and George wanted to go and cheer him up.*

> *Socializer hostess: A likely story. Don't tell me you believe him! George is great at spinning yarns. I wouldn't be surprised if he skipped the party because he got a better offer at the last minute. I'm so mad at him!*

Self-Actualizing Socializers shift their focus from others onto themselves. They no longer have to be the queen bee or the king of the hill, and they recognize when they are covertly manipulating others as a way to reduce their own anxiety. They have come to terms with how their inner "martyr" can hijack them. They consistently work to break the habit of manipulating others. They no longer believe in using their idealized, dehumanized self as a tool to get them through life, and they work to give and take in relationships. They are able to find legitimate ways of feeling loved and cared for without the compromise of "I will help you if you will love me and be grateful for all I do."

Helping Others

Socializers meet their need to be connected by being with people, building networks, and getting involved with the lives of others. Socializers' compassion and interest in others draws people to them, and they are privy to confidential information from those who seek their counsel. They are dependable and responsive to the needs of those around them. Socializers are like cheerleaders when it comes to supporting others and will lavish praise on people when they succeed. They try to make everyone feel like they can do whatever they want to, even though it may be unrealistic. Their special gifts of caring for and serving others, their genuine interest in humankind, and their exceptional intuitive awareness of people make everyone feel comfortable and included.

Self-Protective Socializers have an image of themselves as all-giving, selfless, benevolent, and ever-helpful human beings. They flatter people, thinking that others want praise as much as they do, and they are easily hurt when others don't reciprocate. Because they are so focused on their idealized selves, they have difficulty seeing themselves for who they actually are. Their value is in helping or serving others, which makes Socializers dependent on feedback and gratitude for affirmation. In this episode of the TV series *Desperate Housewives*, we see how Socializer Bree Van de Kamp tries so hard to provide her family with the very best, for their own good.

(The VAN DE KAMP family is seated, eating silently.)

Danielle: Why can't we ever have normal soup?

Bree: Danielle, there is nothing abnormal about basil puree.

Danielle: Just once, can we have a soup that people have heard of? Like French onion or navy bean?

Bree: First of all, your father can't eat onions; he's deadly allergic. And I won't even dignify your navy bean suggestion. So. How's the osso bucco?

Andrew: It's OK.

Bree: It's OK? Andrew, I spent three hours cooking this meal. How do you think it makes me feel when you say it's OK, in that sullen tone?

Andrew: Who asked you to spend three hours on dinner?

Bree: Excuse me?

Andrew: Tim Harper's mom gets home from work, pops open a can of pork and beans, and boom, they're eating, everyone's happy.

Bree: You'd rather I serve pork and beans?

Danielle: Apologize now, I am begging.

Andrew: I'm just saying, do you always have to serve cuisine? Can't we ever just have food?

Bree: Are you doing drugs?

Andrew: What!?

Bree: (angry) Change in behavior is one of the warning signs, and you have been as fresh as paint for the last six months. That certainly would explain why you're always locked in the bathroom.

Danielle: (grinning) Trust me, that is not what he is doing.

Andrew: Mom, I'm not the one with the problem here, alright? You're the one always acting like she's running for mayor of Stepford.

In their minds, Socializers exaggerate how helpful they are and how much more capable they are than other people. By inflating their own value, they can ignore or deny the human qualities that make them feel vulnerable, and even ignore or repress their physical and emotional needs. They work hard to make sure the feedback they get supports their image, ultimately mistaking this imagined self for their authentic self.

Self-Actualizing Socializers stop being martyrs. The biggest challenge for Socializers is to shift away from their habit of becoming martyrs in order to feel needed and valued. Although they still genuinely want to help people, they are more aware of their own needs and they ensure that they are not compromising themselves to get appreciation from others. Their desire to help is rooted in their capacity for unconditional love, of both themselves and others. They no longer try to impose what they think people need just so they can look helpful. They wait to be asked and don't get upset when people refuse their help. Because they are connected to their own emotions and aware of their motives, they can help others in a true spirit of generosity, without expecting to be taken care of in return. Their relationships no longer come with strings attached.

Activators of the Self-Protective System

With their need to be connected and have a network of people around them to help, advise, and otherwise be involved with, Socializers are activated by people and situations that cause them to feel alone, abandoned, and devalued. Their need to be in the know about what's going on with people causes them to feel anxious, worthless, or cast aside when they can't play this role. This feeling is what they fear most, so they will do whatever they can to protect themselves from it.

Time Alone

Without anyone to help, Socializers feel alone and abandoned. Cut off from the perceived source of their power, they often feel incapable of dealing with things. For example, they may want to upgrade their computer skills but can't make a decision about what course to take. They'd rather take the course with a friend because they are anxious about not knowing anyone. No one wants to do it with them, so they join a friend's book club instead.

Others Who Won't Participate

Socializers are confounded when others don't want to attend events with them, especially events they've helped organize. They can take this personally and feel abandoned, annoyed, and hurt. They do not endorse individualism and are not above making others feel guilty for wanting to do their own thing. In an effort to stay connected, they use emotional blackmail or threats, such as "I'll have a terrible time doing this by myself, and it will be all your fault."

Interpersonal Conflict

Any situation in which there is a prevailing feeling of tension or conflict activates Socializers and makes them eager to restore an equilibrium that is not always easily established. When they are unable to avoid the conflict, they either devalue themselves or blame others for making them uncomfortable. They stay in dysfunctional relationships to avoid creating conflict.

When a marital squabble erupts between guests at her book club, Socializer Sue immediately faults herself, thinking, "If only I had put Aunt Enid between Mona and Chris, that argument never would have happened!" But the afterthought is followed quickly by sharp words for Mona and Chris, "Do you really need to ruin my event by airing your dirty laundry right now?"

Of course, the truth is that Sue's seating arrangements are not responsible for the argument, and Mona and Chris probably didn't argue with the intention of spoiling the book club meeting. Because Sue is still in SP mode, her reaction to discord tends to be subjective and speculative. She lets her feelings dictate her actions, which only leads to greater disharmony.

Too Much Time Socializing

Being with others affirms Socializers' self-worth and value. They love to feel needed and included, which makes them reluctant to say no to anyone for fear of letting them down. However, prolonged exposure to others can eventually lead Socializers to exhaustion.

Too Much Intimacy

Socializers love the roses but hate the thorns: they crave connection but fear being hurt, criticized, or abandoned. Their self-protective behavior can be activated by too much personal disclosure by others or the expectation that they do the same.

Not Being Appreciated

Socializers gladly give their time and energy toward helping others, but they tend to have a hidden agenda. They will keep a mental record of what is "owed" to them and will begin to feel desperate for acknowledgment if the payoff is not forthcoming. They can also shift into the long-suffering caricature of the martyr.

Blind Spots
Being Too Idealistic

Socializers create ideal depictions of others and then are disappointed when others don't live up to those ideals. The stereotypical Socializer parent may think her child is failing to be the right kind of son or daughter, has chosen an inferior mate (no matter who the mate is), isn't living up to his or her career potential, and doesn't know how to raise children or even dress them properly.

Taking Things Personally

Socializers take conflict and rejection personally. Interpersonal conflict is a source of great distress, as they tend to blame themselves for the upset of others or to blame others for making them uncomfortable. During conflicts they can let their feelings dictate their actions, which leads to greater disharmony.

Being Taken Advantage Of

Saying no when others need them is a recurrent problem for the Socializer, making them vulnerable to being taken advantage of. They can empathize excessively, losing perspective on the practical aspects of an issue. Socializers make their decisions on the basis of how they feel, which can present a perspective very different from reality.

Manipulating Others

Socializers don't always realize that they manipulate the feelings of others. They focus comments on what others are doing instead of what they are feeling. Should someone not want to come to an event, they are more likely to say, "What's wrong with you? Everyone else is coming. Why do you always have to be so difficult?" rather than "I'm disappointed. It's always more fun when you join us."

Being Critical and Judgmental

Socializers can be very direct and tactless when trying to get people back on track and to correct deviations in expected behavior. Socializers are often unaware that their feedback could be perceived as criticism, which works against them by reducing productivity and stifling cooperation. The short black-comedy film *Guilt* provides excellent examples of Socializers' high expectations coupled with scathing criticism when others fail to rise to the occasion:

Twentysomething Arnie has a problem. His mother is in the hospital with a heart condition and is certain to die if she can't get a replacement heart very soon. Arnie's two Socializer aunts decide that Arnie should donate his heart to his mother. Arnie can't believe they're serious. The aunts lay on the guilt. "There was a time when her heart beat for both of you," one recalls wistfully. "She carried you for nine months," chimes in the other. Even Arnie's girlfriend accuses him of being selfish for not agreeing to give up his heart and take a pig's heart while awaiting a human transplant. The question "What kind of son are you?" rings in his ears, along with the implied answer: "Not a very good one, if you won't give your mother your heart." Pressured from all sides, Arnie eventually gives in and undergoes the surgery, only to be told that his heart was too small to substitute for his mother's! Despite his valiant effort to save his mother's life, he ends up with a pig heart and plenty of grief from his aunts, one of whom admonishes him, "All you had to do was one thing right in your whole life, and you screwed that up too."

Upshifting to Their Self-Actualizing System

For Socializers to upshift to their SA System, they must become more self-aware and begin to redirect their striving energy by doing the following.

Paying Attention to Their Body

Socializers need to practice both self-care and self-discipline. Because they look outside of themselves to see what others need and expect, it's easy for them to ignore their own physical and emotional needs. They do best when they follow a discipline that allows them to stay grounded. Physical exercise—such as jogging, walking, or gardening—or meditating can be critical to keeping their feet on the ground.

Saying No to Others

Socializers need to take time out from being caretakers and organizers; otherwise, they can suffer serious burnout. Using a calendar and getting help to prioritize activities allow them to create a more relaxed, less compulsive way of life and to avoid the sometimes serious health issues that come from running on empty for long periods of time.

Stopping Feeling Guilty

Socializers are vulnerable to having others guilt them into doing things they don't really want or have the energy to do. They often have "free-floating" guilt feelings that emerge from nowhere. Socializers must ensure that their friends take them seriously when they say no the first time and must not be talked out of their feelings and needs. In particular, when Socializers say they need to be alone, they really do need to be alone.

Developing Objective Reasoning

Socializers often need to run things by a more objective friend, partner, or coach, who can help them develop a more rational approach to their lives. They do best when they seek objective and impartial feedback to help them accurately assess the facts, dispassionately and impersonally. This helps them see beyond the immediate situation to the logical consequences of their actions.

Recharging Their Batteries

Socializers can run themselves into the ground when they don't take time out from their commitments to others. They can prevent suffering serious burnout by going into an environment that makes no demands of them. This could be simply a walk in the park, enjoying the outdoors, or getting a massage. Withdrawing from their usual hectic schedule to spend time alone as a part of their regular routine keeps their energy readily available.

Facing Conflict Head-on

Learning to recognize when they are sweeping problems under the carpet to avoid conflict and confrontation helps Socializers deal with conflict as it arises. By reminding themselves that they are not responsible for disharmony and that working through conflict leads to stronger connections, they can wade in further when emotional discomfort wants to keep them in the shallow end of relationships.

Achieving Their Full Potential

Socializers are the "weavers of the social fabric" in families and communities. They easily build and maintain positive relationships with a wide variety of people. They aim to be helpful and are enthusiastic, amiable, outgoing "people people." Their strong need to connect provides others with a delightful companion, an energetic partner, an enthusiastic manager, and a parent willing to invest himself to help a child achieve his or her potential. The Socializer is a Striving Style with tremendous interpersonal strengths and resources, from strong communication skills and charisma to genuine human interest and intuition. When Socializers are able to set boundaries, consider situations rationally, and tolerate conflict, they can change many people's lives—including their own—for the better.

Chapter Eleven
THE ARTIST—STRIVING TO BE CREATIVE

A feeling deep in your soul
Says you were half now you're whole.

—*Barbra Streisand*

ARTISTS CAN BE A little more difficult to spot: their pleasant, friendly outer persona often masks the intense, resourceful, and powerful individual within. Driven by their need to create, they seek authentic self-expression in all that they do and aspire to the ideals that govern their internal worlds. They find their inspiration in nature and in simple, everyday happenings. Their creativity takes many different forms and can be expressed in any occupation: a librarian can be as much of an artist as a dancer or a chef. The authentic expression of artists' creativity lies at the heart of all their actions.

In a world where most people find comfort in belonging and conforming, Artists often stand alone, preferring independence and authenticity. You may recognize them at the edge of the crowd, with a tentative demeanor that suggests a kind of holding back. Yet their clothes, hair, tattoos, and piercings may tell an entirely different story; it is not unusual for Artists to demonstrate their uniqueness through their attire.

Creativity can be defined as moving beyond what currently exists to make something that is new. What this means for Artists is that to meet their predominant need to be creative, they have to be constantly doing new things, meeting new people, thinking new thoughts, transcending the boundaries of their bodies by making love or making music, and generally having the freedom to do things their own way. For Artists, there is no separation between themselves and what they create. They view the creative process holistically. The creator, the materials, the equipment, the actions—and ultimately what is created—are all parts of a whole. The way that our culture defines normal life, with its workaday routines, can be oppressive to them because it conflicts with their desire to tune in to the fresh possibilities of every day.

Consciousness expresses itself through creation…On many an occasion when I am dancing, I have felt touched by something sacred. In those moments, I felt my spirit soar and become one with everything that exists…I keep on dancing, and then it is the eternal dance of creation. The creator and creation merge into one whole-ness of joy. I keep on dancing…and dancing…and dancing. Until there is only…the dance.

—*Michael Jackson*

Artists often say that they aren't really creative because they don't think of themselves in that way. However, they will then go on to talk about the experiences they create for their children, the homes they create, the style of fashion that is so unique to them, and the arts and crafts they do in their spare time. They often work in the helping professions, where they support people's health and well-being in such roles as massage therapist, naturopathic or medical doctor, psychotherapist, nurse, or nurse-practitioner.

What Makes Artists Tick

The Artist Striving Style lives out of the right emotional brain with an inward focus. Everything that happens to Artists is an emotional experience; in fact, they are more concerned with their feeling experiences than they are with what is actually happening in the external world. The primary purpose of this part of the brain is to generate feelings—both present emotions and emotional memories—and Artists have a phenomenal capacity to experience a full range of emotions, from ecstasy to the depths of despair. However, they are stuck in thinking that what they are feeling defines who they are: "I feel, therefore I am." They often live their lives at the mercy of whatever intense emotional experience they are creating. If Artists have positive experiences, they have a positive sense of their value; unfortunately, the inverse is also true: if Artists have negative experiences, they have a negative sense of their value.

Throughout their life, Artists struggle to secure and maintain a sense of their own value. This is because the function of the right emotional brain is to compare, contrast, and assign a value to themselves on the basis of who they are with, what there are doing, and what they experience. If they have positive experiences, Artists have a positive sense of their value, and if negative, vice versa. Because this brain is more likely to create negative feelings, Artists often feel themselves to be behind the eight ball in life, never feeling good enough and always seeing themselves as failing others simply by being themself. Artists are also driven to re-create past feeling experiences over and over again. If the past was one that was fulfilling and desirable, this can be a tremendous asset. However, if their past was marked by events and relationships most people would want to forget, Artists will keep re-creating these kinds of experiences. Their thinking patterns are often distressing and depressing.

Because of the degree of self-consciousness Artists have, they usually appear reserved and are difficult to get to know. Deep down, Artists fear that people or situations are going to overpower or overwhelm them, so they tend to hold themselves apart. People often accuse them of being aloof or standoffish when they are actually self-conscious and anxious about engaging with others. If they choose to go to parties—which often, they don't—they will stay tucked in a corner, looking on. They can seem disinterested, but the simple act of talking to people can start a chain reaction in their heads that works something like this: "compare myself to the person I'm talking to; judge what that comparison says about me; decide that I'm inferior; decide that the other person also thinks I'm inferior." It's no wonder with this self-defeating dialogue that Artists lack confidence in social situations. For example, a behind-the-scenes look at a seemingly innocent party conversation between an SP Artist and a party host might look like this:

Host: "Did you get a piece of the birthday cake? It's amazing!" (Background thought: I hope everyone's having a good time.)

Artist: "No…I…hadn't thought about it." (Background thought: Oh God, you're the relaxed, congenial party host, and I'm the mayor of Moronville. They just sang happy birthday to him, everybody is eating cake, and I'm thinking about what? Wishing I hadn't worn this hideous dress because it makes me look fat.)

Host: "Oh, if you prefer something healthier, we have some appetizers on the counter over there." (Background thought: Not everyone eats cake; good thing we have other food.)

Artist: "Thanks, I might check that out later." (Background thought: Nice. I knew it. Host thinks I'm fat and unhealthy. I knew this dress was hideous! Now my oh-so-capable host is making a mental note: "Strike blasé, clueless guest from future party lists." Why do I bother?)

Although Artists feel that they are unique, they also think of themselves as irreparably flawed. Because they incessantly compare themselves to others, they find more differences than similarities. They fear assimilation—being pulled into the big nasty vat of ordinariness. They run into problems in groups—even groups of friends or family—when they start to feel accepted or included, because the more included they are, the more consumed they feel. They will go to great lengths to reassure themselves that they are still different from others, even if it means devaluing themselves. For example, the Artist who is nominated as her high school's homecoming queen may brush off the distinction, saying, "I'll go to the dance, but when they see my dress, they'll be sorry they decided to put the freak on the list." This unconscious process meets their need to be creative at the expense of work or social contributions.

Please accept my resignation. I don't care to belong to any club that will have me as a member.

—*Groucho Marx*

Relationship Styles of the Artist

I want my boys to have an understanding of people's emotions, their insecurities, people's distress, and their hopes and dreams.

—*Princess Diana*

The love of an Artist is what great romance stories are based on. To be loved by an Artist is to be loved completely and with abandon. Artists have a deep capacity for love and caring, and they do it with the intensity of their whole being. They seek to experience another loving them with the same intensity. Their need to bond and feel at one with others causes them to seek out relationships with just one or a few people. This allows them to form deep, meaningful, and intimate relationships that satisfy their intense hunger for perfect rapport. They don't just want to be known; they want to be known deeply and profoundly. The hallmark of their Style in relationships is authenticity. Artists may claim that they don't need anyone, yet when they are in a relationship, it is intense and consuming. They look for depth and meaningful self-expression with others and have little tolerance for superficiality.

Whether Artists are looking for a partner or a friend, they have a clear idea of the feeling state they wants to create with that person. Artists bond easily when they meet someone who seems to fit their ideal. They seek passion and intensity in the relationship. They also look for someone with whom they can share their "secret self" so that they can be validated and accepted for who they authentically are. At the beginning of their relationships, Artists are blissfully happy because they believe they have found their "soul mate," their heart's desire. They can become walking Hallmark valentines— taking strolls on the beach, staying up until all hours baring their souls, sharing hopes and dreams, and generally creating a heavenly realm in which just the two exist in an exquisite state of oneness.

Who knows what tomorrow brings, in a world few hearts survive?
All I know is the way I feel. When it's real, I keep it alive.

> — *"Up Where We Belong," Jack Nitzsche,*
> *Buffy Sainte-Marie, and Will Jennings*

It is very easy for Artists to feel slighted by others. They are attuned to emotional nuances and are in the habit of assigning emotional meaning to things people say or do. When Artists encounter emotional states of others, they will usually find a way to make the other person's behavior about them. If someone is struggling with his work, the Artist will try to empathize with him but will then become anxious because the Artist doesn't feel helpful enough or doesn't know the right thing to say. The Artist will stop focusing on the need of the other person and will even railroad the conversation by saying how inadequate he or she is at helping and what a terrible friend he or she is. The Artist may even start talking about what a difficult time *he or she* is having at work. Here's an example of how this plays out in real life:

Carol, a Visionary, had been working diligently for months to develop a creative proposal that would help her company land a multimillion-dollar contract. At the same time, her husband Ron (Performer) was experiencing health issues, and when Carol was not at work, she was at home taking care of Ron. Carol didn't talk to friends too much about her personal life because she didn't have the emotional energy. She hadn't realized how fatigued she had become until she started gaining weight and becoming impatient with people and situations. When she recognized that she actually needed some time with a friend to talk things through, Carol made a lunch date with Leslie, an Artist.

At lunch, as soon as Carol brought up the issue of her deep fatigue, her concerns about her husband's health, and her ability to care for him, Leslie burst into tears. She said she felt terrible that she couldn't possibly help Carol because she was going through a personal hell herself. She told Carol the story about how she had been passed over for a long-awaited promotion because her manager felt threatened by her and was holding her back. Her manager said it was because of her repeated failures to manage time and budgets, but Leslie didn't believe that was the reason. Her kids were also driving her nuts by always trying to get out of doing homework or chores around the house. In stunned silence, Carol sat listening to Leslie, regretting that she had chosen her as a confidant, then shifting to empathize and help Leslie problem solve. Carol paid for lunch too, because Leslie said that when she left the house, she was so overwhelmed that she forgot to bring her wallet.

This is an example of the Artist's way of unconsciously meeting her need to be creative at the expense of a relationship. Both women came with different agendas: Carol wanted to share what she was experiencing and get help with staying connected to herself and her own needs. Leslie came to create an experience in which she would get empathy, attunement, and validation for being victimized. She didn't want help with the real issues at work or with her children. Each woman would leave the conversation with a different experience as well: Carol would feel empty and frustrated by her friend's self-involvement, and Leslie would feel that she had created a fantastic bonding experience with her friend, who fully understood and empathized with her pain and suffering. This is why the very people Artists believe are their closest friends may end up avoiding them.

How Artists Satisfy Their Need to Be Creative
Living Aligned with Their Values

There are four questions of value in life…What is sacred? Of what is the spirit made? What is worth living for, and what is worth dying for? The answer to each is the same. Only love.

—*Johnny Depp*

Artists' lives are governed by their personal value system. Their values dominate how they live and how they experience their lives, and aren't swayed by logic or persuasion. They are humanitarian and seek to put their values into practice through activities such as teaching, counseling, health consciousness, saving the planet through living their values, or volunteering time to worthy causes. Because Artists immerse their entire being into whatever they do, they are selective about what or whom they involve themselves with. They look for like-minded people to have relationships with and work situations where there is an alignment of human values. They want their home and work life to reflect their values and their ideals. Anne Shirley, the heroine of *Anne of Green Gables*, is a perfect example of an Artist. While seeking out "kindred spirits" and escaping into daydreams, Anne transforms the emotional life of Matthew and Marilla.

When Anne arrives in Avonlea, she is a stray waif with a pitiable past, but she quickly establishes herself in Green Gables and the Avonlea community.

She is not useful to Matthew and Marilla, her guardians, who wanted a boy orphan to help out on the farm. Still, Anne's spirit brings vitality to the narrow, severe atmosphere at Green Gables. Her desire for beauty, imagination, and goodness motivates her behavior. Although some people, like Matthew, recognize Anne's admirable qualities from the beginning, others misunderstand Anne and think her unorthodox behavior evidence of immorality. The very traits that make Anne unique and enrich her inner life also cause her to act passionately and stubbornly and to bungle chores. Reveries and daydreams constantly absorb her, taking up attention that Marilla feels should be spent thinking of decorum and duty.

As a child, Anne loves and hates with equal fervor. She makes lifelong alliances with people she considers kindred spirits and holds years-long grudges against people who cross her. Anne's terrible temper flares at minimal provocations and she screams and stamps her foot when anger overtakes her. Anne lusts for riches and elegance. She despises her red hair and longs for smooth ivory skin and golden hair. She imagines that which displeases her as different than what it is, dreaming up a more perfect world.

Self-Protective Artists are judgmental. They are intolerant of other people who have values different from their own. If you say to your vegetarian Artist friend, "Will it offend you if I eat this hot dog in front of you?" don't be surprised at a reply along the lines of, "No, as long as you won't be offended by my description of how an innocent, feeling creature was cruelly slaughtered so you could have that artery-clogging, chemical-laden treat." Self-Protective Artists may go to great lengths to tell friends and family the virtues of living an environmentally friendly lifestyle and get upset when everyone doesn't adopt these values (so they are upset much of the time). Self-Protective Artists condemn people who don't aspire to their lofty and often unattainable standards. They can't fathom why everyone wouldn't give up their car and ride a bike to work in subzero temperatures. Self-Protective Artists set themselves up for ridicule by taking fashion stands, for example, going to a black-tie event wearing

Birkenstocks and a beige cotton suit, sporting horrific body odor because they refuse to wear deodorants that contain aluminum, or electing not to cover a Che Guevara tattoo during a job interview.

Self-Actualizing Artists live their lives authentically. Having personal and professional freedom is very important to them, and SA Artists organize their lives so that they can live spontaneously, following their feelings and their need to create. It is not easy for them to do this, as they are generally unassertive and self-effacing. They make sure that they find work in an environment that is both holistic and humanistic, preferably one that is values driven. Artists are not the best match for the fast-paced, competitive corporate world, but that doesn't mean they can't work there. What is important is that they keep their brains focused on what they are doing and not on their personal feelings about the work situation or what might be going on politically or interpersonally with coworkers.

Having the Perfect Relationship

I'd like to teach the world to sing in perfect harmony
I'd like to hold it in my arms and keep it company.
> —"I'd Like to Teach the World to Sing," *Roger Cook,*
> *Roger Greenaway, Billy Davis and William Backer*

Being in a relationship with an Artist can be a wonderful experience. Artists work very hard to make sure that the needs of their partner, family, and friends are met and that others feel well loved and cared for. To them, a relationship is when two people come together and become one blissful unit (perhaps while enjoying a nutritious, organically produced, chemical-free, human rights–conscious beverage— Artists tend to spearhead the green movement). They have a small circle of friends because of the intensity with which they bond with others. When they are with their partners, it's easy for them to disappear into the relationship and become inaccessible to other people in their lives. They abhor disharmony and conflict, which threaten the perfection of the relationship. They easily take responsibility for conflicts that arise and work hard to eliminate them.

Self-Protective Artists create intense emotional experiences. They don't really know how to identify problems objectively; instead, they complain about how difficult their lives are. The real issue becomes secondary to their feelings. They can't stop stewing over how badly they are being treated and how awful the other person is for not knowing what they need. They first suffer in silence, feeling unloved, wronged, and victimized. When they can't keep their feelings in any longer, they dump them out in a dramatic, emotional climax, ranting and sobbing uncontrollably while berating their partner for insensitivity. This type of fighting often takes the place of real emotional intimacy in Artists' relationships. Partners will try hard to help them but give up when they realize that the Artist is never satisfied.

Self-Actualizing Artists express what they need and want, rather than expecting others to "just know." They don't just complain. They identify their need and figure out how to meet it. They talk about their feelings as they occur. They ask others for help without enacting an emotional soap opera. They feel grateful and express appreciation for what they do have, rather than just complaining about what they lack. Artists stop being the creators of their own personal dramas and no longer accuse others of victimizing them. They discard the belief that asking for what they need means there is something wrong with them; instead, they think of it as sensible self-care.

Having Original and Authentic Lifestyles

"I gotta be me" is one of the central values of Artists. Their desire for autonomy is driven by their need to create their own experiences rather than be told what they should be doing. They have little desire to impress or have authority over people, and they expect others to take a hands-off approach in relationships with them. Those who understand and value Artists for themselves will have loyal and trusted friends for life. Other Styles often have difficulty with the Artist's low need to influence or control others. Because freedom is so important to them, Artists would never dream of impinging on the freedom of others, even when it may be in the best interest of the other person to have some boundaries.

Princess Diana was picture perfect and envied by many. Her dress, her looks, and her deeds seemed to embody her need to have beauty around her. No one would have expected by seeing her public persona that this woman suffered as she did. Like many Artists, Diana had the ability to show a calm exterior belying the emotional turmoil and angst that lay within. The stories of Diana's emotionally disturbing inner life, her allegedly suicidal unhappiness, her struggles with depression and self-injury—all are consistent with the Artist Style, which often feels trapped by an inauthentic life.

Self-Protective Artists are absorbed with their own imperfections. They're acutely self-conscious and on a perpetual quest to discover what's wrong with them. Exploring their faults in minute detail seems more compelling to them than building self-awareness and confidence. They're more likely to get down on themselves for not being confident than to use affirmations to build confidence. They're prone to rehearsing conversations in their minds that they will never have with people. By doing this, they deplete their energy and their self-esteem. Self-Protective Artists flock to the offices of therapists and psychoanalysts, where they spend hours exploring their feelings. More than any other Style, SP Artists are in search of their fatal flaw and believe that once they find and heal it, they will attain perfection.

Annie Hall: Oh, you see an analyst?
Alvy Singer: Yeah, just for fifteen years.
Annie Hall: Fifteen years?

Alvy Singer: Yeah, I'm gonna give him one more year, and then I'm goin' to Lourdes (for a healing).

—*Characters' dialogue from the film* Annie Hall

Self-Actualizing Artists accept themselves for who they are. They get past thinking that how they feel is the most interesting thing about them. Instead, they move to action. Like everyone else, Artists need to understand that they can choose to alter their experience through observing and questioning what is actually going on instead of being swept away by what they "feel" is happening. Most Artists have difficulty with the idea that "feelings aren't facts." Self-Actualizing Artists have developed an observing self that provides them with a greater awareness of their excessive focus on their feelings. They learn to discern between *who they are* and *what they feel*, to respond to situations rather than react to their feelings, and to depersonalize others' behavior.

I'm not going to change the way I look or the way I feel to conform to anything. I've always been a freak. So I've been a freak all my life and I have to live with that, you know. I'm one of those people.

—*John Lennon*

Meaningful Self-Expression

Artists seek to express themselves authentically in all they do. They paint pictures with words, complete with their feelings about their experiences. This is a type of self-focused expression, in which Artists seek to have listeners feel what they feel by creating stories that evoke emotion in others. If nothing is going on, they will create an emotional experience by speculating on what might be going on. Artists will discuss their feelings openly and freely, making them the center of the conversation.

Self-Protective Artists can't assert themselves. The gentle, sensitive nature of Artists makes it difficult for them to express themselves, their ideas, or their desires to others. It's as though their nervous systems already felt everything so acutely that they must protect themselves from being overwhelmed by the demands and emotions of others. Self-Protective Artists measure what they will say and do on the basis of people's possible reactions, in the hopes of avoiding criticism or other injury. This means that if someone is very definite about what they want or need, SP Artists will fear the consequences of asserting their own conflicting need. Instead, they will suffer in silence, but the soap opera has already begun.

Mary (Performer) invited her friend Gail (Artist) over for dinner. Mary made a gourmet meal, thinking that Gail would enjoy it and appreciate the effort. Much to Gail's horror, Mary prepared a French meal full of butter and cream—the very things Gail had just given up to address her food allergies. Rather than offend Mary, she ate the meal, made a big fuss about it, and silently vowed never to go to Mary's house for dinner again. She left resenting Mary for not knowing about her food allergies and putting her in this position. But Gail also was angry with herself for not telling Mary earlier about her dietary constraints. She ended up feeling depressed about the whole event.

Unfortunately, SP Artists tend to feel that either they are victimizing themselves or someone else is doing it for them. Their tendency to create drama in response to an unmet need is so automatic that they don't see it until someone points it out to them. They're constantly evaluating, rehearsing, ruminating, and catastrophizing about themselves. They judge what they have done, what they haven't done, what they're not getting around to doing, and everything in between. Much of the time, they're more concerned with what they're feeling than with what they're doing.

Even now when I see my name in the paper, I feel that the world is intruding unduly on my privacy. I ought to be anonymous.

—A. A. Milne

Self-Actualizing Artists communicate authentically. They learn to assert themselves, even when it is difficult to do so. They also recognize when they are inflating events and creating drama in their minds. They use their creativity constructively in their lives rather than destructively to undermine themselves. When emotions become very strong about something, they ask themselves whether the story they told themselves about what was going on might have upset them more than the event itself. Self-Actualizing Artists know when they are holding everything inside and what it costs them to do this. The goal is to live in creative expression—in words, in deeds, and in relationships.

Activators of the Self-Protective System

With their need to be creative and authentic, Artists are activated by people and situations that cause them to have to conform or do things in a way that isn't congruent with their values. They fear being rejected, invaded, or taken over by others because they are somehow inferior or flawed. They feel rejected for who they are and feel they have no choice other than to let themselves be overpowered or invaded by the demands of others for conformity. Feeling this way frustrates their need to be creative and therefore is what they fear most. Artists will do whatever they can to protect themselves from these feelings.

Demands for Conformity

When others so much as imply that Artists need to conform to societal norms, they feel rejected and wounded, even when others are simply giving them advice. It also makes them anxious when they are subjected to sudden changes initiated by others, or when they feel controlled by unpredictable or arbitrary situations that limit their freedom of choice.

Spending Too Much Time Alone

The goal of Artists is to create feelings, so when they spend too much time alone, solitude gives them free reign to create stories, infer meanings, and draw conclusions that have little connection to reality and even less connection to happiness. No one can work themselves into a depressed, anxious, self-indulgent, or self-pitying state faster than an Artist.

Spending Too Much Time with Others

When Artists are with people too much, it's like overeating. They can't digest their experience and start to feel uncomfortable. Rather than understanding that they need some time away, they tell themselves they are being taken over. They become overly sensitive and offended by what others are saying. They are convinced that others are intruding on their space without regard for their personal boundaries.

Conflict

Interpersonal conflict and strong emotional expression adversely affect the sensitive nervous systems of Artists. They find it very hard to function when they are in the presence of conflict or disharmony; they feel the situation as though it was inside of them, and it scares them. They lose their ability to express themselves or to resolve the conflict. If someone criticizes them, they withdraw inside to protect themselves from what they experience as hostility. Should they have to work in an environment that is unfriendly or conflict ridden, it can affect their confidence and cause them to become depressed, immobilized, or even physically ill.

Planning, Scheduling, and Details

When they have to meet goals and objectives or deal with financial details, Artists become anxious, feeling incapable of doing it on their own. They feel inadequate to others who don't have difficulty with these things and spend time thinking about what's wrong with them. They focus on how "bad" they are, creating feelings instead of financial plans, and unbalanced self-images instead of balanced checkbooks.

Taking Action

Although it looks like making a decision is difficult for Artists, what actually activates their SP System is having to do something about their decision. They become anxious when they have to act on what they have decided. Because they believe they are somehow inferior to others, whatever they decide can't possibly be right. They spend days, even weeks, second-guessing themselves and having endless conversations with others about how awful they are at making decisions.

Blind Spots
Making Up Stories

Artists make up stories explaining why they feel the way they do. The story almost always includes a rejection or abandonment theme, which is plausible to the Artist but not necessarily to others. The story may be about an affair the Artist believes his or her partner is having, complete with the identity of the person, how long it has been going on, and how the rendezvous occur. By the time the Artist talks to his partner, he or she can be in a rage, having already "lived" the whole sordid business in his or her head.

Intimidating Others

Most other Styles will find the Artist's perpetual emotional roller-coaster ride too dizzying for their tastes. People often remark that they walk on eggshells around the Artist, whose moods are unpredictable. Artists often have little awareness of the impression they create.

I'm selfish, impatient, and a little insecure. I make mistakes, I am out of control, and at times hard to handle. But if you can't handle me at my worst, then you sure as hell don't deserve me at my best.

—*Marilyn Monroe*

Taking Things Personally

Because Artists take things personally, they make up imagined slights and intrigue, and misread the intentions of others. They accuse others of all kinds of horrible things, as though friends and family members were plotting to destroy or discredit them. They will either withdraw from people or become upset and accusatory.

Being Addicted to Perfection

Artists often accept nothing short of perfection in themselves and others. They can create conflict in their relationships by pointing out even the most subtle flaws and imperfections in others. Their candid honesty may translate into unintended hurtfulness. They can focus so much on what is missing and how others are failing them that they don't see what others are doing to help and support them.

> *Artist husband: Did you pick up my new glasses from the optometrist?*

> *Stabilizer wife: No, I didn't have time. I was getting caught up on the laundry so you'd have enough clean clothes for your trip. And it took longer at the vet than I thought.*

> *Artist husband: Geez, I ask you to do one thing and you don't have time! I thought you loved me. You never think about how I am going to feel when you decide not to do something for me. Now I've got to drop everything and go over there, and it's rush hour. By the time I get back, it'll be late and I've still got to pack and take care of some emails. (He storms away to his office.)*

Score—victimized husband, 0; unappreciated wife, 0.

Fearing and Rebelling against Authority

Artists live according to their own values, even if it means breaking the rules of society. If they think taxes are excessive, they will refuse to pay them. If they believe their manager's policy on personal calls at work is unfair, they will simply not comply. Their fear of being controlled and overpowered by those in authority causes them to blame someone higher up when they can't follow through on their commitments.

Upshifting to Their Self-Actualizing System

For Artists to upshift to their SA System, they need to become more self-aware and redirect their striving energy by doing the following.

Planning and Setting Goals

Artists need to recognize when paying attention to their emotions is interfering with setting and achieving their goals. They also need to break the habit of waiting until they are in the right mood to do something. By facing unpleasant tasks, they become more disciplined and less likely to be pulled off course. They easily recognize when their feelings are calling for attention and can delay responding to them.

Practicing Self-Care

Taking care of their physical bodies by cultivating a disciplined approach to exercise helps Artists build self-esteem and confidence. Body-based activities such as yoga, Pilates, tai chi, walking, or jogging can be very helpful for staying in touch with reality. Practicing mindfulness can also help Artists develop the ability to observe emotions rather than focusing on and giving in to them.

Developing Objective Reasoning

Artists do well when they learn to seek objective and impartial feedback to help them accurately assess the difference between feelings and facts. They need to separate emotional reactions (e.g., anger at a partner's failure to do something for them) and the feeling judgments (e.g., "She doesn't care about me") that often go with them.

Seeking Help

Seeking counseling or therapy—for example, cognitive behavioral therapy—can help Artists see patterns of thinking that lead them to feel anxious or depressed and weaken their self-esteem. They need to talk to a trusted friend or colleague to get a more realistic view of themselves.

Developing an Observing Self

By observing their thoughts and feelings, Artists come to see how dysfunctional it is to complain about what they don't have as a way of trying to get someone to take care of them, to feel their pain, or to deeply empathize with their struggle. When they stop relying on the sympathy of others as a vehicle for getting help, and stop wearing people down with their complaining and helplessness, they will create relationships based on real give-and-take, and not just raw emotion.

Just Doing It

Artists need to catch themselves when they are getting stuck expending energy on ruminating or second-guessing themselves. They stop thinking about what they need to get done and become obsessed with figuring out why they can't just do it. Having supportive friends that tell them that they are spending too much time complaining about themselves often allows them to shift to action and refocus their energy.

Achieving Their Full Potential

It is the "art of living" that is the Artist's true calling. Artists' art capitalizes on the freedom of expression that can create harmony out of disharmony, order out of chaos, joy from tears, and beauty from seemingly random materials. They create their lives as much as they live them. The Artist is a Striving Style with the potential for authentic and creative expression and nurturing of everything and everyone the Artist cares about. These individuals dominate the fields of creative arts, personal service, teaching, and counseling. They hold politicians accountable by insisting on a more holistic approach to government, and this insistence comes from the rock-solid value they place on human life and beauty. When they can hold their values and integrate them with mainstream society, their lives become true works of art.

Chapter Twelve
THE ADVENTURER— STRIVING TO BE SPONTANEOUS

Lookin' for adventure
And whatever comes our way.

— *"Born to Be Wild" Mars Bonfire*

We know when we are in the presence of an Adventurer because the energy in the room increases and the fun begins. Adventurers' enthusiasm and excitement are contagious, and they easily entertain others with story after amusing story. Adventurers are action oriented and make things happen for themselves and others around them. They have an attractive, friendly style and a talent for making even the most mundane events seem exciting. They live for the enjoyment of the moment and work hard to ensure that the moment is never boring.

Adventurers are driven by a need to be spontaneous. With apparent fearlessness, they tread where others dare not go. They may bounce from bungee jumping to foreign travel to tribal drumming classes, just to stay active. Brimming with enthusiasm and excitement, they always have a quality of restlessness about them. They like to "fly by the seat of their pants," often conjuring excitement in an ordinary day, if only to keep things stimulating. They seem to know that despite any trouble they get themselves into, they can easily charm or scheme their way out of it. These abilities make them good at both entrepreneurial enterprises and negotiations.

Often ambitious and competitive, Adventurers are always up for a game of something, or they will turn whatever they are doing into a competition. They enjoying winning and one-upping their friends and colleagues just for the pleasure of beating them. They may argue purely for the fun and excitement of it and turn the simplest conversations into sparring matches. They enjoy the sense of camaraderie that sports and working on a team create as it meets their social needs as well. Their popularity and ambition often help them find their way into roles in management positions that don't always meet their need to be spontaneous. They will take the challenge of throwing their hat in the ring and when they win, they really don't want the prize.

Larry was not prepared for the amount of bureaucracy and planning that the job of captain of his fire station required. When he had first been approached to apply for the position, he was told that he would have the opportunity to make changes for the good of the fire station and to influence his superiors on behalf of his team. It wasn't too long before he realized that his decision to take the job was impulsive, that he hadn't really listened when he was told about the administrative, repetitive, and time-sensitive aspects. In addition, he was now management and had to deal with a very adversarial union that put him at odds with the men and women he considered both his friends and colleagues.

After two months in the role, Larry found himself becoming more and more resentful about being told how to work, what to do, and when to do it. He found the chain of command oppressive and would frequently leave his office to chat or play cards with his former peers. His superiors were shocked when Larry made them look bad by failing to follow through on several commitments and not letting them know that he wasn't going to do so. Instead of working, he spent time planning to leave his job and undertake an expedition to climb Mt. Kilimanjaro. Everyone was angry and frustrated but couldn't put their finger on what the problem was.

Larry's direct superior brought me in for a joint coaching session to try to help Larry before he self-destructed. We spoke at length about the need satisfiers and dissatisfiers of the Adventurer, and Larry quickly realized what the issue was. Larry admitted that the job was not giving him any satisfaction and that he saw no other way of resolving this issue but getting out. We began exploring options for positions that would allow Larry to avoid being demoted and also leverage his leadership and crisis management skills. As a result, Larry continued in the captain's role for another six weeks, until the job as the head of a crisis unit became available. He still plans to do the climb but is no longer obsessed with using it as an escape hatch from his life.

Spontaneous and flexible, Adventurers are great when it comes to dealing with whatever the world might throw their way. No matter what the situation or how bad it is, they always seem to land on their feet, even when the odds are against them. They enjoy life and are rarely caught up in others' drama, but neither are they critical of drama when it occurs. These confident individuals often like to think of themselves as "players." Whether male or female, and regardless of the forum (social, political, business, show business), Adventurers like to be in the heart of the game and where the action is. Like Jerry Maguire before his crisis of conscience in the movie of the same name, they seek the thrill of the win, regardless of the cost to others.

What Makes Adventurers Tick?

Adventurers don't just tiptoe to the edge of life; they dive in headfirst. They thrive on experiencing sensations and are energized by doing things that stimulate them. They live mainly from their left emotional brain—the part responsible for producing and reproducing familiar sensations—and reexperiencing these sensations helps them maintain emotional security. In other words, the Adventurer's goal is to feel on a physical level what he or she has felt before, whether pleasant or unpleasant, right or wrong, good or bad, useful or not useful. Adventurers don't think about the emotions that may be evoked by the chosen activity. They look at what they are doing in relation to what they have done before, and they re-create experiences, often attempting to increase or prolong the intensity.

Adventurers tend to do things in a structured, mechanical, detailed, and sequential way, although this might not be apparent to others. Because they're always looking for experiences that excite and stimulate their senses, they can appear to be simply reacting. However, their emotional security comes from the ability and freedom to take action in response to their environment. They prefer to engage in activities where they have some experience because the sensations will be predictable. They make tremendous athletes, gymnasts, and dancers because they don't mind practicing the same thing again and again for hours—after all, the goal is to keep those familiar sensations coming. Consider ballet dancers, who in the course of their careers will spend thousands of hours performing the same set of warm-up exercises at the barre.

An art exhibit that featured Degas's paintings of ballet dancers included an actual ballet barre as part of the installation. One dancer who visited the exhibit couldn't help but hike a leg up and give it a stretch on the barre. Her explanation: "You can't just walk past it. I see a ballet barre and I just have to do something. [It's] kind of an addiction."

The left brain produces sensations, not feelings. As a result, Adventurers don't see the point of spending time feeling emotions and especially not talking about them. Like Houdini, they are escape artists when it comes to dealing with interpersonal conflict, and they can also be very uncomfortable when they are asked to express their emotions. If someone tries to get them to talk about their feelings or expresses upset with them, they want out. They don't know what to do and feel backed into a corner. Adventurers will cut and run when they feel they are out of options and don't know what the other person wants them to do. When someone gets upset with them, Adventurers may not even stay around long enough to find out why. They are just as likely as not to drop that person from their large roster of friends and move on.

The Adventurer is a thrill seeker who is always trying to turn up the "volume" on the intensity of what he or she is experiencing. Having to follow routines with no relief from the monotony of the activity is a huge challenge for Adventurers. When others are quiet, Adventurers want to shout at the top of their lungs, just to see what will happen. They have great difficulty when others try to curb their enthusiasm or expect them to conform to social norms. They often find that living with others becomes too complex with unwanted obligations and personal entanglements. When this happens, Adventurers can become rebellious, both actively and passively resisting all attempts to restrict their actions.

The widder's good to me, and friendly; but I can't stand them ways. She makes me get up just at the same time every morning; she makes me wash, they comb me all to thunder; she won't let me sleep in the woodshed; I got to wear them blamed clothes that just smothers me, Tom; they don't seem to let any air git through 'em, somehow; and they're so rotten nice that I can't set down, nor lay down, nor roll around anywher's; I hain't slid on a cellar-door for—well, it 'pears to be years; I got to go to church and sweat and sweat—I hate them ornery sermons! I can't ketch a fly in there, I can't chaw. I got to wear shoes all Sunday. The widder eats by a bell; she goes to bed by a bell; she gits up by a bell—everything's so awful reg'lar a body can't stand it.

—*Huckleberry Finn, from* The Adventures of Tom Sawyer

The Relationship Style of the Adventurer

Fun and excitement are always prominent features in relationships with Adventurers, and they make great friends and playmates. If you are looking for an exciting time on the town, your Adventurer friend is the person to call. With their joie de vivre, they are game to do or try anything that you suggest, as long as the energy keeps moving.

Adventurers are positive, optimistic people with an undefeatable can-do attitude. They make supportive and encouraging friends and mates who believe that you can do anything you want to do. They accentuate the positive in people and situations, and for them the glass is always half full. They're the friend you call when you've just broken up with someone and want to lighten up or be distracted. They'll keep you entertained with stories and jokes until your sides are splitting. Adventurers give freely of themselves to their friends, adding fun, laughter, and unpredictability to the lives of everyone around them. Laughter follows Adventurers, as they have an endless supply of amusing anecdotes.

Although they are acquainted with many people and are generally very popular, Adventurers do not always have deep, committed relationships, as they like to keep their options open. They will do anything for their friends, often putting their families' needs second. They will also form conditional relationships based on what they are doing and what they can get out of it. Like politicians, they are always negotiating with others for the best possible deal for themselves. When used effectively, their talent for negotiating can be useful for creating win-win situations for everyone. However, they are just as likely to use this talent to get themselves out of sticky situations. They will charm their way out of trouble by making up stories or being so outrageous that you succumb to their charm. Consider Puss in Boots as he tries to worm his way out of a difficult situation in the movie *Shrek*:

> *Please, no,* por favor, por favor, *please no, I implore you. I was doing it for my family! My mother she's sick and my father, he lives off the garbage. The king offered me much money and I have a little brother…*

In Adventurers' relationships, there is never a dull moment. Adventurers do many things to generate positive experiences. Even when they are fighting with their partners, they optimistically believe that "this too will pass," and they can be annoyingly quiet when they have done something wrong. They can hardly wait for their partner to get over it, as they don't like to delve too deeply into their motivations for their behavior. To end the fight, they may use diversionary tactics such as changing the subject, remembering something they have to do right away, pretending to agree, or just leaving the situation. They are also thoughtful and generous, showing their affection with frequent telephone calls and thoughtful cards and gifts to show they are thinking of others. In return, they expect little and do not keep score of the countless kindnesses they do. Their mischievous side leads them to play practical jokes or pranks on others, which don't always amuse those on the receiving end.

For his first wedding anniversary, Todd the Adventurer wanted to do something his wife Becky would never forget. He loved to surprise her and would go out of his way to pull stunts that made her laugh. This time, he'd come up with a real doozy. Todd had been divorced from his first wife Cherie for about four years and they had maintained a good friendship, so he asked Cherie to help him pull a prank on Becky. Cherie, an Adventurer herself, agreed. She wrote a letter to Todd and sent it via certified mail. In the letter, she claimed that because of an administrative error in the paperwork for their divorce, it was never finalized. Cherie added a little extra shock value to the letter by suggesting that perhaps this error was destiny's way of giving the couple one more chance. Unfortunately, Todd failed to recognize that Becky would be upset by the letter. Even after he revealed it as only a prank, she was so disgusted with his idea of an "anniversary surprise" that she stormed out of the house and didn't return until well after midnight. Todd mistakenly had assumed that Becky would appreciate the trouble he had taken to arrange this elaborate prank and that she'd be happy and relieved when it was exposed as a joke.

Adventurers will stay in a relationship as long as it excites and otherwise stimulates them. As long as their partner is not trying to "tame" them and continues to enjoy their childlike exuberance, they are in. However, they have difficulty staying faithful to their mate if their relationship has become mundane or routine. Adventurers have difficulty tolerating the quiet and slow aspects of family life and will look for distractions to escape the tedium. Their quick wit and direct style are attractive to potential mates, friends, and employers in the beginning but can also cause problems when Adventurers can't seem to get serious. Their attachment to the other person is based on the intensity of the sensations produced by their partner. Whether these sensations come from intense lovemaking or fighting really doesn't matter. The Adventurer wants to *experience* the other person, not just be with them.

How Adventurers Satisfy Their Need to Be Spontaneous
Having Fun

Adventurers love to laugh, and their high spirits turn the most ordinary situations into happenings. There is a theatrical quality about Adventurers that most people find attractive. Adventurers love to get people going and will act outrageously, if they must, to make things happen. They want to experience excitement, to *feel* as much as possible, so they create a lively atmosphere wherever they go. They like to tease others and be playful, and they have a low tolerance for people who seem overly serious and don't have time for a laugh. If you coax Adventurers into the public library, it won't be long before they find some mischief to pursue, like reading aloud from *The Joy of Sex*, adding personal commentary and cajoling a reprimand from the librarian. They seem extraordinarily comfortable in their own skin and often have an endless supply of stories and jokes. A prime example of the Adventurer is TV's *NCIS* character Anthony (Tony) DiNozzo, a streetwise, promiscuous former homicide detective.

In the series, Tony seems incapable of maintaining a serious relationship with just one woman, preferring to flirt with almost every woman he comes in contact with. Most of the other characters see him as chauvinistic and either are offended by his inappropriate comments or dismiss him and don't take him seriously. With a strong belief in his charm and good looks, and that it is easier to ask forgiveness than permission, Tony goes about invading his coworkers' personal effects, rifling through desks and bags, taking their food when he is hungry, and listening in on private phone calls. Displaying an enduring sense of juvenile humor, he finds amusement in the direst situations or at the expense of others. He is not above name-calling, teasing, and childish pranks, which are mostly directed at his coworkers.

Self-Protective Adventurers want to live like Peter Pan. They are like kids who never want to grow up. Like Peter Pan, they act as if they are entitled to do what they want, and they allow others to pick up the slack for them. In an attempt to keep doing what gives them pleasure, they act without consideration of the repercussions on their personal or professional lives. Adventurers either make and break commitments easily or simply refuse to commit to anything. When pressed, they can pay lip service to an agreement but will do what they want despite the promise they have made. They charm, bluff, and otherwise persuade others to let them off the hook, putting their energy into getting out of things. They tend to practice avoidance or escape when these conditions arise, rather than deal with them. This often leads to bigger problems. A conversation between Wendy and Peter Pan demonstrates the Adventurer's distaste for growing up.

Peter: Love?
Wendy: Love.
Peter: I have never heard of it.
Wendy: I think you have, Peter. And I daresay you've felt it yourself. For something…or…someone?
Peter: Never. Even the sound of it offends me.
(Wendy tries to touch his face, and he jumps away.)

Peter: Why do you have to spoil everything? We have fun, don't we? I taught you to fly and to fight. What more could there be?

Wendy: There is so much more.

Peter: What? What else is there?

Wendy: I don't know. I guess it becomes clearer when you grow up.

Peter: Well, I will not grow up. You cannot make me!

Self-Actualizing Adventurers take responsibility. Self-Actualizing Adventurers take time to consider the impact of their actions and decisions on people's feelings. They learn to see the bigger picture and to understand the relationship between choices in the moment (e.g., the impulse to fly away at the thought of growing up) and their impact on the future (never experiencing a deep connection with someone). As they self-actualize, Adventurers recognize that there is more to life than the pursuit of pleasure. Their growth comes from being able to stay in the present moment and persist through difficult times without escaping into activities that satisfy their need for instant gratification.

Thinking on Their Feet

Adventurers are at their best when solving problems and thinking on their feet. They don't stop to reason or think through an issue beforehand; instead they believe a solution is inherent in every problem, and that by taking the first step they will soon find the facts to help them come up with the right solution, even when they are in new situations and don't know what they are doing. Should your car break down, Adventurers will be under the hood without any concern that they don't know anything about engines. They are confident that they can figure it out. With common sense as their compass, they quickly analyze what is needed on the basis of what is immediately observable in their environment, and without any fanfare, they get to it. Their quickness to take action means they may not take the time to investigate the root causes of situations. They stay optimistic by moving on, leaving behind problems that prove too difficult to solve.

Self-Protective Adventurers create crisis. Self-Protective Adventurers don't like it when nothing is going on and will look for mischief to make or something engaging to get into. If they commit to doing something, they might break that promise because someone had an urgent crisis that they needed their help with. Like the time you asked your Adventurer husband to pick up your dress from the cleaners the afternoon of your daughter's dress rehearsal. He didn't get back until a half hour before you had to leave because he stopped to rescue a dog that had been struck by a car. Adventurers don't think to call and let you know what's going on, because whatever they are doing consumes them. So by attending to a physical crisis, they create an emotional one. They're so easily distracted and tempted by whatever may be going on around them that they let their work, commitments, and responsibilities suffer.

Frank went out to the garage to clean it, after two months of nagging from his wife. Melissa was gratified when, two hours later, Frank was still outside. She assumed he was hard at work and had really immersed himself in the cleaning. She decided she would bring him some refreshments. When she got to the garage, Frank was nowhere to be found and the garage was still a mess. When he came into the house an hour later, Frank told an enraged Melissa that shortly after he went to the garage, his friend Tom had come by and asked for some help cutting wood. Frank, preferring company to the solitary task of cleaning the garage, immediately jumped into Tom's car and left—without considering what Melissa's reaction might be.

Self-Actualizing Adventurers learn to tolerate and follow through on commitments. When they develop this capacity, SA Adventurers are able to get an amazing amount of things accomplished. They are able to focus their substantial energy toward making things happen. They no longer need a crisis to activate them. Rather than reacting impulsively in the moment, they learn to respond to the needs of the moment. They learn to manage the frustration they feel when they feel locked in to doing something and another thing they would rather do comes along. They take responsibility for how much they can hurt others by failing to follow through when others are counting on them.

Action, Action, Action

Adventurers meet their need to be spontaneous through perpetual activity. They are at their best when there is intensity in their lives, and they are easily bored by routine. Adventurers pride themselves on their boldness, bravery, endurance, adaptation, and timing. They make things happen for themselves and others around them. They seem as though they are brimming with enthusiasm and excitement and always have a quality of restlessness about them. They like to "fly by the seat of their pants," often flitting from activity to activity just to keep things stimulating. They seem to know that despite any trouble they get themselves into, they can easily charm or connive their way out of it. Action energizes Adventurers, and stillness does not come easy to them at the best of times. They will often refuse to rest until they literally crash.

Self-Protective Adventurers catastrophize. They keep themselves in perpetual motion, as though they were fleeing from the boredom they fear. When anything gets in their way or if they aren't able to move to action, their usual upbeat personality becomes uncharacteristically moody, irritable, and pessimistic. It's as though they plummet into their emotions, where they find themselves overwhelmed by their feeling experiences. They are frightened by their feelings because they are unable to make heads or tails out of them. Unknowingly, they make things worse by being afraid, catastrophizing and ruminating, creating worst-case scenarios about what is happening to them. Normally, Adventurers do not reflect; they just act with confidence in their abilities. When forced to ease off the gas pedal and slow down, they transform from outgoing, enthusiastic go-getters to fatalistic, hopeless catastrophizers.

Self-Actualizing Adventurers get to know their feelings and become connected to their physical needs. Instead of sitting around contemplating what disasters are about to befall them, they take the time to get to know their feelings and to tolerate them. They listen to the messages that their emotions are sending in any given situation. They accept emotions as being normal and they don't catastrophize. They learn to work with uncomfortable feelings and access their genuine emotions, instead of just generating restlessness and anxiety. By acknowledging their true feelings, they can stop going from activity to activity to avoid the emptiness they tend to feel inside. They get the rest their bodies need and take time to just "be" in their lives.

Risk Taking

Hook: And now, Peter Pan, you shall die.
Peter: To die would be an awfully big adventure.

—Peter Pan, *J. M. Barrie*

Adventurers meet their need to be spontaneous by taking risks. They enjoy taking physical risks just to see whether they can do something. Many of them are athletes, like Sam Wakeling, who holds the Guinness world record for greatest distance traveled by unicycle in a twenty-four-hour period (more than 281 miles). Some practice a different form of "athleticism," like Ashrita Furman, who set a record by crushing eighty eggs with his head in one minute. Whatever the feat of daring, it satisfies Adventurers' need to experience sensation. They pride themselves on their boldness, physical endurance, and sense of timing. It's as though their motors are always revved up, waiting for action. Adventurers don't fear what they may lose by taking risks. If there are not enough naturally occurring risks in their lives, they may stir up situations or create risks to achieve the intensity of experience they thrive on. They have a tendency to follow their impulses wherever these might lead, which can propel them to the next big adventure or directly into trouble.

Self-Protective Adventurers put themselves in harm's way. Their escalating need to experience greater levels of sensation can lead SP Adventurers to do things that are dangerous and illegal. These Adventurers don't know when to stop and are prone to excesses in eating, partying, and overstimulating their nervous system. They may pursue the highs of gambling, drinking, and drugs; or they may cut corners at work, just to see if they can get away with it. They are reckless with their bodies, their money, and their relationships. They have no way of discerning what they really need and, as a result, are unable to say no to impulses that tantalize them. If their tendency toward and capacity for risk taking go unchecked, Adventurers are prone to follow their impulses down destructive paths, like Randle McMurphy does in the film *One Flew over the Cuckoo's Nest*.

Randle McMurphy (Jack Nicholson) was a rebellious young man who grew up never staying in one place for long. He wound up in prison having been charged with battery and gambling. McMurphy orchestrated a transfer from the prison work farm to the mental hospital, thinking he would be able to serve out his sentence in comfort. McMurphy felt no need to conform or to follow the rules of the hospital and openly rebelled against things that other patients feared. In the end, McMurphy violently fights Nurse Ratched's rule, which costs him his freedom, his health, and ultimately his life.

Self-Actualizing Adventurers take calculated risks. They consider the consequences of their actions before doing something. They often have to experience the loss of something or someone they valued before they come to terms with how destructive their behavior can be. Recklessness is replaced with reasoned caution and they develop cause-and-effect thinking—for example, "If I have sex with that hot guy who is checking me out, it will wreck my marriage," rather than "Oh my God, I hope my husband doesn't find out!" They have come to terms with the fact that they are human and that their unrestrained behavior can hurt themselves and others, despite this realization being a great source of frustration to their need to be spontaneous.

Activators of the Self-Protective System

With their need to be spontaneous and free to seek excitement and engaging experiences, Adventurers are activated by people and situations that cause them to be afraid of their freedom being taken away from them. They feel confined or backed into a corner when others insist they do things their way or hold them to time lines or commitments. Feeling this way frustrates their need to be spontaneous and therefore is what they fear most. They will do whatever they can to protect themselves from these feelings.

Spending Too Much Time in Activities

Although they love being around people, too much physical or social activity makes Adventurers become even more impulsive than usual. They don't have a natural filter for what they say and do at the best of times, and when they are stressed, they can go beyond the bounds of good taste and behaving outrageously, which can result in negative consequences. They become increasingly impulsive and run the risk of acting or appearing irresponsible.

Spending Too Much Time Alone

To Adventurers, their inner world is like a cage—once inside, they can't get out. When they spend too much time alone, they can get trapped catastrophizing about the future. They move from being bored and restless to becoming prisoners of their depressive and hopeless imaginings. Like flowers in the desert, Adventurers need the life-giving water of human company to keep them from wilting.

Being Forced to Make Commitments

To Adventurers, commitment equals captivity, and it frightens them. Having to show up at a scheduled activity can activate their SP System because it takes away the freedom to act spontaneously if something better comes along. Even something as simple as making a commitment to go to the movies can provoke the impulse to flee. Being expected to show up at social and family events that they don't consider fun will also activate the SP system.

Spreading Themselves Too Thin

Like Peter Pan, if they are having a great adventure, Adventurers just continue doing so and won't deny themselves or impose any restrictions on how much they take on. If someone asks them to do something that sounds like fun, they'll agree, even when they know they have something else planned. They reckon they will figure it out on the fly. Adventurers end up trying to do everything, and the situation can easily get out of hand and completely drain their energy.

Planning, Brainstorming, Theorizing

Nothing is quite as agitating to the Adventurer as when they have to talk about things that currently don't exist. Speculation, theorizing, or figuring out the meaning of something causes them to feel trapped. Their ability to act spontaneously has no place in the realm of the theoretical. One just can't do anything there; one can only think about things. If Adventurers can't figure something out fairly quickly, it's no fun to deal with at all.

Imposed Limitations

"Don't fence me in" is the motto of the Adventurers and nothing frustrates them more than having their freedom restricted. A perceived restriction might be anything from having to sit through long meetings at work or lectures at school to attending children's plays or sporting events—situations in which they can't take action, only watch. If you're going somewhere with an Adventurer, don't bother trying to generate a Google map and turn-by-turn directions to your destination—a set route would be too confining for the Adventurer.

I live for CAN-ing other people's can'ts.

—*Steven Tyler*

Blind Spots
Ignoring the Consequences

Adventurers have a blind spot around the ways that their dislike of planning affects their lives. This leaves them at the mercy of their need for instant gratification. They have difficulty managing their impulses, particularly where there is the promise of excitement. They prefer to live in the moment and for the moment without thinking about the consequences of their actions. They act first and reflect afterward, if at all.

Being a Barrier to Their Own Success

Adventurers are often ambitious and set their sights on being the best in their chosen career. They are often hampered by their fun-loving personalities. They run into problems when they let their social lives take priority over their career pursuits. Adventurers invented the candle that burns at both ends. Should they suffer a missed opportunity or other loss because of others' perceptions of them as irresponsible or unreliable, they tend to divert blame or pretend that what they lost really wasn't that important.

Conflict Avoidance

Adventurers sometimes focus more on the avoidance of difficult feelings than they do on the achievement of pleasure. They have a blind spot about how failing to deal with conflict, or to meet it head-on, causes them to create greater pain and upset in their relationships or at work than the original issues themselves did.

Taking Excessive Risks

Adventurers have a blind spot around how dangerous something actually is; they often seem as though they are fearless. Activities such as mountain climbing, heli-skiing, and white-water rafting are popular with Adventurers because they demand immediate responses to unpredictable, difficult, and often tense situations. But there is a fine line between fearless and reckless, which Adventurers don't really consider.

I thought I was bulletproof or Superman there for a while. I thought I'd never run out of nerve. Never.

—*Evel Knievel*

Absence of Boundaries

In their pursuit of greater levels of sensation, Adventurers can take excessive risks and act like the law doesn't apply to them. Gambling, stock and financial swindles, counterfeiting, confidence rackets, and other "sting" operations are all manifestations of Adventurer talents that have gone bad. Adventurers can get so caught up with their need to be spontaneous that they constantly flirt with imprisonment and punishment for their actions.

Here's to the fear of being trapped.

—*Thomas Crown, from the film* The Thomas Crown Affair

Upshifting to Their Self-Actualizing System

For Adventurers to upshift to their SA System, they must become more self-aware and redirect their striving energy by doing the following.

Facing Conflict Head-On

Adventurers stop reacting to perceived restrictions from others and learn to negotiate to get their needs met. They recognize when they have the impulse to get away and stop themselves from running away from feelings and conflict.

Sharing the Floor

Adventurers recognize when they are monopolizing the conversation to keep things stimulating. They stop talking and entertaining and start listening to others. The act of conversation can be a one-sided event for them, and Adventures have to learn to refocus their attention, making sure they aren't talking more than they listen. Reminding themselves that others also have needs and want to be heard is important to their relationships.

Checking In with Themselves

Adventurers need help in distinguishing those activities and friendships that take them away from their home base, so they can pare away the ones that are less important. They need to be able to see when they are pursuing immediate gratification at the expense of their closest relationships. Slowing down and considering the bigger picture allows them to respond skillfully instead of reacting impulsively to invitations and requests.

Cultivating Discernment

Adventurers need to learn to distinguish quality of experience from quantity of experience. A missed opportunity will often arise again, and responding to everything that presents itself is not always a good idea. Some possibilities that sound exciting are actually harmful in the end, so Adventurers must learn to realize that a quick rush toward pleasure can produce long-lasting pain.

Using a Time Management System

Adventurers need a way to remind themselves of their commitments. They need to remain aware of all they have to lose by being impulsive, to think about the potential consequences of every action and the impression they may be making on others. Learning organizational and time management techniques is often useful, because these skills do not come naturally to Adventurers.

Practicing Mindfulness

Although Adventurers live for the present moment, they need to develop conscious awareness of the choices they are making. The practices of mindfulness and self-reflection can help them develop the habit of observing their impulses rather than giving in to them. It helps them to develop an observing self that can monitor and manage impulses that are most likely to carry them into self-destructive behaviors.

Achieving Their Full Potential

It is through "being in the world" that Adventurers light up the lives of others and bring fun and enjoyment to all they do. Tolerant, unprejudiced, and open to new experience, they seek the freedom to approach each new day as an adventure. They inspire others to live their lives in the present moment with optimism and enthusiasm. The Adventurer is a Striving Style with potential for making the lives of everyone around them more exciting through their vibrant, entertaining, and action-oriented personality. Their ability to respond to problems and crisis, create a not-to-be-missed event out of an informal gathering, and negotiate and mediate among conflicting interests are only a few of the talents that emerge from Adventurers when they are consistently able to meet their need to be spontaneous.

Chapter Thirteen
THE STABILIZER—STRIVING TO BE SECURE

Well pick up your feet
We've got a deadline to meet.

— *"Working for the Man," Roy Orbison*

WE ALL KNOW SOMEONE who is a Stabilizer—a dependable, reliable friend who is always there when you need him or her and willing to lend a hand. As industrious and orderly as worker bees, Stabilizers toil to create and maintain a secure life for themselves and those they care about. Stabilizers are the pillars of society, demonstrating a strong sense of commitment, duty, and responsibility, and doing whatever it takes to make them and others secure. Their actions are always practical and sensible, guided by a set of rules that they apply relentlessly to keep everyone in line. Cautious and traditional, they show how much they care by protecting and serving others.

Their overarching need is to be secure, so anyone who appears keen to change them is seen as a threat to their security. They consider a threat even well-meaning suggestions like "Have you ever thought of wearing your hair short?" or "Could we spend one day of our vacation just winging it, without a plan?" Maintaining security is their mission, their reason to exist. You will easily recognize the Stabilizers at your high school reunion: they've stuck with the same company, relationships, and neighborhood for years, with none of the restless desire that makes others long for change. "Why change?" they ask, and in the absence of a very solid reason, they don't. Their steadfastness (or perhaps, rigidity) extends to their daily activities and thoughts. If you're looking for someone to play hooky from work with, Stabilizers will decline with words of caution about being caught. They're rarely impulsive in their actions, preferring instead to weigh their options carefully before responding.

It was probably a group of Stabilizers who invented the work ethic. They believe in work for work's sake, and for building character. They also believe that greater effort is rewarded with recognition, positions of greater responsibility, and ultimately, financial security. Their need to do things for people is much greater than their need to relate to them. Once they commit to something, they stay with it until they fulfill their obligation. So if your own restless streak causes you to start a new home improvement project every year, while it will bewilder your Stabilizer friends, they will be the ones who actually show up to help you and will leave only when the last piece of tile is neatly glued to your new kitchen countertop. Stabilizers don't question their motives for being the way they are; they simply do what is expected of them.

The Queen of England stood in the Guildhall in London on the fortieth anniversary of her ascent to the throne. Over the rims of her glasses, she peered at the audience gathered together to celebrate her long reign. "1992 is not a year on which I shall look back with undiluted pleasure," she said. "In the words of one of my more sympathetic correspondents, it has turned out to be an Annus Horribilis." That year, three of her children were divorced or separated, her renegade daughter-in-law published a tell-all book, and Windsor Castle caught fire. It was, indeed, a horrible year.

By nature, Queen Elizabeth II was well-suited to her role as monarch in an era of immense change and upheaval, serving as an anchor for a country in flux. Despite questionable fashion sense, the Queen's predictable, composed, and emotionally controlled demeanor has always engendered loyalty in her people, and her ability to maintain her dignity despite the many public and private humiliations the monarchy has endured over the past half century is admirable. She, like other Stabilizers, believes that work builds character and that being productive while in the service of others is reward enough in itself.

Stabilizers are traditionalists who maintain a sense of history and continuity in their lives. They need a place where they feel they belong, whether it's a personal or professional relationship or a community of friends. They value ritual and ceremony, and they are often the preservers of traditions in their homes. You probably have a Stabilizer to thank (or blame) for the yearly events that are deeply embedded in your family history. Like the guards at Buckingham Palace, Stabilizers are there to make sure that what exists is preserved and that what is new, foreign, and therefore dangerous never gets in. Their job is to ensure that everything happens in the proper order and sequence so that life is predictable. Just the way they like it!

What Makes Stabilizers Tick?

End of the road…nothing to do…and no hope of things getting better. Sounds like Saturday night at my house.

—*Eeyore, from* Winnie the Pooh

Stabilizers live from the left emotional brain, where they focus their attention inwardly toward ensuring they feel secure. Stability is achieved when everything feels safe inside of them and they are free from anxiety or upset. They are constantly looking at how the outer world affects their inner security. Because this is the goal of this part of the brain, Stabilizers order, organize, and sequence experiences, and sort things into categories, like "good" or "bad" and "right" or "wrong." This sorting process helps them predict which people, events, and situations are likely safe and which ones aren't. For example, if you ask Stabilizers to describe an experience they've had, they'll declare it either good or bad. Martha Stewart, for example, is well known for ending a segment of her show with the phrase "and that's a good thing." Tell Stabilizers about something unusual that happened to you, like the time you had an unexpected two-day layover in Iceland, or the time you met the president in an elevator, and they'll ask, "Was that a good thing, or not?"

For Stabilizers, there's a simple rule for evaluating any experience: "If it upsets me, it's bad; if it makes me happy, it's good." Once they know where something fits in the "good" or "bad" categorization, they know how to respond to it. Stabilizers don't get overly concerned with the subtler meanings of things, including their own feelings; from their point of view, it's sufficient to conclude, "That's just the way I am." Every new possibility is viewed relative to what came before it, which helps to minimize surprises. When trying something novel, Stabilizers will act only after working out a series of separate steps. Until that time, they don't feel that it's safe to do anything.

The brains of Stabilizers are wired for easy recall of facts and details, rote learning, and solving technical or mechanical problems. They store information in a semantic (logical) system without attaching personal baggage to it, so they can produce necessary information on demand. If you're one who likes to tell tall tales, beware! Stabilizers not only use their excellent command of facts and detail to make their own stories more credible, but they'll also use their precise memories to challenge the accuracy of other people's stories—like our Uncle Hedley who would trap us in the corner and recount his last twelve euchre hands, including each play he made and why. If Stabilizers aren't sure of the facts, they tend to keep quiet. They aren't the type to share your fish stories with, but if you want honesty and a straightforward worldview, be assured that Stabilizers say what they mean and mean what they say.

Because their brain is wired to keep things the same, Stabilizers are tenacious and stubborn. They pick up the slack for others and stay until everything has been finished, because that's the right thing to do. They will not quit, even if what they are doing—whether activities, jobs, or relationships—makes them unhappy, unless experience tells them they are wrong to continue because they believe, in some way, it will be worse to leave.

Manuel is a forty-three-year-old, first-generation Canadian. He works in his father's butcher shop, which he'll soon take over when his father retires. Over the past five years, their neighborhood has changed. Many of their friends have moved to the suburbs to join a growing Spanish-speaking community. The old neighborhood was close to downtown and its houses were being bought up by young professional couples. The Spanish flavor of the area was disappearing, and the butcher shop was suffering because of the change.

Maria, Manuel's wife, missed her friends and community and wanted to move. When she first raised the subject, Manuel simply said no, left the room, and went out to his workshop. Showing his true Stabilizer colors, he was already catastrophizing about the butcher shop, imagining a scenario in which a large "Going out of Business" sign was on the front door, for all the family to see as they passed on their way to the welfare office. He could not begin to consider the thought of moving and the disasters that would surely follow. Maria, unperturbed by such doom-and-gloom scenarios, continued her campaign to convince Manuel to move. She threatened, pleaded, and even tried painting him a rosy picture of how their lives would change for the better—but to no avail. The more she went on about change, the angrier he became, eventually refusing to speak to her at all.

Manuel's brother, who was using the Striving Styles at his workplace, had already figured out that Manuel was a Stabilizer. He noticed that his brother spent longer hours at work despite the decrease in customers. He also sensed the tension between Manuel and Maria and suggested that they work with me, his coach, to help them through the business challenges. After much resistance, Manuel agreed.

Stabilizers like Manuel don't tend to show their need for a strong leader, so it's important that their friends and family members intervene when Stabilizers are shutting down in distress. Unable to cope with the magnitude of major life changes, they can freeze in place like the Tin Man from *The Wizard of Oz*, helpless to move in any direction. It takes a lot of soothing of their anxiety to convince them to move again. Once this happens, they can start to take small steps in a well-organized plan to guide them during change.

During the coaching sessions, Manuel immediately connected with what I told him about Stabilizers and how they catastrophize and carry the responsibility for everything on their own shoulders. We compared his current experience to that of his father's struggle to immigrate to Canada, away from all that was familiar, and how successful he was ultimately. We systematically began separating his fears from reality and looked at the consequences of doing nothing. Manuel was also reminded of the duty of a man to do what's best for his family. He had not heard that the new Spanish neighborhood didn't have a butcher shop, which soothed his fear that there would not be enough customers for two shops. After many sessions, Manuel had worked out all of the steps he needed to transition both their business and their households to the new neighborhood.

Relationship Style of the Stabilizer

Stabilizers are solid, dependable friends and mates. Relationships with Stabilizers develop slowly, but once they commit themselves to a relationship with their boss, coworkers, friends, or loved ones, they are in it wholeheartedly, through good times and bad. Like everything else in their lives, Stabilizers take their personal relationships very seriously. If they say they are going to do something with you, even if it's going out for wings and a beer, they will be there. In their community, they tend to rely on and uphold traditions and all things familiar. They protect and defend the people and traditions they care about. They have a strong sense of family and community responsibility, and they show their caring by bringing order and structure into the lives of others. Stabilizers are more likely than any other Style to remain in dissatisfying relationships out of duty and obligation.

Stabilizers are intensely private people who rarely demonstrate to others what is going on underneath their calm exterior. While

Stabilizers often feel positive and warm toward people, they fail to express their emotions and therefore leave people in the dark as to what they feel. They are more concerned with what they are doing than what they are feeling; they don't find spending time thinking about or expressing emotions particularly useful. They are equally ill at ease when forced to deal with the emotions of others, withdrawing further into themselves when faced with a situation that calls for it. Most people consider Stabilizers to be emotionally unavailable; most Stabilizers are hard pressed to even know what that means. They feel very unsafe when they have to share themselves with others. Their need for privacy makes it difficult for others to know what they feel or even understand them.

Their uncommunicative approach can sometimes create very serious interpersonal problems in relationships. Very easily, they may be seen as insensitive or harsh because they often use judgment rather than empathy in their responses to others. They can steamroll less assertive people when demanding that everyone conform to their way of doing things. Stabilizers can also take the fun out of relationships by being so controlling and predictable, insisting that everything be done their way. They may even resort to sulking when asked to do things differently, using the silent treatment to communicate their upset for having their routine changed. They can also act like a stick in the mud, taking the playfulness out of the relationship.

Stabilizers take a no-frills approach to their relationships. Once they have wooed and won their partner, there is no reason to keep the romance going. They are pragmatic and unimaginative when it comes to thinking of new ways to make the relationship interesting. However, they do value tradition and don't want to disappoint or upset their partner because they failed to do what was expected. Because of their difficulty with expressing their emotions, they take full advantage of everything Hallmark has to offer, buying sentimental or romantic cards for special occasions, hoping that they won't be expected to actually say anything more than that. They let their actions speak for them.

How Stabilizers Satisfy Their Need to Be Secure
Building a Secure Foundation

Stabilizers believe that hard work and consistent effort are cornerstones of security. Before climbing the career ladder, they try to find a line of work that has security, a good retirement plan, and a history of stability, such as accounting or inventory management. They are not likely to initiate career changes, nor do they consider a lack of job satisfaction an adequate reason to do so. They stick with what they know and work hard to keep things the same. They make sure they are financially secure, especially for the proverbial rainy day that they feel is sure to come. The more Stabilizers save, the better they feel. In fact, Stabilizers get anxious when they spend money, as if every penny spent is one more brick removed from their financial foundation.

Only the wisest and the stupidest of men never change.

—*Confucius*

Self-Protective Stabilizers say no. They have absolute faith that there will be "rainy days" because they have spent so much time catastrophizing and thinking about every possible disaster that could befall them. Self-Protective Stabilizers say no before even considering something; they are more inclined to decline than to invest in trying new things for their own enjoyment or benefit. They fail to enjoy their hard-earned dollars, sacrificing pleasure in the present for security in the future. Because their fear of losing everything they've worked for is just another emotion they don't discuss, others may see them more as downright miserly than as thrifty. Stabilizers will say no even to things they would like to do or experience, because their knee-jerk reaction is simply to deny themselves anything that would upset their carefully crafted sense of stability. They are the people who win the lottery and show up for work the next day. They are deeply satisfied with the security that comes from the familiar, even when it becomes severely restricting.

Ling (Stabilizer) is a risk manager for a financial services company. He likes his job and makes a good living. On his way home from work one night per week, he eats dinner at the same inexpensive Chinese restaurant. Often, as he eats, he wishes that he had a nice woman to keep him company, but as soon as he starts to imagine this woman, his dream turns into a nightmare. It turns out that she doesn't like his family, spends money like it grows on trees, and complains bitterly when he has to work overtime. By the time he's finished his dinner each week, Ling has decided he is definitely better off without a woman.

By anticipating only negative outcomes of a hypothetical experience, Ling has not only sabotaged his chances with an imaginary woman, he's also reduced his odds of finding happiness with a real woman, and he's done all this in the course of a single meal!

Self-Protective Stabilizers stop catastrophizing. They let themselves step back and see situations for what they are. Instead of denying themselves everything, they include a certain amount of their budget to spend on doing things that please them. Once they let themselves feel the anxiety that they normally react to, they can start calming themselves before they react. They can become aware of their tendency to reject anything that doesn't agree with their carefully ordered world and work toward lessening it. With increasing self-awareness, they begin to pause on the verge of saying no and instead ask questions and gather more information. These simple acts of pausing and gathering information help them build their tolerance to anxiety by not saying no immediately.

Taking Care of Others

Stabilizers feel it's their responsibility to provide for the physical needs of the people they care about. Loyal and quietly supportive, they are deeply committed to taking care of their "tribe" in either an active or a behind-the-scenes fashion, protecting and serving, and working hard to become solid members of society. They prefer friends who, like themselves, are modest, quiet, and genuine. They express their feelings through action much more frequently than through words. They are very self-effacing, avoiding the limelight and preferring to stay in the background, where they can contribute in a steady, practical manner. Stabilizers are the go-to people when help is needed. In their families, they will do their duty and take responsibility when no one else will. Katniss, a character in the book *The Hunger Games*, gives us insight into how the Stabilizer takes care of her family.

Ever since the death of her father in a tragic coal-mining accident, Katniss has taken on the role of her family's head of household. While Katniss's mother was unable to cope with the loss, falling into a deep depression, Katniss stayed focused and took charge. Filling her father's shoes, she became the chief cook and bottle washer, bringing home the food and income that would save the family from starvation. Katniss is the stalwart rock of her family. Hunting, foraging, and providing for her mother and sister Prim are at the very core of her identity.

Self-Protective Stabilizers become withdrawn and uncommunicative. When "doing it all" is impossible, SP Stabilizers become singularly focused. Once overwhelmed, they narrow their focus to getting things done and become increasingly uncommunicative, unable to tolerate even simple conversations. They refuse to sit down and talk about what is going on with them, leaving those around them in the dark. Because they feel overwhelmed, they can't see how they are ever going to get anything done and believe that talking just gets in the way. When in this state, Stabilizers can get so caught up in trying to keep their emotions under control that they are unable to see solutions to problems. They work compulsively, spending long and lonely hours keeping busy until they feel they are back on top of things.

Self-Actualizing Stabilizers learn to trust. No longer fixated on usefulness and duty as their sole sources of worth, Stabilizers can feel secure knowing that others love them and want to take care of them in the same way that they take care of others. Self-Actualizing Stabilizers know they belong and no longer have to prove themselves repeatedly by being useful. They realize that people, including their employers, aren't going to get rid of them if they are sick or unable to solve a problem. They learn to practice methods for calming themselves in the face of their own anxiety. They also learn how to be more direct in communicating their feelings and needs to others and not rejecting others who attempt to find out what is going on with them. By learning to trust themselves and others, SA Stabilizers can stay balanced and centered in their lives.

Assuming a Role

Stabilizers feel more secure when everyone's roles—especially their own—are clearly defined. They maintain a black-and-white view of people's duties or stations in life and believe that everyone should stay within these stations. They excel at followership, because when they know the expectations of their role, they fulfill them to the letter. They relate more easily to roles than to people, adapting their behavior toward others accordingly. If you are the Stabilizer's boss, parent, or a high-ranking government official, you will be treated with respect and a sense of duty. If you are a son or daughter, your Stabilizer parent will provide you with the physical necessities of life. Stabilizers don't see the point in trying to understand what another person is like; rather, they think of what the person should be according to experience and knowledge they have accumulated about the person's role. When people behave in accordance with the expectations of their role, they earn Stabilizers' trust and foster feelings of safety.

Henry loves to cook. His wife, Sara, is also a good cook, and he had always assumed that she loved cooking too. But he begins to notice that Sara is avoiding his suggestions for trying new recipes or cooking something together, particularly since she quit her job to stay at home and take care of their new baby. If he says he wants to cook, Sara immediately says, "That's great," and gets busy doing something else while Henry gets the meal ready.

Sara is a Stabilizer. She believes that her role and responsibility is to take care of her husband and child, especially now that she is at home full-time. It makes her feel anxious when Henry wants to cook because she interprets this as making her somehow useless and "bad." She doesn't see the cooking experience in the same way Henry does, as a way for the two of them to spend quality time together. In fact, she finds it annoying to cook with Henry because he strays from the recipes and is always under foot as she tries to follow her normal routine.

Self-Protective Stabilizers see everyone as unsafe. They can be hypercritical and judgmental of everyone, including themselves. The role they have depended on for their sense of stability eludes them and everything feels chaotic and frightening as they project their perceived weakness and inadequacy onto others. They start sorting everyone into negative categories, according to perceived failures and flaws. Self-Protective Stabilizers call them names—no good, lazy, stupid, and so on—and they lash out critically at people who are close to them. Even those who are unfamiliar to them may be seen as incompetent at best and threatening at worst.

Self-Actualizing Stabilizers enjoy people for who they are. They no longer expect everyone to perform solely according to their roles. They stop judging and sorting people to figure out which ones are safe; instead, they become curious and learn why they do this. Self-Actualizing Stabilizers work at not judging others; rather, they try to put themselves in other people's shoes to understand others' feelings and actions. Their tendency to be opinionated and unreasonable in their expectations is replaced with a softer, more human approach. Although adhering strictly to their role may continue to be a challenge, they understand that they sometimes get run down, overcommitted, or ill, and deadlines may go unmet. Their belief in judging others solely according to the performance of their expected roles begins to loosen, allowing them to let people into their lives. They also attain peace through accepting that individuals are not easily categorized, and that the shadowy area between black and white is often what gives life its richness and intensity.

Following the Rules

Stabilizers have clear rules for just about everything in their lives, including their personal relationships, and they take these rules very seriously, seeing it as their duty and responsibility to follow them. They aren't particularly tolerant of others who don't. Because order is so important to them, they can serve as both caretakers and drill sergeants in their families. Although work comes first, when that is done, they put time and effort into their family and recreational lives. Rules and regulations are freely imposed on family members and should be followed without question or exception. Stabilizers have a firm idea about the right way to run a household, and they keep everyone and everything in line with routines and schedules. They will try to make sure to conform socially to the status quo. Stabilizers truly believe that people should behave as their station in life dictates, and they do not appreciate people who put on airs or project an image of being better than they actually are.

Carmen (Stabilizer) and Michael (Visionary), both in their early twenties, met when they were taking a night course at the community college. They went out a few times and hit it off. Over the following two months, things started to get more serious and Michael asked Carmen to spend a weekend at the beach with him. Carmen, who comes from a conservative Catholic family, was offended by the idea, especially since Michael had not met Carmen's parents and she had not been introduced to his parents. Carmen now feels that Michael has breached an important, if unstated, rule of their relationship: before things get too intimate, the parents must meet the potential boyfriend or girlfriend. To do otherwise, in

Carmen's view, shows a lack of respect for the family. Carmen now begins to have second thoughts about all aspects of her relationship with Michael.

Self-Protective Stabilizers become emotional, insisting others conform. When these expectations are not met, Stabilizers can become very anxious. This anxiety has a destabilizing effect, which in turn manifests as disapproval and anger. If someone says he is going to do something, he should do it. If he says he will be somewhere at a certain time, that is when he should arrive. If Stabilizers can keep their commitments, everyone else should be able to as well. They accept no excuses. The same effects can occur if the rules are suddenly changed, forcing Stabilizers to behave differently or to accept something without having adequate time to stabilize themselves internally. Once in a state of emotional reactivity, SP Stabilizers respond in a way that is out of proportion to the situation. They may make hurtful comments, lash out in anger, and express open criticism of just about everything. It is as if an emotional dam has burst and a tide of feelings and judgments crashes over those unfortunate enough to be in its path.

Conformity is the jailer of freedom and the enemy of growth.

—*John F. Kennedy*

Self-Actualizing Stabilizers challenge their self-imposed limitations. When they start to self-actualize, Stabilizers are no longer slaves to doing things "by the book." They stop policing others to ensure conformity to standards. Their relationships are more rewarding, playful, and enjoyable. They know the importance of maintaining personal relationships and they plan social activities. They live their lives creating solid comfort, taking care of their families, their friends, and themselves. They appreciate having beauty around them and care deeply for their physical surroundings. They create a nestlike environment in their homes, where they can go to be alone and feel safe, warm, and secure. In this sanctuary, they can recharge their batteries after being with others. Although they are accustomed to expressing love through their strong sense of responsibility, they now find romantic and even sentimental ways to show how much they care. With their excellent memories they can recall and attend to details that endear them to their loved ones, such as important anniversaries.

Activators of the Self-Protective System

With their need to be secure and maintain everything the way it's always been, Stabilizers are activated by people and situations that cause them to feel useless, unsettled, or insecure. Their need to have their world ordered as it "should" be causes them to fear anything that causes uncertainty. They are prone to worry or catastrophize, which fuels their fears and anxiety. This way of thinking and feeling frustrates their need to be secure and therefore is what they fear most. They will do whatever they can to protect themselves from these feelings.

The Unknown

Stabilizers feel anxious and are easily activated by anything new. If a novel activity hasn't been sufficiently planned for, Stabilizers view that as a threat that they must resist in order to keep things stable. However, just thinking about engaging in a new experience is enough to cause them anxiety. The Stabilizer's logic is, "If I haven't done it before, why do it now?" For example, if a Stabilizer isn't happy with where she is living because it is too small and she can afford a larger space, she may convince herself that all places in the area where she wants to live are unsafe, bug infested, and dangerous.

Spending Excessive Time Thinking

Stabilizers enjoy their own company; however, they can spend so much time worrying that they work themselves into a panic attack. They become consumed by obsessive thoughts, catastrophizing about everything that might go wrong. The more they predict catastrophic events, the more physical distress they feel. They can easily work themselves into a depression this way.

I've developed a new philosophy...I only dread one day at a time.
—*Charlie Brown, "Peanuts"*

Inability to Schedule Everything

Not being able to secure the steps or timing of activities causes Stabilizers' anxiety to escalate. They tend to overextend themselves, preferring to be productive rather than idle. To accomplish what they have to, they become increasingly mechanistic in their approach, trying to get some distance from their feelings while at the same time forgetting that they are human beings. However, like a machine when it hasn't been serviced, they can cease to function.

Inability to Perform Their Role

When Stabilizers become sick or hurt in a way that makes them unable to enact their roles, they become emotionally distressed, fearing the worst—that they will become useless or a burden to others. They find it hard to relinquish their role and to let others provide for them instead.

Not Following Rules

Stabilizers tend to see the world as a "machine" in which all the moving parts must work in a specific order and sequence in order for everyone to feel secure. Family members not showing up for celebrations, rituals not adhered to, people arriving late—all these behaviors cause the Stabilizer to feel anxious and fear the catastrophic outcome of the "machine" not functioning as it should.

Batman: "Robin, you haven't fastened your safety bat-belt."
Robin: "We're only going a couple of blocks."

Batman: "It won't be long until you are old enough to get a driver's license, Robin, and you'll be able to drive the Batmobile and other vehicles. Remember, motorist safety."
Robin: "Gosh, Batman, when you put it that way."

— *"The Purr-fect Crime,"* Batman *episode*

Multitasking

Stabilizers become overwhelmed when they have to deal with competing priorities and too many things coming at them at the same time. They lose their ability to sequence and prioritize their activities and look to others for direction. When none is forthcoming, they try to stabilize their anxiety by attending to one thing at a time and ignoring everything else.

Blind Spots
Rigidity and Inflexibility

While others see Stabilizers this way, they don't see it themselves. They believe that everyone will benefit from their steadfast efforts to keep things the same. As they strive to maintain stability on every level, they can get so caught up in keeping things the same that they get in the way of necessary change. They can easily become stuck in a rut, holding on to "the way things should be done." They limit themselves and others and get in the way of achieving their potential.

Doing Everything

Stabilizers have a hard time seeing how talking to others can help them problem solve. They believe they're responsible for fixing whatever is wrong and making sure everything that needs to get done is done. Their imagination runs amok with negative consequences of epic proportions should they not get things back in order.

Impact of Their Behavior on Others

Stabilizers see themselves as providing a necessary service: guarding and protecting. They can't see how harsh and judgmental they are when doing this. They don't tend to reflect on the impact their harsh words and criticisms have on themselves and others. Even when they are told, they can dismiss the other person as being too "soft" or lenient.

Blind Obedience

Stabilizers have a blind spot around the benefit of challenging rules. They don't realize that by blindly following rules, they are failing to get to know themselves. Their sense of security remains dependent on the consistency of events outside themselves, which they must constantly try to manage because they have not learned to find a source of security within themselves.

Rules are for the obedience of fools and the guidance of wise men.

—*Douglas Bader*

Inability to Say No

Stabilizers have difficulty saying no when asked to do something for someone in need. They quietly support their colleagues and friends, helping them in practical and tangible ways. They can do so much for others that they are easily taken for granted. This characteristic can be difficult and frustrating for people who care about the Stabilizers when they see how others take advantage of them.

Upshifting to Their Self-Actualizing System

For Stabilizers to upshift to their SA System, they need to become more self-aware and redirect their striving energy by doing the following.

Picking Battles

Stabilizers need to learn to know when something is worth fighting or upsetting others about. They tend to "sweat the small stuff," treating minor breeches of protocol with the same degree of upset as a major transgression. Stabilizers can upshift to where they see the impact of their behavior on other people. Taking a moment to actually feel what they are inflicting can stop them in their tracks.

Practicing Self-Soothing

Stabilizers need a mechanism inside of them to calm their anxiety so that they can shift to the SA System. They can also get others to put things in perspective. Although Stabilizers' behavior can seem frightening to others, they need to be soothed out of their anxious state. Over time, they will develop their own mechanism for recognizing when they are in this state, but a good friend, partner, or colleague needs to reach out to help them so that they don't destroy their relationships.

Asking for Help

Talking to others and letting them know what is going on with them can help Stabilizers get perspective. They need to learn to trust others and become less suspicious of others' motives for helping them. They need to be reminded that worrying isn't a solution and that sometimes the best action is to relax and float, and let the stream support them.

Taking a Time-Out

Quiet time to reflect and calm their anxiety is often a key to Stabilizers upshifting to their SA System. This lets them consider, order, and make sense of what is going on. Being alone often helps this happen. Stabilizers need time on their own to stop reacting to their anxiety, to actually understand what they are saying no to. It is often surprising to others how quickly they can shift if they are not pushed.

Getting the Steps Straight

If they take time to consider the sequence of steps required to make them feel safe doing a new activity or learning a new skill, Stabilizers gain the ability to say yes to novelty. Having someone help them put the steps in place greatly reduces their anxiety. They can also upshift by talking to trusted friends and family who have experience with similar activities or situations, and who can convince them that there are possible outcomes other than the worst imaginable ones.

Practicing Mindfulness

Stabilizers need to be able to take stock of what they are experiencing and reacting to. They think of themselves as practical, rational people and don't realize that they are reacting to their fear. In fact, if you asked them they would tell you they aren't afraid! The practice of mindfulness helps them to develop an observing self that can monitor, recognize, and manage their fear-based reactions so that they can act from their SA system.

Achieving Their Full Potential

Steadfast, reliant, and true of heart, Stabilizers are the "backbone of society," intent on building a solid foundation upon which they ensure physical safety for themselves, their families, and their community. Seeming to bear the weight of the world on their shoulders, Stabilizers will not stop working until they are spent. Then they will get up and do it all over again. They are loyal, trustworthy, and capable. When Stabilizers learn to meet their need for stability without becoming rigid and to do what is expected of them socially and professionally without undue fear of failing, their considerable assets shine.

PART III
BECOMING YOUR BEST SELF

There's a difference between interest and commitment. When you're interested in doing something, you do it only when circumstances permit. When you're committed to something, you accept no excuses, only results.

—*Art Turock*

RECENTLY, WE MET WITH a group of angel investors to discuss investment money for the Striving Styles Personality System (SSPS). In response to our pitch, they told us that unless we were offering people something that would give them immediate results or a quick fix, it wouldn't be successful, because that is what people want. Two of the three people to whom we were pitching told us that people really couldn't do anything about their unproductive habits and behaviors because "it's human nature." Needless to say, we didn't get any investment money from them.

This example shows the beliefs and attitudes people have that get in the way of change and growth. Although there is truth to what the angel investors said, that it's human nature to want things to be easy (Self-Protective System), it is also human nature to want to self-actualize (Self-Actualizing System). We make up all kinds of excuses when we give in to our fears and impulses, instead of holding our minds steady and staying on course. We say things like, "It's too hard. There has to be an easier way." "I'm not ready. I have to be in the right space to do this" or "I'm too undisciplined to do this. I probably don't deserve to be happy anyway."

There are all kinds of excuses we can use for not putting in the *sustained* effort it takes to live life as your best self. This section gives you the tools and strategies for developing self-awareness, starting with the awareness of where you are right now. It helps you identify and work through self-limiting beliefs and fears and teaches you how to face head-on the excuses (resistance) you are likely to put in the way of living life as who you are meant to be. It guides you to chart a course for your own development so you can stop living from your Self-Protective System and become who you are meant to be.

CHAPTER FOURTEEN
HOW TO BECOME YOUR BEST SELF

What this power is I cannot say; all I know is that it exists and it becomes available only when a man is in that state of mind in which he knows exactly what he wants and is fully determined not to quit until he finds it.

—Alexander Graham Bell

WHILE WE LOVE TO learn about how to improve and develop ourselves, taking in such information is a passive activity, whereas actually changing our behavior is an experiential one. These two activities are governed by different areas of the brain, and as much fun as an aha moment is, it usually doesn't take us anywhere in our lives. The purpose of part 3 of the book is to provide you with a step-by-step approach to becoming who you are meant to be based on your Predominant Striving Style. It takes you from simply learning about your Predominant Style through all the actions and experiences necessary to break your emotionally driven behaviors and unconscious habits of mind that get in the way of achieving your potential.

Step One:
Get to Know
Your Brain

Step Two:
Chart a Course
for Development
(Set Your Goals)

Step Three:
Move to
Action

This chapter introduces the SSPS Roadmap for Development, which is a three-step process that helps you repattern your brain and achieve concrete behavioral changes that can make an immediate difference in your life. This chapter also takes you through a series of exercises to let you get to know your brain (step 1) from the insights you've gained from parts 1 and 2 of the book. In chapter 15, you will complete the Who Are You Meant to Be Planner, which helps you to articulate and then achieve your specific development goals (step 2), as well as exercises intended to support your ability to move to action (step 3).

By the end of part 3, you will know in which areas of your life your predominant need is being met and in which it is not. You will understand why your need is not being met and the consequences for you in terms of how you feel and behave. As well, you will have charted a course for getting your need met that enables you to shift out of self-protection and to strengthen your Self-Actualizing System in order to achieve your potential. You will be armed with all the tools and practices you need to become your best self by routinely meeting the need that is at the root of your Predominant Style.

SSPS Roadmap for Development

We all want progress, but if you're on the wrong road, progress means doing an about-turn and walking back to the right road; in that case, the man who turns back soonest is the most progressive.

—*C. S. Lewis*

For our brains to lay down new patterns of behavior, we must follow a conscious process that begins with understanding our Predominant Striving Style and its need. The Roadmap for Development gives you the experiences you require to develop and helps you tolerate the difficult emotions that are a natural part of growth. Actions don't always follow intent, so the Roadmap has been designed to ensure you move to action and are able to sustain it by directly addressing the tendency to revert to familiar self-protective behaviors, which is a predictable part of resistance to change. It helps you break through these stubborn habits of mind that inhibit development by identifying them in advance and deciding what you will do when they are triggered.

The Roadmap provides you with clear directions for living life as your best self. It gets you to explore how you are currently experiencing your life and whether you are living out of the Self-Protective (SP) System of your Predominant Style. It helps you "shake up" your existing neural pathways by having you check in with yourself through reflection on your thoughts, feelings, and behaviors. It shows you how to challenge your assumptions and beliefs, and create new experiences that break old patterns. The Roadmap gives you directions on how to identify the activities and practices necessary to build your Self-Actualizing (SA) System, allowing you to break long-standing habits of mind and deal with the impulse to do what you "feel" like rather than what your intention is. It facilitates the process for you to get on the road to achieving your potential.

Each of the steps in the Roadmap builds on the others, so resist the impulse to skip through without completing all of the exercises and reflections. Remember, development is a biological activity that happens in your brain, not just through abstract thinking, awareness, or knowing. Developing your brain and learning to live from your SA System is not something that you can do without self-knowledge, self-awareness, and a great deal of reflection and introspection. Nor can you do it without facing your fears, trying new behaviors, and having experiences that change the neural connections in your brain. Make sure you give yourself the time you warrant to complete each step of the Roadmap.

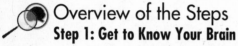

Overview of the Steps
Step 1: Get to Know Your Brain

It's important to spend some time thinking about your brain and your current state in preparation for creating your Who Are You Meant to Be Planner. The experience of immersing yourself in you helps you to embody the information, not just know it. For this reason, this first step provides you with activities to help you get to know your Predominant Striving Style, including its self-protective and self-actualizing behaviors. It instructs you to reflect on your current behaviors, because before you can start defining what actions you want to take, you have to first undertake an honest assessment of where you are today. This step also includes activities to examine the extent to which your predominant need is being met and ways in which you need to strengthen your SA System.

Step 2: Chart a Course for Development

In this step, the Who Are You Meant to Be Planner leads you through a clear process to create your personal Roadmap for achieving your potential. To begin, you envision your desired future state and set goals for yourself including what it will look and feel like. From there, you explore the fears and underlying beliefs that will get in the way of achieving your vision so you can be prepared when they are triggered. Next, you define your plan of action to achieve your goals and then the specific steps that you must follow to be successful.

 ## Step 3: Move to Action

In this final step, you learn about the key practices for ensuring your success in executing on the action plan created in step 2 of the Roadmap. As well, you define how you will put these practices to work for you to sustain forward movement toward your goals.

Getting Started

Now that you understand the steps of the Roadmap, it's time to get started. The following pages include structured activities for you to complete along with the space to do so. You can either complete the exercises directly in the book or use your own paper or journal. Copies of the blank forms are also available for download at www.whoareyoumeanttobe.com if you want larger-sized versions. It doesn't matter how, but it does matter that you put your answers in writing. This is not a mental exercise—it has to be experiential—so doing it in your head doesn't count.

If you find yourself not wanting to write down your answers, recognize this as a form of resistance to your own development that you need to problem solve before you can get started. For example, you might feel more energized to do this as a shared experience rather than doing it alone. One solution might be to ask a trusted friend to do it with you. This makes the process more fun and social for Styles like the Socializer, Performer, or Adventurer. Styles like the Artist and Stabilizer often need someone to get them started because of their fear of what they might uncover through the exercises. Writing down any fears or underlying beliefs that might get in the way of starting can help keep you moving along. The Leader, Intellectual, and Visionary might run into trouble because they think the process is a waste of time, so it helps them to note all their judgments and critiques of the process and get them out of the way before moving on. Remember, feelings are the biggest barrier to growth and development, so write them down and keep going.

You can also become more familiar with your patterns of resistance by thinking of the things you normally skip when you read self-help books or participate in a development program. As you work through the exercises in the book, when you notice the tendency to want to do the same thing, try a different approach. Know that your resistance or hesitation is influenced by your Predominant Style, and depending on the quadrant involved in the activities, some are going to require a bit more energy or self-encouragement to stick with. This is particularly true if your Predominant Style is located in your right brain. That's because defining, making things real and tangible, and moving into action are all left-brained activities. That doesn't mean you won't encounter resistance if your Predominant Style resides in your left brain: many of these activities involve examining feelings and emotions, and being in process, which can create resistance from that perspective as well.

The important thing is to notice whatever resistance you experience and to do the exercises anyway. You don't have to give yourself a hard time for what is naturally challenging to you; your challenge this time around is to experience the resistance and still choose to do the activities. Approach the questions and your resistance to them with curiosity and understanding rather than judgment and criticism. If you notice yourself being critical of yourself or the process, simply choose to shift to a kinder, more supportive position. For example, try a few words of encouragement to keep you moving along rather than giving way to feelings of frustration or impatience.

Should you notice yourself getting tired or thinking of it as too much effort, give yourself permission to take a short break while making the commitment to come back to it, or simply remind yourself that its natural to feel some resistance and keep going. This just might be the most important project of your life, but doing it will naturally test and discover all the ways you may be living in self-protective, self-limiting, and self-critical patterns. It will bring to light the relationship you have developed with yourself, so adopting an attitude of interest, curiosity, and openness to discovery is your best approach to success.

You will notice that chapters 14 and 15 focus solely on your Predominant Striving Style. This is because it is most important that we get our predominant need met first by learning about its self-actualizing behaviors and practicing them. Once you feel that you have mastered using your Predominant Style and are getting your predominant need met consistently, repeat the same approach when you begin work on your Associate Styles, making sure that their needs are being met in all aspects of your life. Remember, you have only one member of your Squad in each area of the brain, so it's important that you work all four Styles throughout this process. If you have any questions about your Squad and want to validate your Associate Styles, you can complete the full assessment online at www.whoareyoumeanttobe.com.

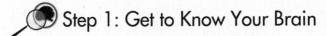 Step 1: Get to Know Your Brain

Where are you right now?
What are you experiencing?

The first step in the Roadmap ensures that you fully understand the mechanics of your own mind as well as your current state so you can build your development plan in step 2. This will be based on your Predominant Striving Style, its need, and the extent to which you are getting this need met in your life. Before you can ensure you are getting your predominant need met, you must first become conscious of what it means to get this need met, including a familiarity with the self-actualizing behaviors you demonstrate when it is being met. Armed with this information, you can define the steps necessary to get your predominant need met in your life and shift to living from your SA System.

While the overarching goal is to live your life as who you are meant to be, no two individuals will take the same path to achieve this even if they have the same Predominant Style. Planning for your development requires you to be able to chart a path from your current state of being to your desired state. To change your patterns of behavior, you have to know what those patterns are. Assessing your current state openly and honestly allows you to examine where your need is being met, how you are using your Predominant Style, and what is activating your SP System.

We have provided you with information on what quadrant of the brain is most effective in coming up with the responses to the questions. If the quadrant you need to use is not one you tend to use as frequently, give yourself some extra time to consider your responses, or ask someone for help.

To complete this section of the Planner, consider what is actually happening in your life today. By answering the following questions, you will become aware of the extent to which you are getting your needs met, living in your SP System versus living in your SA System.

Tips for Completing This Step:

This activity needs to be performed by the left rational quadrant of your brain (Leader, Intellectual). Depending on your Predominant Style, you will find this exercise easy or you will experience different challenges in your attempts to complete this section.

Here are some tips based on your Predominant Style:

Leader or Intellectual: You may have a tendency to believe that if you think it is so, then it is so. Think about how frequently you actually do what you claim, not just your idea or concept of you. Take some time to reflect and find examples that illustrate what you think about yourself, and include any experiences that may or may not support your view. For example, you might find that you aren't using your self-actualizing behaviors as much as you think you do when you actually stop and reflect on it.

Performer or Visionary: You will have a tendency to see yourself in terms of your potential, rather than as you are. Reflect on your experiences and what you actually do, and then record the facts in order to see yourself as you are. Envisioning it can feel as though it is real and that you are already experiencing the things you see. If you don't see your self-protective behaviors as clearly as your potential, ask someone to help you out. Don't forget to make sure you take the time to write down your answers without skipping over the exercises.

Socializer or Artist: Know that you may resist defining yourself because you tend to value yourself as either "good" or "bad." You will tend to describe your current reality based on how you are feeling. This means that if you are feeling terrific, you may record all of your self-actualizing behaviors without identifying any self-protective ones. If you are feeling low or discouraged, you may record that you are self-protective in all areas of your life. In either case, you may be unrealistic about the picture you paint, so it's important to make sure you remind yourself to be objective.

Adventurer or Stabilizer: You may not see the point to this activity at first, so if you need to, look ahead through all the exercises and see that the steps are in place and lead to a particular outcome. To get started, refer to the chapter on your Predominant Style and the examples of self-protective and self-actualizing behaviors. Take each behavior and see if you can find examples from your experience that match what is being asked for.

My Predominant Style: _____;
I Need to Be _____

I get my predominant need met by the following behaviors, circumstances, and/or other means:

[Note all the ways in which your predominant need can get met and consider all aspects of your life. What is happening? What activities are you pursuing? What behaviors are you demonstrating? What actions are you taking? What circumstances are in place? What are your experiences in your relationships, your career, or your other pursuits?]

_____

_____

_____

_____

_____

_____

_____

On the basis of my Predominant Style, when I am living in my Self-Actualizing System, it looks like this:

[Note all the behaviors you demonstrate, the activities you engage in, and/or the circumstances that are present in your life if you are living from your SA System.]

_____

_____

_____

_____

_____

_____

_____

On the basis of my Predominant Style, when I am living in my Self-Protective System, it looks like this:

[Note all the behaviors you demonstrate, the activities you engage in, and/or the circumstances that are present in your life when you are living in your SP System.]

_____

_____

_____

_____

_____

_____

Currently, I am using the following talents and abilities of my Predominant Striving Style and I am demonstrating the following self-actualizing behaviors of my Predominant Striving Style:

_____

_____

_____

_____

_____

_____

Currently, I am NOT using the following talents and abilities of my Predominant Striving Style and I am NOT demonstrating the following self-actualizing behaviors of my Predominant Striving Style:

_____

_____

_____

_____

_____

_____

Assess the extent to which your predominant need gets met.				
	Never	**Some**	**Often**	**Always**
At home and in my relationships with my partner, family, and/or children	❑	❑	❑	❑
At work in my job, with my boss and team, in my company, or at school	❑	❑	❑	❑
In social activities, with my friends	❑	❑	❑	❑
In leisure, through my hobbies and other interests or involvements	❑	❑	❑	❑

Identify where you are living in your Self-Protective System on the basis of your Predominant Style, as well as where you are NOT utilizing the talents and abilities of your Predominant Style.

Living in SP System and/or not utilizing:	Yes	No
At home and in my relationships with my partner, family, and/or children	❑	❑
At work in my job, with my boss and team, in my company, or at school	❑	❑
In social activities, with my friends	❑	❑
In leisure, through my hobbies and other interests or involvements	❑	❑

Currently in my life, I am demonstrating the following self-protective behaviors of my Predominant Style that I would most like to shift:

At home and in my relationships:

_____

_____

_____

_____

_____

_____

At work in my job or at school:

_____
_____
_____
_____
_____
_____
_____

In social activities:

_____
_____
_____
_____
_____
_____

In leisure:

_____
_____
_____
_____
_____

The following are possible reasons my predominant need is not being met, including any activators of my Self-Protective System that I am currently experiencing:

[Note: in addition to reasons such as environmental factors or behavior of others, consider your fears (e.g., "I am afraid of looking incompetent or being rejected"), your underlying beliefs (e.g., "I am lazy or undeserving"), and innate patterns of behavior.]

At home and in my relationships:

_____

_____

_____

_____

_____

At work in my job or at school:

_____

_____

_____

_____

_____

In social activities:

_____

_____

_____

_____

_____

In leisure:

_____

_____

_____

_____

_____

_____

Some of the actions I could take so that I am more fully utilizing the talents of my Predominant Style or living from the Self-Actualizing System of my Predominant Style include:

[Consider changes that you might make or things you could ask of others so your predominant need gets met; what you might give up, such as being a martyr or the hero; new activities you might pursue.]

At home and in my relationships:

_____

_____

_____

_____

_____

_____

_____

At work in my job or at school:

_____

_____

_____

_____

_____

_____

_____

In social activities:

_____

_____

_____

_____

_____

_____

_____

In leisure:

_____

_____

_____

_____

_____

_____

On the basis of the above assessment, I need to focus on the following areas of my life as my predominant need is not being met (answered **Never** or **Some**), I am living in my **Self-Protective System** and/or I am not fully utilizing the talents and abilities of my **Predominant Style** (select all that apply):

❑ Home/relationships

❑ Work or school

❑ Social/friends

❑ Leisure

Strengthening Your Self-Actualizing System

The best years of your life are the ones in which you decide your problems are your own. You do not blame them on your mother, the ecology, or the president. You realize that you control your own destiny.

—*Albert Ellis*

Living from our SA System is key to becoming who we are meant to be. It must be strengthened before we can do any other development, and it does not just develop on its own. You can't just say, "I'm not going to do that anymore," or "Now I know what to do. I just have to…" Therefore, it's important to know exactly how to do it. With new experiences and by making different choices for how you think and behave, you can develop the neural pathways connecting your three brains in order to start living from your SA System. This takes constant attention and practice. If we aren't using the connections between the brains, those pathways will be pruned away, leaving us to our automatic behaviors that don't support us in our attempts to live life as our best selves.

Think of your rational brain as your conscious self. It is aware of what is happening and what is possible. It sees the future, pictures what can be, knows how to identify what your issues are, and can create solutions to your problems. Now think of your emotional brain as your experiential self. It wants to feel physical sensations, communicate through emotions, and do what gives it most pleasure, right now. It's easy to see the different agendas of the two parts of the brain. The old example of the devil on one shoulder and an angel on the other is a perfect illustration of our brain in conflict:

Don't listen to him. He's trying to lead you down the path of righteousness! I'm gonna lead you down the path that rocks!
—*Kronk's shoulder devil,* The Emperor's New Groove

If you are one of the Styles that primarily lives out of the rational brain (Visionary, Leader, Performer, Intellectual), don't think that you have any less of a challenge and that this only applies to those who have Styles housed in their emotional brains. You are so busy thinking about and working toward the future that you forget to check in and see what you are experiencing. As you read in the third chapter, the rational brain can assume the role of policing and controlling emotions or detaching from what is realistic. Take time to recognize the things that you aren't experiencing—sensations or emotions—and what you might be missing as a result.

When the agenda of each of the brains is not aligned, it presents us with an inner conflict. Take Max, an Adventurer, who goes to the gym to work out for two hours, five times a week. He loves the experience of feeling strong and pushing to greater levels of physical power. Night finds him out clubbing, drinking to excess, and eating junk food. While the SA System of the Adventurer holds the discipline, a lack of a strong connection with the rational brain will cause the emotional brain to override all his hard work, and he ends up acting against himself by going for instant gratification instead.

The following are the key activities that promote the use of our SA System, especially when we find ourselves reacting to our emotions. They support us to develop and strengthen the required neural pathways. With practice, these activities become automatic and your brain will no longer default to the behavioral patterns of the SP System. You need to understand these activities—what they are, why they are important, how to use them—as well as assess the extent to which you are able to practice them in your life today. If you have not developed the ability to perform these activities, then demonstrating them regularly needs to be included in your development plan.

Instructions: Read the description of the activity and then rate the extent to which you do it in your day-to-day life. Complete the practice exercise to strengthen your SA System and ensure that you can do it (rather than just "know" how to do it). If it is not an activity for which you answer Always or Mostly, you will want to include it in your Planner in step 2 (chapter 15) as part of your development plan to strengthen your SA System.

Build self-awareness: Self-awareness is the ability to observe oneself and recognize thoughts and feelings as they occur. It is the ability to see the self separate from what is experienced and therefore recognize what we want to pay attention to. This means you don't have to listen to yourself complain about your teenage daughter for hours on end, thinking the same negative thoughts, and giving yourself ulcers! With self-awareness, we are able to define ourselves and then observe our behaviors and how they align with our self-definition. We are aware of a self that experiences feelings rather than defining ourselves by them, that is, "I feel anxious; therefore, I am an anxious person." It involves acknowledging and accepting your feelings, especially those that are difficult. With self-awareness, you become curious rather than judgmental about yourself and your behavior, eliminating negative self-talk that triggers the SP System. Self-awareness also helps you build a realistic self-concept and self-image without needing to inflate or deflate it.

Self-awareness also includes self-care, which is the ability to be aware of your physical, mental, and emotional needs, and to attend to them in a consistent fashion. It is the realization that you have a self that you must be conscious of and not ignore or neglect. If you don't take care of your physical and emotional health and well-being, it can end up undermining your development. It's like going on a grapefruit diet. Sure you'll lose weight, but in the process you will negatively affect your health. When the diet is over, you put the weight back on.

Extent to which I use this activity:
❏ **Always** ❏ **Mostly** ❏ **Periodically** ❏ **Rarely** ❏ **Never**

Practice: Identify a couple of current situations that are triggering difficult feelings for you. List the feelings you are actually experiencing as well as any negative self-talk about the situation or the feelings that you notice (e.g., "I said yes to helping my friend with his move even though I need to spend time with my children"; "I am angry with myself and tell myself I am a chicken for never saying no to anyone.") Notice how being upset with yourself becomes the focus of your attention and how you judge yourself. _____

_____

_____

_____

_____

_____

_____

_____

_____

_____

Practice reflection and insight: The rational brain is the only brain with insight into itself. Without it, we don't have the ability to ask ourselves why we are reacting to something with such anger or upset. Many blame other people for making them feel the way they do. However, our feelings are a direct reaction to a stimulus and not the fault of the other person. By reflecting on our feelings, our behavior, and our impulses, we gain insight into ourselves and develop self-awareness. It also strengthens the connections between the three brains, making it easier the next time the same activator occurs to respond in the new way. The more we use this self-questioning approach, reflecting on our emotional experiences and reactions, the more we are able to meet and negotiate to get our needs met.

> ### Extent to which I use this activity:
> ❏ **Always** ❏ **Mostly** ❏ **Periodically** ❏ **Rarely** ❏ **Never**

Practice: List a few situations in which you are currently blaming others for the way you are feeling. Try to identify why you are reacting the way you are.

_____

_____

_____

_____

_____

_____

_____

_____

_____

_____

Learn from your experiences: Even though we get stuck in patterns of behavior that result in making similar mistakes, we have the capacity to learn from our experiences to avoid doing this. If we are operating from our SP System, we are more likely to repeat mistakes, as stress has a negative impact on our ability to learn. If you get upset at yourself for repeating a pattern, you are more likely to repeat it again, especially if you don't identify a new behavior to replace the unwanted one. It's of greater benefit to write down your pattern, what you have learned from the experience, and what you will do differently in the future, instead of lamenting the fact that you're human and make mistakes.

Extent to which use this activity:
❑ **Always** ❑ **Mostly** ❑ **Periodically** ❑ **Rarely** ❑ **Never**

Practice: Write down one to two key patterns along with a recent example of each pattern at work in your life. Record what you learned from the experience and what you will do differently the next time.

_____

_____

_____

_____

_____

_____

_____

_____

_____

Practice mindfulness: Mindfulness is the practice of paying attention to your immediate experience and to develop the capacity to focus attention where you want it to go. It enhances the experience of being in your life, alerting you to when your thoughts are in the past or the future. The practice of mindfulness keeps you in touch with what you are experiencing and helps you recognize and accept your emotions without reacting to them or judging them. It helps you recognize automatic negative thinking patterns so that you can refocus your attention where you want it to be.

Practicing mindfulness on a daily basis is one of the most profound things you can do to support your development. In fact, research institutions, including UCLA, have conducted studies showing that mindfulness meditation changes the brain itself, laying the foundation for new patterns of thinking, feeling, and behaving that lead to greater self-awareness and the ability to notice your thoughts and feelings instead of getting tangled up in them. The practice of mindfulness allows us to observe, manage, and direct our attention, choosing self-actualizing behaviors over self-protective ones.

There is more right with you than wrong with you.

—*Jon Kabat-Zinn*

Extent to which use this activity:
❑ **Always** ❑ **Mostly** ❑ **Periodically** ❑ **Rarely** ❑ **Never**

Practice: Think about one or two recent occasions on which you found yourself reacting negatively to a situation or person. How did you react? What did you tell yourself about the situation or person (what assumptions did you make)? What were you feeling at the time? What thoughts did you think in response to those feelings? How did your reaction affect the situation or the relationship?

How would you respond differently if you had the chance to do it over again? _____

_____

_____

_____

_____

_____

_____

_____

Harness your emotions: This involves knowing what you are feeling and using your rational brain to decide how you will behave. It lets you be conscious of when you are rationalizing feelings or keeping them to yourself because you are afraid of what might happen when you share them. It shifts you from putting your energy into controlling or ignoring your needs and emotions to understanding what causes your feelings and finding ways to handle fears and anxieties, anger and sadness. You also learn to tolerate your feelings so they are expressed in appropriate ways.

Extent to which I use this activity:
❏ **Always** ❏ **Mostly** ❏ **Periodically** ❏ **Rarely** ❏ **Never**

Practice: Write down feelings that you tend to struggle with expressing in a constructive fashion or even feeling. Make a note about how you deal with them (e.g., "Whenever I feel angry, I smile so that no one knows." "Whenever I feel afraid, I tell myself I'm stupid and shouldn't feel that way." "I laugh when I feel uncomfortable to hide it."). Write down what you will do instead the next time you are experiencing this emotion. _____

_____

_____

_____

_____

_____

_____

_____

_____

_____

Solve issues, not emotions: When the SA System is engaged, we separate issues or frustrated needs from what we feel about them. We are curious, we ask questions, and we negotiate to get our needs met. The SP brain, however, doesn't want to problem solve; it just wants to survive. By acknowledging our emotions, identifying the actual issue, and negotiating to get our needs met, we strengthen our SA System and get a better result for everyone involved. When our SA System is fully engaged, it decides the best way to deal with the issue. When you find yourself judging something that is happening, notice how it does little more than add fuel to the fire of your emotions. Asking questions will shift you from your reaction to understanding what is happening and doing something constructive about it.

Extent to which I use this activity:
❑ Always ❑ Mostly ❑ Periodically ❑ Rarely ❑ Never

Practice: Write down some recent examples of when you couldn't separate issues from feelings. List the feelings you were focusing on as well as the actual issue(s) (e.g., "angry, left out—I did not get to have a say in the plans"). Identify what you might do differently in the same situation next time to get at the issues (e.g., questions you might have asked, what you might have negotiated for, rephrasing what you heard to ensure it is what was meant). _____

_____

_____

_____

_____

_____

_____

_____

_____

Respond, don't react: Not all emotions, feelings, or impulses are really worth responding to. However, when we react as though they are, we can create a great deal of emotional drama without anything actually going on. When our three brains (rational, emotional, and instinctual) are working together the way they should, we ask ourselves whether we are reacting to our emotions or to the situation. Instead of letting our feelings determine our behavior, we think about what the best action is in the face of disappointments, setback, and conflict. When we are upset, we don't just lash out, burst into tears, or call everyone we know to defame the other person. Instead, we let the rational brain name what the issue is instead of making our emotions the issue.

Extent to which I use this activity:
❑ **Always** ❑ **Mostly** ❑ **Periodically** ❑ **Rarely** ❑ **Never**

Practice: Write down some of the things you usually react to that you would like respond to more effectively (e.g., "I always react when my son doesn't tell me about projects in time to get them done." "I get mad at myself when I don't tell others what I want." "I cut the other person off when I feel hurt or disappointed."). Indicate what you will do the next time to respond rather than react.

_____

_____

_____

_____

———————————————————————————

———————————————————————————

———————————————————————————

———————————————————————————

———————————————————————————

A Final Look at Where You Are Today

By three methods we may learn wisdom: First, by reflection, which is noblest; second, by imitation, which is easiest; and third by experience, which is the bitterest.

—Confucius

The purpose of this chapter was to encourage reflection—on life at home, at work or school, socially, and during leisure—to determine whether you are getting your predominant need met and the extent to which you are living in your SP System. Before moving on to chapter 15 and the next steps in the Roadmap, review your notes and consider the following questions:

- Did you skip completing any section that made you feel uncomfortable?
- Did you withhold writing down any of your thoughts or experiences?
- Did you try to tell a particular story about yourself, presenting either an overly positive or an overly negative view?
- Did you find yourself being dishonest with yourself when you answered the questions?
- Was there anything that you didn't understand or were confused about?
- Did you find yourself becoming frustrated, agitated, or judgmental with the process (e.g., did you find yourself thinking,

"This is stupid, what's the point? Can we just get on to the actions I need to take?")?

- Did you find it difficult to stay focused on doing the exercises, or were you easily distracted by your environment?
- Did you find yourself bored, disengaged, or disinterested with the activities?
- Did you find yourself discouraged or tell yourself this was too hard?

If you answered yes to any of the above, write down the fears or underlying beliefs that might have contributed to your resisting these activities as well as the impact on your behavior in this step of the Roadmap (e.g., "I avoided doing all the exercises"; "I did not write down everything that came to mind"). Getting more familiar with the way your brain resists these activities can be extremely useful, as your resistance is a part of your SP System and activated by a fear. The good news is that becoming more aware of the way you tend to resist things will make this behavior easier to spot the next time it comes up in your daily life. Remember that change is "the devil we don't know," and even when the change is something that will result in getting your needs met, your SP brain will still wave the red flag indicating a potential threat. It's up you to recognize it for what it is.

By becoming conscious of these emotionally driven, instinctual habits of mind that keep you living from your SP System, you can choose to shift to self-actualizing behaviors. By doing this, you will keep moving in the direction of your potential, seeing resistance for what it is—a barrier to becoming who you are meant to be. Resistance will fall away over time as you learn to simply acknowledge that it is there and, without judging it or focusing on it, keep doing the exercises!

Fear or Underlying Belief Triggered While Completing Step 1	Impact on My Behavior/ How I Completed the Step 1 Exercises

Thinking about the impact you noted in the chart, go back through the step 1 exercises and complete them, staying in your SA System. Once you have finished this final look at where you are today, you are ready to move on to step 2.

Chapter Fifteen
PLANNING ON BECOMING WHO YOU ARE MEANT TO BE

"Would you tell me which way I ought to go from here?" asked Alice.
"That depends a good deal on where you want to get," said the Cat.
"I really don't care where," replied Alice.
"Then it doesn't much matter which way you go," said the Cat.
                                    —Alice's Adventures in Wonderland, *Lewis Carroll*

THIS CHAPTER INCLUDES THE Who Are You Meant to Be Planner. It provides a highly effective approach to helping you articulate, stay focused on, and then achieve specific goals for your development (step 2). By following all of the exercises laid out in the Planner, you will set out a clear Roadmap for becoming who you are meant to be based on your Predominant Striving Style. It will guide you, step by step, in defining the experiences that will build your Self-Actualizing (SA) System and chart a course for fulfilling the needs of your Predominant Style in all areas of your life.

Writing down your plan, rather than just thinking about it, ensures that you will work through all the elements of the planning process, including how you will stay with your plan despite the frustration, fear, anxiety, and other emotions that may arise during the development process. It provides you with a means of checking your progress as well as for celebrating your successes along the way. Your written plan allows you to move from intention to action and ensures you shift from inactive knowing to active knowing by providing your brain with the experiences it needs to create new neural pathways and live from your SA System.

Achieving your potential requires a well-defined plan that starts from where you are now and gives you a clear Roadmap to follow based on your Predominant Style and how your brain develops. If you don't have a plan of what you are trying to accomplish and how you are going to accomplish it, you can end up expending energy in many different directions. Or, you can end up not doing anything at all.

Step 2: Chart a Course for Development
Who Are You Meant to Be Planner

He who fails to plan is planning to fail.

—*Winston Churchill*

Step 2 in the SSPS Roadmap for Development uses the Who Are You Meant to Be Planner, a comprehensive planning approach that builds on the insight you gained about your Predominant Style and your current state in step 1. The Planner is divided into four sections that engage your whole brain in the planning process as follows:

Section 1: Envision Your Desired Future
Right rational brain: *Where do you want to go? What does it look like when you get there?*

Section 2: Confront Your Fears and Underlying Beliefs
Right emotional brain: *What fears do you need to face? What underlying beliefs do you need to challenge?*

Section 3: Define Your Plan
Left rational brain: *What needs to happen for you to move to action? What barriers will you encounter?*

Section 4: Sequence Your Specific Steps

Left emotional (experiential) brain: *What are the specific steps? How are you progressing against your plan?*

The Planner will remind you which part of the brain you need to be using as you work through each section and provide tips to help you complete it based on your Predominant Style. You need to make sure your Predominant Style doesn't take over when you need to be using one of the less developed quadrants of your brain. If you just use your Predominant Style to complete your plan, you may end up with a plan that is sure to get the one need met at the expense of exercising the other functions and therefore limiting your development. For example, if you only use your Performer, you will envision your future state without setting the specific steps you need to follow to get there. You'll probably tell yourself you don't need to bother, because you are excited and you just want to get to work. Or, if you only use your Artist, you could easily get caught up in thinking about why you are afraid and lamenting the fact that you are and always have been. You think about all the times that fear has gotten in your way. By now, you are totally overwhelmed and can't possibly finish the exercise because you are too upset. You don't make your way to Leader so that you can define your course of action.

Also, check to ensure that you are responding from your SA System and not your SP System. For example, a Self-Protective Intellectual may want to skip the step of using the right emotional brain to explore his fears, insisting that there is nothing he fears. Or, a Self-Protective Stabilizer may get stuck catastrophizing all the reasons why the plan won't work or the future state can't be achieved, stopping her from sequencing the specific steps to follow.

Planner Section 1: Envision Your Desired Future State

Where do I want to go?
What does it look like when I get there?

Our brain is naturally oriented toward creating worst-case scenarios as a self-protective mechanism. However, it is capable of creating best-case and desired future states as well. Envisioning your desired future state requires you to fully engage your right rational brain (Visionary or Performer). It involves creating an idealized view of yourself, based on living in the SA System of your Predominant Style. This desired future state is meant to be a long-term view that concentrates only on the future—*what it will be like when you have become and are living who you are meant to be.*

If you try to use any of the other parts of your brain to complete this section, you are more likely to get distracted with limiting beliefs, such as "I don't deserve this," "I will never be able to achieve that," or other self-protective responses. When you start using your imagination without limitations, it's normal to be interrupted with automatic negative thoughts and feelings, especially fear and anxiety. You need to be aware when you're censoring your thoughts or ideas and not writing down what you really want. It's like having a brainstorming session with yourself in which you are just generating ideas. All ideas are welcome, and no criticizing or judging the ideas is allowed. At this stage, you want to ignore thoughts about how possible or impossible your vision seems.

To be effective, your future state must provide you not only with clear goals ("to overhaul the education system in my state by 2014") but also with a vivid description that reflects the reality of achieving them ("I will create a system in which the learning and emotional needs of children are attended to through their experience of school.

This system will take X amount of time to complete and X number of people to work with me on it…"). You need to talk about it as though it were happening now, using the present tense and describing what it looks like as well as what it feels like. Without imagining yourself in your scenario and seeing how it would feel, you are bound to your survival thinking patterns, in which nothing ever gets any better.

Tips for Completing This Section Based on Your Predominant Style:

Leader or Intellectual: Give yourself time to produce the possibilities without moving into structuring or planning how you will achieve them. Don't dismiss anything as overly emotional or too far fetched because it is not logical. You may find yourself questioning, "What is the point of this?" and miss out on your own desires and aspirations in the process.

Performer or Visionary: This will likely be an exercise that you will enjoy or that may come more easily to you. Be aware of the tendency to try to police or critique your ideas, or attempts to contain your expansive thoughts. Dreaming can seem like you've experienced it, so it's important for you to get your ideas down on paper in order to turn them into plans of action.

Socializer or Artist: Allow yourself to come up with ideas without evaluating them subjectively or judging yourself for having them. You may find that your secret dreams, desires, or ambitions may put you outside your comfort zone because they mean putting yourself first. You may be surprised that you have such ambitions at all! Don't devalue them or yourself for having them.

Stabilizer or Adventurer: Get help. Don't try to do this on your own. Be willing to listen to what others have to say without getting into a lot of "yeah, buts," and resist the temptation to dismiss anything that seems to be too far fetched, unreasonable, or frightening. This exercise is about exploring ideas, aspirations, and possibilities; it does not have to "make sense," so don't censor or edit things as you go along. Just get it all down.

Brainstorm Your Future State

Start by brainstorming elements of your desired future state by considering things you would like to change, emotional states you want to experience, possibilities you imagine, and/or dreams you have. Use the information from "Step 1—Get to Know Your Brain" (chapter 14) to help with completing this activity.

- Changes—What frustrations in your life would you like to eliminate (what do you complain about)? What self-actualizing behaviors would you like to demonstrate instead of your current self-protective behaviors? What would you do differently in the future from today? What would you do more of or less of? What new habits of mind would you establish, and what existing habits or underlying beliefs would you eliminate?

_____

_____

_____

_____

_____

_____

_____

_____

_____

- Possibilities—If there were no limits, what would be your ideal future? What possibilities can you brainstorm for yourself? What do you want for yourself? What ideas for a future different from today you can you play with? What would you do if you won the lottery? What feeling state would you live in? What might you try or experience if you believed it were possible to do so?

_____

_____

_____

_____

_____

_____

_____

_____

_____

_____

- Dreams—What ambitions or hopes do you have now for yourself that you are not pursuing? What dreams did you hold when you were younger but have since given up on? What do you most wish for in your life? What secret desires or ambitions do you hold for yourself or your life that you don't share with others but wish would come true?

_____

_____

_____

_____

_____

_____

_____

_____

_____

Set Out Your Specific Goals for Your Future

Next, take the inputs from your brainstorming and state them as specific goals to be achieved in your desired future state. Then describe what each goal looks like and feels like when you have achieved it by following the instructions below. Again, its not enough just to set the goal; you have to envision what the experience will be like and how you will feel as though it were actually happening today. Try closing your eyes and describing out loud what you see and feel if you get stuck trying to write down your descriptions. Remember to be aware of when you are censoring your thoughts or ideas and not writing down what you really want.

Here is an example from Heather's Planner:

Goal for my future. Define what you would like to achieve in your future state in all areas of your life. Your goal may be a behavior you want to demonstrate, experiences you want to have, or accomplishments you want to achieve.

To be a leader of consciousness and guide people to become who they are meant to be by speaking to audiences all over the world.

What does it look like? Using the present tense, describe exactly what it would look like—what would exist and what would not, and what you would be experiencing—so that you know when you achieve your goal.

- *Keynote speaking at least 2x/week, and teaching at least 1 day/week*
- *Traveling every other week to new cities to speak to new groups*
- *Packed houses (sold out) and standing ovations, laughter*
- *Letters from people about how it's impacted their lives*

What does it feel like? Using the present tense, describe how it will feel—all of the emotions you will and will not experience—when you achieve your goal.

- *Excitement and thrill*
- *Compassion and hope*
- *Strong, confident, and powerful*
- *Joy, love, and passion*
- *Won't feel scared, hesitant, or like I am not entitled*

Goal for my future. Define what you would like to achieve in your future state in all areas of your life. Your goal may be a behavior you want to be demonstrating, experiences you want to be having or accomplishments you want to achieve.

1.

2.

3.

4.

What does it look like? Using the present tense, describe exactly what it would look like—what would exist and what would not, and what you would be experiencing—so that you know when you achieve your goal.

1.

2.

3.

4.

What does it feel like? Using the present tense, describe how it will feel—all of the emotions you will and will not experience—when you achieve your goal.

1.

2.

3.

4.

Remember that it's okay to dream big during the brainstorming portion of the Roadmap. When setting your goals, it's important for you to be realistic. Don't get caught up in thinking that you can become something that won't satisfy your Predominant Style or is not realistic given your physical reality. For example, you may love horses, spend hours around them, and feel a burning desire to be a professional jockey. That would be a fantastic goal if you weren't 5'10" and weighed 210 pounds. Realistically, you might consider training jockeys or finding a clubs where members race. Otherwise, you set yourself up for disappointment. Like the old joke:

Patient: Doctor, will I be able to be a concert pianist after the operation?
Doctor: Yes, of course.
Patient: Fantastic. I never could before.

Planner Section 2: Face Your Fears and Underlying Beliefs

What fears do I need to face?
What underlying beliefs do I need to challenge?

In this section, you need to use your right emotional brain to uncover any fears that could be potential barriers and to acknowledge any underlying beliefs that will limit your thinking and get in the way of becoming who you are meant to be. You'll also need to figure out in advance what will help when you're experiencing these fears and beliefs so that you'll be prepared to tackle them when they threaten to hijack you in your developmental process.

Tips for Completing This Section Based on Your Predominant Style

Leader or Intellectual: This may be the most uncomfortable exercise for you, but don't dismiss your fears or deny that you have any. As difficult as it is for you to experience the feeling of fear, building tolerance for it is critical to your development as it anchors you in your body. Start by focusing on fears involving your predominant need, including loss of power, isolation, others attempting to have power over you, feeling vulnerable, feeling incompetent, and so on.

Performer or Visionary: Your natural optimism and idealism may make you want to avoid exploring fears, preferring to believe you don't have any. All this does is disconnect you from your experiential brain. Think about your predominant need and look for things that relate to loss of approval of others, not coming in first or being ahead of others, being told you can't do something, how you might be perceived by others, or how your ideas may be received by others.

Socializer or Artist: Although you can think you know what your fears are, you might have one you tell yourself about that is more tolerable than the real fear. For example, you fear and believe that you aren't loveable and have a self-protective pattern of behavior that has you always taking care of others. Like the Canadian comic Red Green used to say, "If they don't find you handsome, they find you handy." You believe you focus on and do things for others to be loved. The actual fear is to be yourself and independent. Make sure you scratch below the surface to emerge your real fear.

Stabilizer or Adventurer: Don't get stuck catastrophizing. Thinking about what you are afraid of can make you feel like it is actually happening. Also, it's one thing to feel afraid, but admitting it by putting it on paper can feel embarrassing, triggering the belief that you shouldn't be afraid. It can be helpful to think about what beliefs you might have about trying new things, making changes, or attempting to pursue your life goals.

Fears You Have to Face

There is nothing to fear but fear itself.

—*Franklin D. Roosevelt*

This quote sums up the biggest barrier that we have to living our life in the fulfillment of our potential and letting our fear define us and our experiences. We've heard this so many times over the years as we have offered people solutions to their problems. "I won't do that because it's too scary." People stop themselves from moving beyond their limitations and experiencing the pleasure of achievement because they don't want to feel discomfort. This is why emotions continue to be so dominant in our lives. We fear being out of control, abandoned, confined, or insecure. Whatever our dominant fear, we can either live with it or live for it. Living with it, we notice it's there and keep right on forging ahead. Living for it, we make our lives smaller and more limited, never putting ourselves in situations that take us out of our comfort zone. Saying yes to our fear before exploring why we are afraid, or knowing the consequences of not doing something because of the fear, is actually saying no to life and to our own potential.

Anne has always been afraid of talking in front of an audience, yet she has repeatedly said yes throughout her life to any opportunity to speak. The first time she spoke was to a group of five hundred teenagers on the emerging topic of stress in 1978. Over the years, she has appeared many times on television and radio, and frequently lectures and gives workshops. Each time she does, at the beginning of the talk her mind is calm and her body shakes like a leaf in the wind. Because she pays no attention to it, it passes.

Facing our fears is critical to the process of becoming who we are meant to be. If we put our energy into avoiding people, situations, and events that make us feel afraid, we continue to live in a self-protective fashion, missing out on our potential. By knowing the predominant fear of your Striving Style, you can face it head-on. Although you may be aware of having more than one fear, as many of us do, you will readily see that you have a cluster of fears that are associated with your predominant need and therefore more easily activated.

The following table shows the predominant fears for each Striving Style. As you complete this section of the Planner, consider these fears as well as any other fears that might be triggered through this development process.

Striving Style	Predominant Need	Predominant Fears
Leader	In control	Weak, helpless, or powerless
Intellectual	Knowledgeable	Incompetent, irrelevant, or dominated

Performer	Recognized	Humiliated, worthless, or disappointed
Visionary	Perceptive	Limited, ridiculed, or diminished
Socializer	Connected	Alone, abandoned, or devalued
Artist	Creative	Rejected, invaded, or inferior
Adventurer	Spontaneous	Confined, restricted, or imprisoned
Stabilizer	Secure	Insecure, useless, or uncertain

List all the fears that will get triggered and why, as you move toward your desired future state. Consider the key fears of your Predominant Style as well as any others you are likely to experience. You can try imagining yourself living in your desired future state and then write down any fears that surface. Or, think about how others might think about you living in this fashion and notice your reaction. Consider what will help when you experience these fears so you can be prepared to act when they are triggered.

What is my fear?	What triggers the fear?	What will help me?

Beliefs You Have to Change

Whether you believe you can do a thing or believe you can't, you are right.

—*Henry Ford*

It can be challenging for us to unearth the beliefs and assumptions that are running the dysfunctional patterns of our lives, for they are often buried in our emotional memory along with the feelings we experienced that led to the belief. If we believe we can't change, are lazy, are stupid, or will never amount to anything, well, then those things will come true. But if we become aware that our beliefs limit our day-to-day behavior and what we allow ourselves to feel and experience, as well as what we teach our children, it encourages us to dig below the surface to see what is actually at the root of our beliefs. Most of the time, beliefs about ourselves come out of our childhood and are the conclusions that our young brain drew about our experience. You need to exterminate any negative beliefs that cause you to stay in your SP System, especially when they aren't true.

A young girl is watching her mother prepare a ham for Thanksgiving. Before the mother puts the ham into the pan, she cuts about six inches off of the end of it and throws that piece away. The daughter asks the mother why she cuts the end off the ham. The mother replies, "I'm not sure, but that's how my mother did it."

So, knowing that all the family is gathered in one place, the young girl approaches her grandmother. She asks her grandmother why she cut the end off the ham before preparing it. Her grandmother replies, "I'm not sure, but that was how my mother did it."

In one final attempt, the young girl approaches her great-grandmother. She asks why she cut the end of the ham before cooking it. Her great-grandmother replies, "We only had one pan to cook with in our day. I had to cut the ham so it would fit in the only pan we had."

This story illustrates what happens when we don't question our beliefs, assumptions, and the stories we tell ourselves about why we can't achieve what we want to. However, we have the choice to use self-limiting beliefs to keep us safe or to go after our potential by facing our fears and challenging our beliefs.

List all the underlying beliefs that will get triggered and why as you move toward your desired future state. These include any assumptions you hold about yourself or your world, as well as the stories you tell yourself that keep you in your SP System. Consider what will help when you experience these underlying beliefs so you can be prepared when they are triggered.

What is my underlying belief?	What triggers the underlying belief?	What will help me?
I believe I should always take care of others first.	Thinking about saying no to a friend's request for help. Thinking about spending money on a new dress when my daughter has asked for a new pair of running shoes.	Tolerating feeling guilty when I do something for myself. Asking for the things I need and learning to feel entitled to being helped and taken care of.

Recognizing the Impact of Fears and Underlying Beliefs

If you believe that feeling bad or worrying long enough will change a past or future event, then you are residing on another planet with a different reality system.

—*William James*

While you completed section 1 of the Planner, envisioning your desired future state, your fears and underlying beliefs could have been triggered. Before you move on to the next section, make sure that they did not have a negative or limiting impact on what you wrote down for your desired future. This next activity gives you an opportunity to strengthen your SA System by building self-awareness and practicing reflection.

List all the fears and underlying beliefs that surfaced as you created your desired future state. Consider things you were saying to yourself or any fear-based emotions you experienced. Identify the impact these fears and underlying beliefs had on the picture of your desired future state, for example, "was not completely honest," "told myself it will never happen so aimed lower."

Fears and underlying beliefs triggered while envisioning my desired future state	Impact on my desired future state (what I recorded in my Planner)
I was afraid my siblings would laugh at me when I told them that I envisioned myself a thought leader.	I found myself writing that I was going to be a well-known author.

Note: You may need to revise your desired future state if your fears and beliefs diminished what you wrote. Challenge yourself to not let your fears or beliefs limit your description of your desired future state.

Planner Section 3: Define Your Plan

What needs to happen for me to move to action?
What barriers will I encounter?

In this section, you need to use your left rational brain to define how you are going to move from your current state to your desired state. This includes defining the strategies you will focus on (what) and the specific actions, experiences, or activities you will complete (how) in order to achieve your goals. You also have to identify the barriers or resistance you are likely to experience as you move to action so that you are prepared to address them. Use your notes from step 1 to complete this section, particularly those on possible actions to take to fully use your Predominant Style. This ensures the likelihood of your predominant need being met. It also identifies the activities that you need to demonstrate more frequently in order to strengthen your SA System.

Consider the following as you complete the "what" of your plan:

- **Change:** Identify ways to help get your predominant need to be met. If you can't get it met by making major changes in a specific area, for example, your job, think about what self-actualizing behaviors you might use at work instead of behaving in a self-protective fashion. Or, you can look to other areas of your life to satisfy your predominant need so that you feel more in charge of your life.

Max (Leader) had expected to get the branch manager role when his boss retired, but instead senior management brought someone in from a branch across the city. For the past several months, Max did everything he could to show management that the guy they brought in was a total loser. Max interrupted him in meetings to show how much more he knew than his boss and was always giving his opinions to coworkers about how incompetent management was because of way they made their decisions. He was convinced he knew best.

Max was blindsided when he was called in to his manager's office and told that if his attitude and behavior didn't change, he would no longer be on the management track. Waking up from his self-protective stupor, Max finally realized that he felt that his career was out of his control and he was acting out his anxiety. He knew that he needed to find a way to get his need to be in control met, and decided he could first get some control over his attitude. He volunteered to lead an office reorganization project, and at home he volunteered to coach his son's soccer team.

- **Shift:** Determine the actions you can take to stop living from your SP System and start demonstrating the self-actualizing behaviors of your Predominant Style, for example: "I will not lose my temper (self-protective) the next time my mother says she doesn't like what I am wearing, I will manage my emotions (self-actualizing), I will restate her comment and reinforce what different tastes in fashion we have, I am not a victim, and she is not attacking me."

Consider the following as you complete the "how" of your plan:

- **Experiential:** Define actual experiences you will have so that your brain can lay new neural networks, for example, "I will practice my listening and empathy skills by asking coworkers about their personal time and how they spend it." Pick activities you can repeat over and over again in order to strengthen these new pathways.
- **Simple:** Break the "what" into small, simple actions that you can start doing immediately, for example, set a time each day to practice the self-actualizing behavior. The more complex the "how," the less likely you will be to complete it.

- **Challenging:** Make sure your activities have the right amount of challenge to engage your brain without making it too hard, thereby activating your SP System. Set challenging yet realistic goals for yourself, as your brain functions optimally when it's appropriately challenged. Without enough challenge, the brain falls asleep and you will lose focus and downshift.

Consider the following as you identify the "barriers" to your plan:

- **Resistance:** Changing behavior causes resistance from the SP System in the form of anxiety, fear, embarrassment and vulnerability, and so on, which no one really wants to feel. Not understanding that behavioral change involves feelings of discomfort, and resistance derails many of our good intentions. What emotions are you likely to experience when you move to action on your plan?
- **Emotional buy-in:** As soon as you feel discomfort, you may rationalize why the change isn't that important or allow emotional self-indulgence to take the place of emotional self-management. You need to figure out how you will tolerate your emotions and use them to drive toward your goals rather than allowing them to hijack you.

Tips for Completing This Section Based on Your Predominant Style

Leader or Intellectual: Your Predominant Style possesses a natural confidence and arrogance about its abilities, so be aware of the tendency to do this entire exercise from this quadrant of the brain, and the possibility of being hijacked by the needs of your Associate Styles should you not take them into consideration (e.g., not acknowledging emotional barriers or how to handle them).

Performer or Visionary: Acknowledge any resistance you may feel to defining your plan and making it "real," noticing how it can affect your mood, and then proceed with the activity anyway. Resist the urge to think you are above "limiting" yourself by developing a plan to follow. Your brain will benefit and grow so much when you hold yourself to the planning process instead of resisting and jumping from one thing to another.

Socializer or Artist: Make sure you factor yourself in. People of these Styles can have difficulty putting themselves first for fear of being considered selfish or unhelpful. Defining your goals objectively may mean putting limits on behaviors and relationships patterns you have tolerated in your life. Push past your resistance by remembering that the changes you make will enhance the quality of all your relationships.

Adventurer or Stabilizer: Focus on identifying the overall actions and objectives that you want to achieve, knowing that you will detail the steps of how to do this in the next section. If you can't figure out the necessary action, get someone to help you. When defining actions and activities, don't simply do those that are easy or that allow you to avoid pain or discomfort.

At Home

Consider changes in the way your relationships work, how you behave with others or what you expect from other people, the role you play in your personal life, how you parent or interact with your children, and/or how you negotiate to increase the frequency with which your predominant need is met. Consider how you will shift from your SP System and/or strengthen your SA System to achieve your desired future state in your personal life.

Here is an example:

What I am going to do? Record your approach to achieving your desired future state.

Increase the extent my predominant need as a Performer gets met in my primary relationship.

How I am going to do it? List specific activities you will do or experiences you will seek to develop your brain's neural pathways.

1. *Make a list of which actions would meet my need.*
2. *Communicate to my spouse about my need to be recognized and what it looks like if he is meeting it.*
3. *Show appreciation when he does something to reinforce his behavior.*

When I am going to do it? Write down dates so you can monitor.

1. *By end of week*
2. *By end of month*
3. *Each time my need gets met*

Barriers I am likely to encounter. Identify what will get in the way and how you can address when it happens.

1. *Discomfort disclosing I have this need—acknowledge my feeling; be prepared.*
2. *Habit of saying "you shouldn't have" when someone does something; catch myself and add, "but I am glad you did"…*

What I am going to do? Record your approach to achieving your desired future state.

1.

2.

3.

How I am going to do it? List specific activities you will do or experiences you will seek to develop your brain's neural pathways.

1.

2.

3.

When I am going to do it? Write down dates so you can monitor.

1.

2.

3.

Barriers I am likely to encounter. Identify what will get in the way and how you can address when it happens.

1.

2.

3.

At Work or School

Consider changes in your current role, what you do (job) or who you do it for (company), how you interact with your boss or team, or how you negotiate for more opportunity to get your need met at work; or, if at school, what you study and how you participate, that would allow you to better get your predominant need met. Consider how you will shift from your SP System and/or strengthen your SA System to achieve your desired future state at work or at school.

Here is an example:

What I am going to do? Record your approach to achieving your desired future state.

1. *Shift my Stabilizer out of the SP System so I can get more enjoyment from work.*
2. *Practice mindfulness, and become aware of my negative self-talk.*

How I am going to do it? List specific activities you will do or experiences you will seek to develop your brain's neural pathways.

1. *Make a list at the end of each day of my wins or successes, and post them.*
2. *When people ask about work, answer with positive responses for at least thirty seconds.*
3. *With new tasks, check if they frustrate my need to be secure and figure out how to feel safe while performing them.*

When I am going to do it? Write down dates so you can monitor.

1. *Start now*
2. *Start now*
3. *Each time asked to do something*

Barriers I am likely to encounter. Identify what will get in the way and how you can address when it happens.

1. *Habit of judging myself and calling myself names as a result—say something positive when I do.*

2. *Own resistance to change—acknowledge the feeling and identify what I need.*

What I am going to do? Record your approach to achieving your desired future state.

1.

2.

3.

How I am going to do it? List specific activities you will do or experiences you will seek to develop your brain's neural pathways.

1.

2.

3.

When I am going to do it? Write down dates so you can monitor.

1.

2.

3.

Barriers I am likely to encounter. Identify what will get in the way and how you can address when it happens.

1.

2.

3.

In Social Activities

Consider changes in your social activities. Think about who you spend time with and what you do when you spend time together, what role you play with your friends, and how you interact in social settings. Think about what you might do to increase the frequency of getting your predominant need met. Consider what you can do to shift from self-protective to self-actualizing behaviors when you are with your friends and/or how you could strengthen your SA System through your social activities.

Here is an example:

What I am going to do? Record your approach to achieving your desired future state.

Use my SA Socializer so I can have more consistency and intimacy in my relationships with friends.

How I am going to do it? List specific activities you will do or experiences you will seek to develop your brain's neural pathways.

1. *Plan a social activity each week with a friend.*
2. *Share information about myself and my life with friends and family.*
3. *Ask for help when I need it.*

When I am going to do it? Write down dates so you can monitor.

1. *Start now*
2. *Every Monday*
3. *Each time I am with someone*

Barriers I am likely to encounter. Identify what will get in the way and how you can address when it happens.

1. *Discomfort with initiating social contact. I tell myself I am too busy or wait until last minute to see how I feel—have my husband remind me each Monday.*
2. *Discomfort I feel when I share personal information about myself—be prepared with things I want to share.*
3. *Embarrassed to ask for help—Ask my daughter to help with gardening.*

What I am going to do? Record your approach to achieving your desired future state.

1.

2.

3.

How I am going to do it? List specific activities you will do or experiences you will seek to develop your brain's neural pathways.

1.

2.

3.

When I am going to do it? Write down dates so you can monitor.

1.

2.

3.

Barriers I am likely to encounter. Identify what will get in the way and how you can address when it happens.

1.

2.

3.

In Leisure

Identify changes in what you do in your leisure time, such as hobbies, interests you might pursue, or volunteer roles you might take on, that would increase the opportunity for you to get your predominant need met and shift from your SP System.

Here is an example:

What I am going to do? Record your approach to achieving your desired future state.

Meet my Artist's need to be creative through the hobbies I pursue.

How I am going to do it? List specific activities you will do or experiences you will seek to develop your brain's neural pathways.

1.   *Quit activities that don't meet my need to be creative to free up time.*
2.   *Sign up for the photography lessons I have always wanted.*
3.   *Set aside a specific time each day to take pictures.*
4.   *Learn Photoshop.*

When I am going to do it? Write down dates so you can monitor.

1.   *By end of week*
2.   *By end of month*
3.   *Today 15 min.; 45 min. by end of month*

Barriers I am likely to encounter. Identify what will get in the way and how you can address when it happens.

1.   *Feelings of guilt for taking time for myself to practice and take lessons— acceptance of this feeling.*
2.   *Tell myself I am not very good so why bother—write down why I am doing it (to enjoy the art of photography, not to be good) and how it meets my need.*

What I am going to do? Record your approach to achieving your desired future state.

1.

2.

3.

How I am going to do it? List specific activities you will do or experiences you will seek to develop your brain's neural pathways.

1.

2.

3.

When I am going to do it? Write down dates so you can monitor.

1.

2.

3.

Barriers I am likely to encounter. Identify what will get in the way and how you can address when it happens.

1.

2.

3.

Planner Section 4: Sequence Your Specific Steps

What is the sequence of steps for me
to complete my action plan?
How am I progressing against my plan?

In this section, you need to use your left emotional brain to create a sequence of activities that you will do during the following month. This will help break the activities down into smaller steps so that you can then take action. The form also provides you with the ability to monitor your progress against your plan, noting your achievements, any challenges you experience, and any other reflections you have as you work through the development process. Once completed, this form must be kept somewhere that you will see it regularly to remind yourself to follow through on the specific steps and to note your progress as you go. Remember, out of sight means out of mind when we are working to break long-standing patterns of behavior.

Using your plan from section 3, write down the steps you are going to take over the next week toward completing the "what" and "how" from your plan as well as any actions to address your barriers. Support your success by balancing out how challenging the activities are with how many you list. You will need to repeat this section each week until your goal is achieved.

Tips for Completing This Section Based on Your Predominant Style

Leader or Intellectual: You may just want to move into action at this point, but you need to take the time to identify the steps that address each component of the plan in a detailed way. Resist the urge to skip planning around relationship and self-awareness activities, as having specific steps will make it easy for you to practice and strengthen the lines of communication to this part of your brain.

Performer or Visionary: Dealing with detail is not your idea of a good time, so take your time when doing it, reviewing it once it's done to see if you can think of anything you've missed. Or enlist the help of a Stabilizer to help you with the steps. While this level of detail can be an irritating activity for you, don't skip over

Weekly Planner for:

Activity from Plan	Target Date	Progress	Notes—Achievements, Challenges, or Reflections
Quit activities that don't meet my need to be creative to free up time.	*Friday*	*Completed*	*Got it done! Some easier than others; Jane was upset when I told her I wasn't going to hot yoga anymore. Made me feel guilty. Had to remind myself why I was doing it.*
When I feel guilty, tell myself I am practicing self-care, which I am entitled to.	*Daily*	*50%*	*Realized how often I feel guilty! Briefly felt compassion for myself and then felt guilty again. Need to keep monitoring and reflecting on this next week.*
1.			
2.			
3.			
4.			

it or rationalize that you don't need to do it to change, as it can prevent you from squandering your energy or giving up on your plan altogether.

Socializer or Artist: You may need some assistance with working out the details and prioritizing the activities. You may find that your fears arise around losing or alienating people, so push past those and focus on the factual steps required, whether it is you working the plan or someone else.

Adventurer or Stabilizer: This section will be relatively easy for you to complete given your talents for sequencing. Recording these activities may be an easier task for Stabilizers who love to plan and make lists. For Adventurers, this may be a little more difficult because you simply like to move into action, so be patient with the process of writing them down.

Step 3: Move to Action

The people who get on in this world are the people who get up and look for the circumstances they want and if they can't find them, make them.

—*George Bernard Shaw*

Now that you have developed your Roadmap to become who you are meant to be, it is time to move to action. Your Planner provides you with the sequence of steps to follow; however, you need to be prepared to maintain your momentum and avoid getting derailed at this step in the Roadmap. When establishing a new behavior pattern, the challenge arises because the existing pattern is physiological and the result of decades of reinforcement. This is why you can't expect to read a book and change your brain, or go to a workshop and think that because you gained insight into why you do something, you'll automatically be able to change it.

You need to prepare yourself to succeed. In this final step in the Roadmap, the focus is on supporting your success by managing your expectations of what you will experience, getting the support you require, and monitoring your progress so you can celebrate your wins. The activities in this step of the Roadmap ensure you are ready to move into action and are prepared to stay the course despite the resistance and setbacks you will naturally experience.

Prepare Yourself to Succeed

I don't sing because I'm happy; I'm happy because I sing.

—*William James*

Before you even get started on the execution of your Planner, you need to know what to expect as you take action to develop and shift from your Self-Protective System in order to achieve your potential and become who you are meant to be.

Expect to struggle. Most people give up after they experience frustration when their new behavior doesn't get the results they expected or doesn't happen as quickly as they thought it would. It's just easier to give up and give in to the existing pattern than to keep struggling. Then you can phone a friend and talk about what a hard time you are having so that you can get some sympathy. Perhaps your friend will tell you not to bother because it's too hard and let you off the hook. But that's not really what you want; it's just a habit. Many still hope that an epiphany will bring substantial change, but the truth is that stepping out of our comfort zone means that we are going to be uncomfortable. In other words, you can expect to experience feelings that will trigger your SP System, so just keep on working the new pattern anyway. Don't pick up the phone and complain! You have to truly accept and believe that if you want to change your behavior, you have to change your brain. Repetition and reinforcement are the only ways to do this, so expect to struggle and recognize when you are so that you resist the impulse to simply give up on your plan.

Complaining adults are the same as whining children. Both expect someone else to kiss the boo-boo and take care of them.

—*Anne Dranitsaris*

Know what you have to give up. Our brains are not supposed to stay stagnant and are actually predisposed to change and develop. By becoming self-aware and making our beliefs and patterns of behavior conscious, we can change automatic thoughts and reactions. New experiences create neural pathways that override the ones that were created by past experiences. However, we develop them only when we stop doing what we have always done and do something else. If we don't give up the security of keeping things the same, we can't build something new. If you want to be a kinder, more compassionate person, you have to give up bad-mouthing your ex. If you want to be an effective leader, you have to give up being "one of the boys." You can't get what you are striving for without giving something up. That something, in most cases, is an outdated belief or habit of mind or behavior that is no longer serving you. Be sure you know what you have to give up and notice when you are resisting doing so.

Be prepared for what you will feel and experience. Behavioral change is possible no matter what age you are. But it's not as easy as thinking you will do something different or changing a habit. Anyone who has tried to create a new routine—exercise, healthy eating, not yelling at his or her children—will attest to this. The intention is there, but the old pattern of behavior is still wired into the brain, so we just keep doing what we have always done in the past. Our emotional brain reflexively causes us to behave in ways that we sometimes can't believe ourselves. We observe ourselves acting the way we were determined not to and feel helpless that we can't do anything about it. The brain is simply wired to respond a certain way once psychological equilibrium has been set.

As much as a person will say that he or she loves change or exploring new things, the reality is that those things are probably not within the person's comfort zone. For example, Adventurers may love new activities that give them the sought-after rush of sensation, but suggest a team-building session in which they can share their feelings, and they head for the hills! Socializers may love to travel to a country that others wouldn't dream of, but suggest that they go to a silent meditation retreat and it brings their anxiety levels through the roof. Each of the Styles has a different fear that is activated when the person with that Style has to change or develop his or her brain. When we know what to expect, it makes it easier to trust the process and tolerate the emotions that naturally arise during the process.

Stay the Course

We are what we repeatedly do. Excellence, then, is not an act, but a habit.

—*Aristotle*

As you move to action, there are certain disciplines and new habits of thinking that will support your success no matter what plan you set out in your Planner. You need to consider how you will integrate each of these habits into your way of being as you execute your plan. It's not enough to merely have the idea of doing something; you must commit to exactly how you will make each of these become a habit in order to support your ability to stay the course through the process of becoming who you are meant to be. It's like the bumpers they put in the gutters in bowling alleys. Even when your ball goes off course and hits the side, you know that it is still likely to hit a few pins. Make sure that you have your bumpers or boundaries in place to keep you on the straight and narrow.

Practice, practice, practice. It takes determination, discipline, and a lot of regular practice to change your brain over time. Sports analogies help us see the amount of practice that goes into developing a new physical skill and give us an idea of the work that we must commit to, but the development of our brain, self-care, and relationship skills are much more complex than sports skills and take longer to wire into the brain. Think about how long it takes a baby to walk or how long it took you to learn to swim. You have to be prepared to dedicate yourself to your own development, in the same way your mother or primary caretaker dedicated him- or herself to your care while growing up. And if that person didn't set a good example for you, it's time to move beyond where he or she left off and challenge yourself to do it differently.

Tiger Woods and others who have achieved great success as a professional athlete are examples of what it takes to change neural patterns. Tiger, following a less-than-stellar year in 2004, decided to make some changes to his swing because he wasn't having the experience he desired. He worked for an entire year before the new patterns kicked in, substantially improving his game and ultimately winning two postseason tournaments back-to-back. In 2005 he won his fourth Masters, placed second in the U.S. Open, and won the British Open. He finished the year with six victories, ranking first in the world and winning about $10 million in tournaments alone. His need to experience the perfect swing and to be the best golfer in the world fueled his disciplined approach. He was willing to invest the time, effort, and money into becoming who he was meant to be: a world-class golfer.

New habit: *Write down how you will ensure you get the time you need to execute your plan and practice in order to establish new neural pathways in your* *brain (e.g., "Every Sunday, I will block time in my calendar for the week. I will get up before the kids each day so I have the time.").*

_____

_____

_____

_____

_____

Monitor your progress. It is not enough just to set the plan. You have to follow it, consistently monitoring your progress against the plan, reflecting on what is going well and where you are struggling or avoiding moving to action. At the end of each month, you will need to reset your monthly plan, acknowledging your accomplishments and identifying new actions or experiences to keep you moving forward to become who you are meant to be.

New habit: Identify how you will monitor your progress against your plan—how, when, and where. What will you do to flag if you are falling off track so you can adjust your plan, rather than abandon it? (E.g., "I will review it each Sunday morning, and will complete that day anything missed from the prior week.")

_____

_____

_____

_____

_____

Talk about your successes. Pleasurable experiences are stored in our working memory in the rational brain. For them to register, you actually have to experience them and hold them in your conscious awareness for at least ten to twenty seconds. To the brain, if you have a pleasant experience and just move on, it's like it never happened. The brain is wired to throw up painful or "negative" emotional memories faster and with greater frequency, which is why people complain more than they talk about their successes and joys. Refocusing the brain on pleasurable experience requires slowing yourself down and taking the time to share your experiences with others so you can build confidence, self-esteem, and optimism. It also requires you to discard that old belief that talking about your achievements is "bragging" or "blowing your horn."

New habit: Write down how you will talk about your successes and other pleasurable experiences with others (and yourself), rather than complaining (e.g., "If I have something negative I want to share, I have to share a success or pleasurable experience before and after.").

_____

_____

_____

_____

_____

Create a positive-focus activity. Another thing you can do is to develop a positive-focus activity. Our family has one called "The Best Part of the Day." It is often driven by our children, who want to recount the fun things that they have done. We go around the table and everyone says what he or she has enjoyed and why. At work, we start our weekly planning meeting with the "wins, achievements, and things that made us feel proud." Making this conscious effort allows us to get excited about what we are doing and to share the experience with others.

New habit: Identify what positive-focus activities you can do in your life to regularly reflect on the things that are bringing you enjoyment and a sense of pride (e.g., "I will create a "wins" board in my kitchen where I can write down throughout the week all of my wins.").

_____

_____

_____

_____

_____

Leverage Relationships

Our brains are especially open to change through relationships. Current brain research has demonstrated that the brain is a relationship organ and that our interactions with others are critical to changing our brain. Relationships provide us with the opportunity to meet our predominant need as well as develop our SA System. They have the capacity to enrich our lives, deepen our self-awareness, and provide us with the love, recognition, and support we need. You need to define how you will leverage relationships in order to support your success.

Don't do it alone. You can't develop in a vacuum, nor can you develop when you are trying to prevent everyone from seeing what you feel is wrong with you. Development won't happen as long as it is an intellectual exercise. You have to get past the discomfort of letting others in on your plans so that they can support you.

New habit: Identify the people in your life you will share your plans with and engage their help as well as the specific type of help you would like from them (e.g., "My sister—help me to stop complaining about my ex by letting me know when I am and asking me something that helps change the subject.").

_____

_____

_____

_____

Seek professional help. Coaching, counseling, psychotherapy, or cognitive behavioral therapy are all approaches that provide a safe, nonjudgmental environment for building self-awareness and getting in touch with your emotions. These professionals help support our emotional and mental health in the same way that a chiropractor supports the health of our spine. This type of support can help you to identify and eliminate automatic negative thinking and patterns of behavior that get in your way. The purpose is to leverage the help of others so you can become more aware of your thoughts and feelings and be supported to live more authentically. Think about seeking professional help to help you build self-awareness or to guide you to achieve the more challenging parts of your plan. Our rule of thumb is, if you need help, ask for it.

New habit: Define your support system by considering what other resources you might need based on the development goals of your Planner. Determine how you will access them. For example, if a career change is included, then a career counselor or some type of career workshop might be needed for you to move forward on this aspect of your plan, especially if you are unsure how to do so on your own. Ask friends if they can recommend someone.

_____

_____

_____

_____

_____

Prepare for the resistance of others. Be prepared to deal with other's feelings and judgments about what you are doing, as it is part of the process. Sometimes we expect others to be as excited as we are about making changes and are deflated when someone is critical instead. As much as they love you, friends and family don't always like it when you start to change. Prepare yourself for criticism, skepticism, or even blatant sabotage. You may have to help others adjust to your new way of being and lifestyle, and let go of those who can't. Most important, don't let anyone talk you out of doing what you know in your heart is the right thing for you.

New habit: Identify the people in your life who may resist your efforts to become the person you are meant to be. Write down how they are likely to behave—what they might say or do—and how you will respond when these situations arise (e.g., "My husband is likely to tell me I am great the way I am. I will thank him and tell him I am doing this for me.").

_____

_____

_____

_____

_____

A Final Look at Your Planner

No horse gets anywhere until he is harnessed. No stream or gas drives anything until it is confined. No Niagara is ever turned into light and power until it is tunneled. No life ever grows great until it is focused, dedicated, disciplined.

—*Harry Emerson Fosdick*

The purpose of this chapter was to chart your Roadmap for becoming who you are meant to be based on your Predominant Striving Style. This Roadmap is intended to set out your desired future state, engage you to face your fears and underlying beliefs, and define your plan of action as well as the specific steps you will take. Before moving on, review your Planner and consider the following questions:

Did you complete all the sections including those that made you feel uncomfortable?

- Were you completely honest with yourself?
- Is it clear what you will do, when you will do it, and how you will support your success as barriers arise, including your own natural resistance?

- Are you ready to move to action by creating the experiences you need to get your predominant need met and strengthen your SA System?

If you answered no to any of these questions, reflect on what fears, underlying beliefs, or patterns of behavior may be at play for you. Identify things you can do or support that you can access to help you to fully complete your Planner and prepare to move to action. Go back through your Planner and make the necessary changes, noting when your resistance surfaces and simply acknowledging it without judgment. Then finish the work necessary on your Planner.

If you answered yes to all of these questions, **congratulations!** You are ready to start your journey to becoming who you are meant to be. It's time to move to action following the steps set out in your Planner.

Conclusion
THE END OF THE BEGINNING

Your time is limited, so don't waste it living someone else's life. Don't be trapped by dogma—which is living with the results of other people's thinking. Don't let the noise of others' opinions drown out your own inner voice. And most important, have the courage to follow your heart and intuition.

—*Steve Jobs*

WHO ARE YOU MEANT to Be? provides an introduction to the process of achieving your potential. As we conclude the book, we want to congratulate you for taking this step for living life as your best self. Every day we show up in our lives and we have the ability to generate the experiences we want to have; to feel the joy of being alive, loving, and loved; to be the authors of our own lives and to authentically express ourselves as we go about doing this. This journey really begins with your commitment to yourself, as who you are meant to be. You won't achieve your potential just by reading this book, but by spending time with it, going through the exercises, and waking up daily and thinking about what you want to experience, whose lives you want to touch, and what you want to create. The daily practice of reflection, exercising the brain, and living life as your best self is truly a worthwhile experience, and over time it will ensure that you will no longer find yourself living in survival but instead moving steadily along the path toward actualizing your potential.

For some people, the best they can do in life is just survive. But for most, the capacity for self-actualization is already available to us—we just need to learn how to access it. We have a choice as to whether or not we live our lives feeling at the mercy of situations and people. We can say no to adventure, challenges, and new experiences for fear it will cost us our security, or we can say yes. Having the courage to meet our needs, to grow, develop, and prosper—to be the person we are meant to be—may mean that we live our lives without a safety net.

The SSPS offers you the opportunity to become self-aware and to develop a faster, smarter brain. There is no time like the present to learn to help your brain become more efficient and to develop more advanced skills. Even though we can damage our brain and its cells through neurotoxins caused by drugs, alcohol, and environmental pollutants, if we continue to use it, we won't lose it. Brain connections that are stimulated and used repeatedly grow stronger, whereas unused connections wither away. The more time we spend giving ourselves new and challenging activities and experiences, the more the capacity of our brain is increased.

Reading this book and completing your Roadmap to becoming who you are meant to be is really just the end of the beginning of your journey toward your conscious life. We are excited about the books to come, including those on the following:

- **Relationships.** This book will be for everyone who wants to create a fulfilling relationship. It will show how use a need satisfaction approach to living and working with, and loving, others.
- **Careers.** This book will be for people wanting to chose a career that is most likely to satisfy their needs. It will demonstrate the work environment and the need satisfiers and dissatisfiers that will influence how they feel about themselves at work.
- **Parents.** This book will help people parent consciously, aware of the impact of their Striving Style on their children and of

what their needs are, so that they can raise them to know their brains and the biology of their best self. It will also give insight into why children frustrate their parents needs just by being themselves and how parents can get their needs met despite this.

- **Children.** This book will teach children the mechanics of their mind and their personality. It will help them learn about their behavior and how they behave when they are trying to get their predominant need met. It will help them understand how their brains are organized, what their needs are, and what their behavior means.

- **Educators.** This book will be for educators who want to teach students consciously. It will help educators become aware of the different learning needs of their students and how to teach to all four quadrants of the brain. It also will show how individual Striving Styles influence how teachers manage their classrooms and the need that they must have met to be fulfilled in their roles.

- **Leaders.** This book will identify how the different Striving Styles lead others. It helps people lead authentically from their Style. It also shows them how they are most likely to organize their teams and employees to achieve their potential and that of the organization.

Don't Stop Here!

This book is just the first milestone on the road to becoming who you are meant to be. Learning about your Predominant Style and charting your course for shifting from your Self-Protective System is only the beginning. There is much more you can learn about your Predominant Style to support your development. To fully achieve your potential, you must learn how to engage the other quadrants of your brain, your Associate Styles, in all aspects of your life. Our site, www.whoareyoumeanttobe.com, provides you with all the resources you need to keep moving along the road to living consistently from your Self-Actualizing System.

Deepen Your Understanding of Your Predominant Style

While this book has provided you with a general introduction to your Predominant Striving Style, including its self-protective and self-actualizing behaviors, more resources are available. Learn about the developmental priorities of your Predominant Style to help you with your planner. Find out how you get your predominant need met in all aspects of your life, including relationships, parenting, career, work, leadership, and learning.

Leverage Your Striving Style Squad

As you learned in chapter 2, you have access to the talents and abilities of three Associate Styles that, together with your Predominant Style, make up your Striving Style Squad. When you incorporate the unique abilities and talents of your whole brain in your life, a powerful new way of experiencing yourself will open up for you, a self that is creative, versatile, resilient, and multifaceted. You will likely discover new talents that you never knew you had. This process starts by understanding how to use all four of the Striving Styles on your Squad and by not limiting yourself to using only a portion of your capacity.

Take the full SSPS assessment, available at www.whoareyou meanttobe.com, to discover the four Styles in your Squad as well as the extent to which you are using each of the four quadrants of your brain. Use the information in this book to better understand each of your Associate Styles as well as how to fully leverage your Squad to achieve your potential. Download the *SSPS Development Workbook* and complete the activities related to leveraging your Squad.

Get in the Driver's Seat

The SSPS accelerates the process of becoming conscious by helping you understand the mechanics of your mind. Self-awareness begins when you realize that you have an authentic self that defines, understands, relates, and experiences. This self has the potential for growth, happiness, fulfilling relationships, realization of talents, and more. Knowing that you—your self—are different from your Predominant Style and Associate Styles puts you in the driver's seat and allows you to develop the capacity to lead and manage all of the members of your Striving Style Squad.

Complete the full SSPS Roadmap for Development set out on our website, which provides you with additional learning resources to build your foundation for living from your Self-Actualizing System and guides your further development according to our five building blocks for achieving potential. From our website, you can also access support from an SSPS practitioner or from our live webinars, so that you can stay the course, change your brain, and achieve your goals.

Get Out of Your Own Way!

The great end of education is to discipline rather than to furnish the mind; to train it to the use of its own powers, rather than fill it with the accumulation of others.

—*Tyron Edwards*

You're never too old to become the person you were meant to be and get back onto the track you detoured from many years ago. However, as adults, learning to think and behave differently tends to activate our Self-Protective System. We are afraid of making mistakes, feeling embarrassed, failing, or being judged or disapproved of. To become who you are meant to be, you need to get out of your own way.

You can't just decide to be different without working at it. You have to expect things to be hard. You have to act the part before it becomes natural to you. This is the part that trips up most people because it doesn't feel natural in the beginning. Prepare to feel anxious, embarrassed, and uncomfortable as you try new behaviors. You may feel discomfort, but accept it and don't give up. Learn to stop paying so much attention to the feelings that hijack you so that you can focus on what you are trying to achieve.

A Final Thought

If you take only one thing from this book, let it be this: As humans we are meant to develop from the inside out. However, most of us have been conditioned to develop from the outside in. Take some time to look inside and don't hurry the process. The potential inside of you that you've been denying, the needs that have been frustrated, and the desired life that you have been too cautious or afraid to live are there for you to embrace, nurture, and fulfill.

And the great news is that the power is ours. Any one of us can become who we are meant to be.

ACKNOWLEDGMENTS

We wrote this book about people, for people, and we couldn't have done this without our collective experiences. We are grateful for everything we have learned from our spouses, Blake Taylor and Jeff Hollefriend; our children and grandchildren, Ben, Emma, and Paige; and our extended family and friends. In particular, we are indebted to those who joined us in our petri dish over the past five years (as though they had any choice) while we tested our theories and development strategies and who continue to allow their lives to be turned into examples for our books and anecdotes for our seminars.

We are grateful to all of those people who stood beside us, believing in what we were doing and helping us with their time and their caring. To friends Melanie Faye Reeve and Stephen van Beek, for their curious minds and generous feedback. To Thom Boehlert, Tim Baker, Bonnie Mah, and Kirk Fernandes for backing us financially from day 1. To clients who used the Striving Styles with their employees and their families, just because they believed in us.

We would like to thank the editors and writers who contributed to the proposal for the book: Jill Stern, Jacob Moore, and Katrin Schumann. Their work helped give shape to the organization of the book. A special thanks to Bonnie Lynch, whose use of humor and ability to convert our writing into everyday language has made reading this book a more pleasurable experience. To our literary agent extraordinaire, Jennifer Gates, whose belief in the importance of the book and the insistence of "just having one more set of eyes on it" brought the best out in our work. And finally, deep gratitude to Shana Drehs and our publisher, Sourcebooks, for seeing our potential and taking a chance on us.

Thanks to all of the brilliant minds who did the research and psychometric legwork for us, people such as Carl Jung, Katherine Benziger, Ned Hermann, Jaak Panskepp, Abraham Maslow, and Paul MacLean, whose theories and research provided us with everything we needed to create the Striving Styles Personality System. In addition, we want to thank people like Wayne Dyer, Daniel Goleman, Daniel Siegel, and Jon Kabat-Zinn, who are at the forefront of living life with consciousness. Their work has inspired us, and we continue to follow and grow from it, both personally and professionally.

We would also like to acknowledge Oprah Winfrey and her editorial team, who chose to feature our work on the Striving Styles in *"O", The Oprah Magazine* in November 2009 and who continue to use our materials in Oprah's Life Classes. Oprah's commitment to helping people to be their best self and become who they are meant to be parallels ours. We are honored to have her use the Striving Styles in her work as a leader of consciousness.

And we have saved the biggest thank-you until last! Our most heartfelt gratitude to our sister and aunt, Nancy Dranitsaris, who has worked with us on the Striving Styles since its inception. Her deep and abiding commitment to the SSPS and her contributions through writing and editing, as well as training and coaching with the Striving Styles, have been invaluable to us.

BIBLIOGRAPHY

Ainsworth, Mary D. Salter, Mary C. Blehar, Everett Waters, and Sally Wall. *Patterns of Attachment: A Psychological Study of the Strange Situation.* Hillsdale, NJ: Lawrence Erlbaum Associates, 1978.

Amen, Daniel G., MD. *The Brain and Behavior.* Newport Beach, CA: Mind Works Press, 2005.

Amen, Daniel G., MD. *Making a Good Brain Great.* New York: Three Rivers Press, 2005.

Badendoch, Bonnie. *The Brain-Savvy Therapists Workbook.* New York: W. W. Norton and Company, 2011.

Bar-On, Reuven, and James D. A. Parker. *The Handbook of Emotional Intelligence: Theory, Development, Assessment and Application.* San Francisco, CA: Jossey-Bass, 2000.

Beck, Aaron T., MD. *Cognitive Therapy and the Emotional Disorders.* New York: Penguin Group, 1979.

Beck, Aaron T., MD, and Brad A. Alford, PhD. *Depression: Causes and Treatment,* 2nd ed. Philadelphia: University of Pennsylvania Press, 1972.

Beck, Aaron T., MD, A. John Rush, Brian F. Shaw, and Gary Emery. *Cognitive Therapy of Depression: The Guilford Clinical Psychology and Psychopathologies Series.* New York: Guilford Press, 1979.

Benziger, Katherine, PhD, and Anne Sohn. *The Art of Using Your Whole Brain.* Rockwell, TX: KBA Publishing, 1989.

Benziger, Katherine. *Thriving in Mind: The Art & Science of Using Your Whole Brain,* rev. ed. Carbondale, IL: KBA/LLC Publishing, 2000.

Bowlby, John, MD. *A Secure Base: Parent-Child Attachment and Healthy Human Development*. New York: Basic Books, 1988.

Bowlby, John, MD. *Attachment*, 2nd ed. New York: Basic Books, 1982.

Bowlby, John, MD. *Separation: Anxiety and Anger*. New York: Basic Books, 1973.

Burns, David D., MD. *Feeling Good: The New Mood Therapy*, rev. ed. New York: William Morrow and Company, 1999.

Burns, David D., MD. *The Feeling Good Handbook*. New York: Plume, 1989.

Carter, Rita, Susan Aldridge, Martyn Page, and Steve Parker. *The Human Brain Book: An Illustrated Guide to Its Structure, Function and Disorders*. New York: DK Books, 2009.

Damasio, Antonio. *Self Comes to Mind: Constructing the Conscious Brain*. New York: Pantheon Books, 2010.

Doige, Norman. *The Brain That Changes Itself: Stories of Personal Triumph from the Frontiers of Brain Science*. New York: Penguin Books, 2007.

Dranitsaris, Anne, PhD. *Jung's Typology for the Workplace: Personality and Employee Behavior*. Toronto: Dranitsaris Consulting Services, 2009.

Dranitsaris, Anne, PhD. *Jung's Typology for the Workplace: Personality Type and Leadership Behavior*. Toronto: Dranitsaris Consulting Services, 2009.

Dranitsaris, Anne, PhD. *Jung's Typology for the Workplace: Personality Type and Teamwork*. Toronto: Dranitsaris Consulting Services, 2009.

Dranitsaris, Anne, PhD. *Personality Profile for the ENFJ*, rev. ed. Toronto: Dranitsaris Consulting Services, 2000.

Dranitsaris, Anne, PhD. *Personality Profile for the ENFP*, rev. ed. Toronto: Dranitsaris Consulting Services, 2000.

Dranitsaris, Anne, PhD. *Personality Profile for the ENTJ*, rev. ed. Toronto: Dranitsaris Consulting Services, 2000.

Dranitsaris, Anne, PhD. *Personality Profile for the ENTP*, rev. ed. Toronto: Dranitsaris Consulting Services, 2000.

Dranitsaris, Anne, PhD. *Personality Profile for the ESFJ*, rev. ed. Toronto: Dranitsaris Consulting Services, 2000.

Dranitsaris, Anne, PhD. *Personality Profile for the ESFP*, rev. ed. Toronto: Dranitsaris Consulting Services, 2000.

Dranitsaris, Anne, PhD. *Personality Profile for the ESTJ*, rev. ed. Toronto: Dranitsaris Consulting Services, 2000.

Dranitsaris, Anne, PhD. *Personality Profile for the ESTP*, rev. ed. Toronto: Dranitsaris Consulting Services, 2000.

Dranitsaris, Anne, PhD. *Personality Profile for the INFJ*, rev. ed. Toronto: Dranitsaris Consulting Services, 2000.

Dranitsaris, Anne, PhD. *Personality Profile for the INFP*, rev. ed. Toronto: Dranitsaris Consulting Services, 2000.

Dranitsaris, Anne, PhD. *Personality Profile for the INTJ*, rev. ed. Toronto: Dranitsaris Consulting Services, 2000.

Dranitsaris, Anne, PhD. *Personality Profile for the INTP*, rev. ed. Toronto: Dranitsaris Consulting Services, 2000.

Dranitsaris, Anne, PhD. *Personality Profile for the ISFJ*, rev. ed. Toronto: Dranitsaris Consulting Services, 2000.

Dranitsaris, Anne, PhD. *Personality Profile for the ISFP*, rev. ed. Toronto: Dranitsaris Consulting Services, 2000.

Dranitsaris, Anne, PhD. *Personality Profile for the ISTJ*, rev. ed. Toronto: Dranitsaris Consulting Services, 2000.

Dranitsaris, Anne, PhD. *Personality Profile for the ISTP*, rev. ed. Toronto: Dranitsaris Consulting Services, 2000.

Eccles, John, Sir, and R. W. Sperry, eds. *Bridging Science and Values: A Unifying View of Mind and Brain: The Many-Faceted Problem.* New York: Paragon Publishers, 1985.

Eliot, Lise, PhD. *What's Going On in There? How the Brain and Mind Develop in the First Five Years of Life.* New York: Bantam Books, 1999.

Gardner, Russell, and Gerald A. Cory Jr., eds. *The Evolutionary Neuroethology of Paul MacLean: Convergences and Frontiers.* Westport, CT: Praeger Publishers, 2002.

Goleman, Daniel. *Emotional Intelligence: Why It Can Matter More Than IQ.* New York: Bantam Dell, 1995.

Goleman, Daniel. *Social Intelligence: The New Science of Human Relationships.* New York: Bantam Dell, 2006.

Greensberger, Dennis, PhD, and Christine A. Padesky, PhD. *Mind Over Mood: Change How You Feel by Changing the Way You Think.* New York: Guilford Press, 1995.

Hansen, Rick, PhD, and Richard Mendius, MD. *Buddha's Brain.* Oakland, CA: New Harbinger Publications, 2009.

Hermann, Ned. *The Creative Brain.* Lake Lure, NC: Brain Books/ Atlantic Books, 1989.

Jacobi, Jolande. *Complex/Archetype/Symbol in the Psychology of C. G. Jung.* Translated by Ralph Manheim. Princeton, NJ: Princeton University Press, 1971.

Kabat-Zinn, Jon, PhD. *Coming to Our Senses: Healing Ourselves and the World Through Mindfulness.* New York: Hyperion Books, 2005.

Kabat-Zinn, Jon, PhD. *Full Catastrophe Living: Using the Wisdom of Your Body and Mind to Face Stress, Pain, and Illness,* 15th anniversary ed. New York: Bantam Dell, 2006.

Lawrence, Paul R., and Nohria Nitin. *Driven: How Human Nature Shapes Our Choices.* San Francisco, CA: Jossey-Bass, 2002.

Le Doux, Joseph. *The Emotional Brain: The Mysterious Underpinnings of Emotional Life.* New York: Touchstone Books, 1996.

Maclean, Paul D. *A Triune Concept of the Brain and Behavior* (published for the Ontario Mental Health Foundation). Toronto: University of Toronto Press, 1973.

Maslow, Abraham H. *Maslow on Management.* New York: Wiley, 1998.

Maslow, Abraham H. *Motivation and Personality,* 3rd ed. New York: Addison-Wesley, 1987.

Maslow, Abraham H. *Towards a Psychology of Being*, 3rd ed. New York: John Wiley & Sons Inc., 1999.

Masterson, James F., MD. *Disorders of the Self: New Therapeutic Horizons: The Masterson Approach*. Levittown, PA: Brunnel/Mazel Inc., 1995.

Masterson, James F., MD, et al., eds. *The Personality Disorders through the Lens of Attachment Theory and the Neurobiological Development of the Self: A Clinical Integration*. Pheonix, AZ: Zeig, Tucker & Theisen Inc., 2005.

Maultsby, Maxie C., Jr., MD. *Help Your Happiness: Through Rational Self-Counseling*. New York: Institute for Rational-Emotive Therapy, 1975.

Maultsby, Maxie C., Jr., MD. *Rational Behavior Therapy*. Appleton, WI: Rational Self-Help Aids/I'ACT, 1990.

Maultsby, Maxie C., Jr., MD, and Kathryn L. Burns (illustrator). *Coping Better...Anytime, Anywhere: The Handbook of Rational Self-Counseling*. Alexandra, WA: RBT Centre LLC, 1986.

Murray, Henry. *Explorations in Personality*, 70th anniversary ed. New York: Oxford University Press, 2008.

Panksepp, Jaak. *Affective Neuroscience: The Foundations of Human and Animal Emotions*. New York: Oxford University Press, 1998.

Pascual Leone, Alvaro, Pascual-Leone A, Nguyet D, Cohen LG, Brasil-Neto JP, Cammarota A, Hallett M. *Modulation of Muscle Responses Evoked by Transcranial Magnetic Stimulation during the Acquisition of New Fine Motor Skills*. Boston: Harvard University, 1995.

Pascual Leone, Alvaro. "The Plastic Human Brain Cortex." *Annual Review of Neuroscience* 28, no. 1 (2005): 377–401.

Read, Herbert, Sir, Michael Fordham, Gerhard Adler, and William McGuire, eds. *Jung, C.G. Psychological Types: The Collective Works of C.G. Jung*, Volume 6. Princeton, NJ: Princeton University Press, 1971.

Sperry, R. W. "Lateral Specialization in the Surgically Separated

Hemispheres." *Neurosciences Third Study Program*, Ch. I, Vol. 3, pp. 5–19. Cambridge: MIT Press, 1974.

Schwarz, Jeffrey M., MD, and Sharon Begley. *The Mind and the Brain: Neuroplasticity and the Power of Mental Force.* New York: ReganBooks, 2002.

Siegel, Daniel J., MD. *Mindsight: The New Science of Personal Transformation.* New York: Bantam Books, 2010.

Siegel, Daniel J., MD. *The Mindful Brain.* New York: W. W. Norton and Company, 2007.

Siegel, Daniel J., MD. *The Mindful Brain: The Neurobiology of Well-Being* (audio). New York: Sounds True, 2008.

Siegel, Daniel J., MD. *The Developing Mind: Toward a Neurobiology of Interpersonal Experience.* New York: Guilford Press, 1999.

Sperry, R. W. "Cerebral Organization and Behavior: The Split Brain Behaves in Many Respects Like Two Separate Brains, Providing New Research Possibilities." *Science* 133, no. 3466 (1961): 1749–1757.

Thompson, Henry L., PhD. *Jung's Functions—Attitudes Explained.* Watkinsville, GA: Wormhole Publishing, 1996.

INDEX

ABOUT THE AUTHORS

Anne Dranitsaris and Heather Dranitsaris-Hilliard coauthored *Who Are You Meant to Be?* as a result of their sixteen-year business collaboration. It was also greatly influenced by their personal journey together. Anne gave up Heather at birth for adoption and did not see her again until their reunion when Heather was twenty-seven years old. As they began to forge their relationship, they both recognized how much they had in common despite their separation. They both had a desire to help people achieve their potential and were doing it in different careers. This led to them starting a business together working with their own business model, shortly after their reunion.

Anne Dranitsaris, PhD (Visionary)

Anne Dranitsaris, PhD, brings a lifetime of study, "psychological savvy," and hands-on clinical experience to helping people become who they are meant to be. Her interest in creating mental health, coupled with her interest in personality systems and the dynamics of human behavior, has influenced the development of the Striving Styles Personality System.

Anne has always followed her intuition about education and didn't go the traditional path to a PhD. She has attended a wide range of eclectic learning establishments where participation and experience were both part of the curriculum and aligned with her passion. At the same time, she studied at mainstream universities such as Ryerson (business management), University of Toronto (mindfulness-based stress reduction, religious studies), and ADR Institute of Ontario (alternative dispute resolution). Anne looked for training institutes that would help her integrate the cognitive, emotional, and physical approaches to healing the mind and body. This education included receiving her degree as a registered massage therapist; graduating from the International School for Spiritual Sciences (Montreal); earning a psychotherapy certification from the Centre for Training in Psychotherapy (DipCTP); undertaking studies at the Masterson Institute for Disorders of the Self (New York); and earning a PhD in therapeutic counseling from the Open International University for Complementary Medicine (WHO).

Committed to lifelong learning, Anne has completed postgraduate programs in cognitive-behavioral therapy, spiritual self-schema development, and brain and behavior and emotional intelligence (EQ-i), and she has been a longtime follower of the work of Carl Jung. Anne continues to stay educated and informed through her own research about recent advances in neuroplasticity, brain development, mindfulness, and social intelligence.

A serial entrepreneur, Anne has started several businesses of her own, including the Annex Natural Health Clinic, Dranitsaris Consulting Services, Sage Developmental Resources, and the Centre for Mindful Therapies. She was also instrumental in two business start-ups, Figure & Face and Seroyal International. Anne was one of Toronto's first executive coaches in the late 1980s. She could see the direct application of the therapeutic tools to the corporate world, which drove her to expand her work into that realm. Anne began using the title of corporate therapist to indicate the depth with which she worked with leaders and teams developing emotional intelligence, behavioral competence, and relationship skills in organizations. She has also used her unique approach to work through dysfunctional relationships, partnerships, teams, and boards.

She is a prolific and frequently cited writer on a broad range of topics on organizational dysfunction, behavior, emotional intelligence, and personality styles, and their impact in the workplace. Prior to developing the SSPS, she authored two distinct series of books based on Jung's theory of psychological type (the Personality Profile Series and the Jung Typology series) to support her work with clients. Anne has been working over the past several years on the development of reports for the SSPS, in the areas of leveraging your squad for relationships; leadership, career, and work style; maximizing employee, team, and leadership potential; children and parenting style; and teaching and learning style. She is currently working on developing the manuscript for a subsequent book on Relationship Styles based on the Striving Styles.

Heather Dranitsaris-Hilliard (Performer)

Always curious about what makes people perform and why some people achieve their potential in their lives while others do not, Heather embarked on a journey to understand performance and motivation as well as behavioral change. Her background in organizational and leadership dynamics, coupled with her own experiences as an entrepreneur and parent, has influenced the development of the Striving Styles Personality System.

With a keen interest in business, Heather pursued an education focused on understanding how organizational systems and practices drive performance and the achievement of potential. Attending the Ivey School of Business, she obtained her bachelor's degree in honors business administration. Upon graduating from the university, she completed postgraduate courses in human resources management (HRPAO), as well as compensation management (Canadian Compensation Association/World at Work), organizational development (Linkages), performance systems (University of British Columbia), and management consulting (CMC). In the past, she held a certified human resources practitioner designation as well as her certified compensation professional designation.

Heather started her career working in human resources for a major publishing company in Toronto and then as a consultant in Vancouver, where she designed performance and rewards systems for organizations seeking to increase employee performance. She was the coauthor of a Canada-wide study conducted in 1997 through Mercer HR Consulting on performance management practices in organizations. This study focused on whether or not organizations were able to foster the performance they desired from their employees. Through this work, Heather began to see that—despite well-designed systems—there clearly was something missing in organizational approaches to employee performance. It was at this time that she began working with Anne to learn about the impact of personality and emotions on behavior and ultimately on performance.

Before devoting herself to the development of the Striving Styles, Heather was the driving force behind Caliber Leadership Systems, Vancouver's largest independent leadership and human resources consulting firm. The firm was an evolution of the company that Anne and Heather originally started as a way for them to combine their expertise and develop unique models to expedite results for their clients. Caliber was twice recognized as one of Canada's fastest growing companies (Profit).

Blending systems thinking and behavioral dynamics, Heather has spent the past twenty years guiding clients out of dysfunction, chaos, apathy, and more to achieve higher levels of performance and realize potential at the personal, team, leader, and organizational level. She has worked in the areas of leadership assessment and transformation, organizational effectiveness, strategy, engagement, and culture development for a wide range of local and global firms.

Heather is also a highly recognized and sought-after speaker at professional, business, and entrepreneurial events. Audiences love her unusual, thought-provoking, and often cutting-edge concepts and insights, delivered with both humor and energy. They relate easily to her ideas and feel inspired to take action and improve. She engages audiences with her illustrative and entertaining stories while providing them with the clarity they need to achieve their potential.

Heather has delivered a wide range of courses, workshops, and keynotes to employees, human resource professionals, and leaders. Over the past few years, Heather has begun working with parents and teachers to help them understand and support the emotional needs of children, particularly in situations involving learning or behavioral difficulties.

Find Out Who
YOU REALLY ARE

Who Are You Meant to Be? is an energetic, step-by-step program that helps you move from surviving to thriving. Integrating recent breakthroughs in brain science with a fresh take on how your personality affects your behavior, this book provides a clear roadmap, based on your brain, to break patterns of behavior that get in your way.

THIS BOOK:

○━━ Provides insight into how you can use the abilities you were born with to achieve what you were born for

○━━ Discusses eight personality Styles through highly entertaining and transformative stories

○━━ Allows you to identify which Style is truest to you, and how it influences your behavior

Too many of us live □□□□□□□□□□□□ make it through the day. **Who Are You □□□□□□□□□** offers a way to put us in the driver's seat of our lives, providing a brand-new approach to living authentically and achieving our potential. It's a must have for anyone wanting to understand themselves and others in order to live a more satisfying, fulfilling life.

sourcebooks
www.sourcebooks.com